MARKET AND COMPETITION AUTHORITIES

Market and Competition Authorities

Good Agency Principles

ANNETJE OTTOW
Utrecht University
Faculty of Law, Economics, and Governance

OXFORD
UNIVERSITY PRESS

OXFORD
UNIVERSITY PRESS

Great Clarendon Street, Oxford, OX2 6DP,
United Kingdom

Oxford University Press is a department of the University of Oxford.
It furthers the University's objective of excellence in research, scholarship,
and education by publishing worldwide. Oxford is a registered trade mark of
Oxford University Press in the UK and in certain other countries

First Edition published in 2015

Published in the United States of America by Oxford University Press
198 Madison Avenue, New York, NY 10016, United States of America

British Library Cataloguing in Publication Data
Data available

Library of Congress Control Number: 2014959018

ISBN 978–0–19–873304–1

Preface

This book builds on my work of the last seven years, which started with my PhD on the supervision of the Dutch telecommunications sector. The scope of my work has since broadened, thanks to the combination of my academic work as a law professor at Utrecht University and my membership of the board of OPTA, the Dutch Independent Post and Telecommunications Authority. In April 2013 OPTA merged with the Netherlands Competition Authority (NMa) and the Netherlands Consumer Authority to form the Netherlands Authority for Consumers & Markets (ACM). This example of institution building was a very valuable experience for me and inspired me to conduct further research, while, more recently, my membership of the board of the UK Competition & Markets Authority (CMA) has given me the opportunity to gain greater insight into how independent agencies work and the challenges they face.

Over the years it had become apparent to me that the same basic principles were coming back time and time again when we discussed and sought to understand the framework in which market and competition authorities operated, not only within the Dutch context, but also at a European and an international level. This book identifies five principles: legality (L), independence (I), transparency (T), effectiveness (E), and responsibility (R), which I refer to jointly as the LITER principles. These five principles prove to be fundamental to a framework for agency design and actions, both for the agencies themselves, and also for the actors reviewing the agencies' actions. The book explores theory and practice to provide insight into these fundamental principles and uses several cases, mainly from the Netherlands and the United Kingdom, to draw lessons for and illustrate issues that in my view need to be addressed worldwide. My purpose in identifying the five LITER principles is to enable independent agencies of all kinds, and especially agencies and practitioners responsible for market regulation and competition law enforcement, to apply them in their own specific environments. The book is intended for all those responsible, today and in the future, within the context of an independent agency overseeing markets.

There are a number of institutions and individuals I would like to thank for their help in enabling me to complete this book. I could not have done it without the financial contributions made by the Law Department of my Law, Economics & Governance Faculty, by RENFORCE (the Utrecht

Centre for Shared Regulation and Enforcement in Europe), as well as by 'Institutions', one of the multidisciplinary research programmes at Utrecht University. Writing a manuscript takes time, which was generously granted to me by Utrecht University in the form of a sabbatical leave. I am also very appreciative of the support I received from my Public Economic Law team, and especially the help provided by Anna Gerbrandy. The discussions with my fellow board members at OPTA and CMA, as well as the board of ACM, inspired me every day and indeed continue to do so. Their expert knowledge of and insight into the day-to-day work of independent agencies provided valuable information for the manuscript.

I am grateful to the many people who helped me during the writing process by providing critical comments, suggestions, and advice, specifically Lucky Belder, Sonya Branch, Anna Gerbrandy, Eva Lachnit, Philip Marsden, Benjamin Nunez, Monique van Oers, Mira Scholten, and Adam Scott. My two research assistants, Laurens Venderbos and Aydan Figaroa, found useful material and provided valuable technical assistance. I would also like to express my thanks to Laurian Kip and Alison Gibbs for their excellent language corrections and editing work that helped me to shape the book. A special word of appreciation is for Chris Fonteijn, the ACM chair, for his immense support and advice when commenting on the draft versions of the book. His ideas and insights inspired me tremendously. Above all, I am incredibly grateful to Ton and Anne, my family, who always believed in the project and helped me to keep on going.

Annetje Ottow

Utrecht
September 2014

Table of Contents

Table of Cases

Table of Legislation

FRANCE

INTERNATIONAL

NETHERLANDS

UNITED KINGDOM

List of Abbreviations

AER	Australian Energy Regulator
ACCC	Australian Competition & Consumer Commission
ACER	Agency for the Cooperation of Energy Regulators
ACM	Netherlands Authority for Consumers & Markets (*Autoriteit Consument & Markt*)
AFM	Netherlands Authority for the Financial Markets (*Autoriteit Financiële Markten*)
AID	General Inspectorate of the Dutch Ministry of Economic Affairs (*Algemene Inspectiedienst*)
AMF	French financial markets authority (*Autorité des marchés financiers*)
ARAF	French railway regulator (*Autorité de Régulation des Activités Ferroviaires*)
AVMS	Audiovisual Media Services Directive
BEREC	Body of European Regulators of Electronic Communications
BIS	UK Department for Business, Innovation & Skills
BNetzA	German federal electricity, gas, telecoms, postal and railway regulator (*Bundesnetzagentur für Elektrizität, Gas, Telekommunikation, Post und Eisenbahnen*)
CA	Netherlands Consumer Authority (*Consumentenautoriteit*)
CAA	UK Civil Aviation Authority
CAT	UK Competition Appeal Tribunal
CBb	Dutch Trade and Industry Appeals Tribunal (*College van Beroep voor het bedrijfsleven*)
CC	UK Competition Commission
CDGs	CMA Case decision groups
CERRE	Centre on Regulation in Europe
CMA	UK Competition & Markets Authority
CNMC	Spanish federal markets and competition authority (*Comisión Nacional de los Mercados y la Competencia*)
CPC	Nigerian Consumer Protection Council
CPD	continuing professional development
CPCS	EU Consumer Protection Cooperation System
DNB	Dutch central bank (*De Nederlandsche Bank*)
DGCCRF	French competition, consumer protection, and anti-fraud authority (*Direction Générale de la Concurrence, de la Consommation et de la Répression des Fraudes*)
DTe	Netherlands Office of Energy Regulation (*Dienst uitvoering en Toezicht energie*)
EBA	European Banking Authority

EC	European Commission
ECB	European Central Bank
ECHR	European Convention of Human Rights
ECJ	European Court of Justice
ECN	European Competition Network
ECtHR	European Court of Human Rights (Council of Europe institution)
EGC	European General Court
EIOPA	European Insurance and Occupational Pensions Authority
ERG	European Regulators Group
ERGEG	European Regulators Group for Electricity and Gas
ESAs	European Supervisory Authorities
ESFS	European System of Financial Supervision
ESMA	European Securities and Markets Authority
ESRB	European Systemic Risk Board
FCA	UK Financial Conduct Authority
FCC	US Federal Communications Commission
FERC	US Federal Energy Regulatory Commission
FSA	UK Financial Services Authority
FTC	US Federal Trade Commission
ICARE values	impartial (I), committed to service (C), accountable (A), respectful (R), ethical (E)
ICN	International Competition Network
ILR	Regulatory affairs institute of Luxemburg (*Institut Luxembourgeois de Régulation*)
INDIREG	indicators for independence and efficient functioning of audiovisual media services regulatory bodies
IMF	International Monetary Fund
KFST	Danish competition and consumer authority (*Konkurrence- og Forbrugerstyrelsen*)
KKV	Finnish competition and consumer protection authority (*Kilpailu- ja kuluttajavirasto/Konkurrens- och konsumentverket*)
LITER	legality (L), independence (I), transparency (T), effectiveness (E), responsibility (R)
NEDs	Non-executive directors
NCBs	National central banks
NMa	Netherlands Competition Authority (*Nederlandse Mededingings-autoriteit*)
NMD	Non-Ministerial Department (UK)
NRAs	National Regulatory Authorities
NVWA	Netherlands Food and Consumer Product Safety Authority (*Nederlandse Voedsel- en Warenautoriteit*)
NZa	Dutch Healthcare Authority (*Nederlandse Zorgautoriteit*)
MMS	US Minerals Management Service

MTB	Dutch Consultation Forum of Regulatory Bodies (*Markttoezichthoudersberaad*)
MoU	Memorandum of Understanding
OECD	Organisation for Economic Co-operation and Development
Ofcom	UK Office of Communications
Ofgem	UK Office of Gas and Electricity Markets
Ofwat	UK Water Services Regulation Authority
OFT	UK Office of Fair Trading
OPTA	Dutch Independent Post and Telecommunications Authority (*Onafhankelijke Post en Telecommunicatie Autoriteit*)
ORR	UK Office of Rail Regulation
PD	Plant Pathology Inspectorate of the Dutch Ministry of Agriculture (*Plantenziektekundige Dienst*)
PRA	UK Prudential Regulation Authority
PRC	US Postal Regulatory Commission
Profeco	Mexican Federal Attorney's Office for Consumers (*(Procuraduría Federal del Consumidor*)
SMP	significant market power
SSM	Single Supervisory Mechanism (for EU banking sector)
TEU	Treaty on European Union
TFEU	Treaty on the Functioning of the European Union
VWA	Dutch Food and Consumer Product Safety Authority (*Voedsel- en Warenautoriteit*)
WRR	Netherlands Scientific Council for Government Policy (*Wetenschappelijke Raad voor het Regeringsbeleid*)

1

The Regulatory Space of Market and Competition Agencies

Introduction

Although market and competition agencies supervising and regulating competition and specific sectors in the economy are nowadays seen as an integral and indispensable part of the governmental and institutional scene, market oversight is actually a relatively new phenomenon. Prior to the 1980s it was generally accepted that only the state could oversee public services such as telephony and public utilities. In the late 1980s and early 1990s, however, partly as a result of technological advances, people started believing that these public services could be safeguarded more effectively and efficiently by introducing competition into these markets. Competition was seen as the instrument of choice for eliminating inefficiencies, for promoting technological advances, and for achieving greater prosperity. The state responded by divesting itself of various tasks and leaving these to the market, while at the same time establishing independent agencies to monitor this liberalization process and to promote and oversee fair competition. The state itself was unable to assume this role, given that it continued to hold a share in some of the privatized public services companies being supervised. Many countries created independent agencies of this nature.

Generically, all authorities supervising or regulating markets can be referred to as independent authorities or agencies. In general terms, they can be divided into two types: market authorities and competition authorities. Market authorities have a mandate pertaining to a specific economic sector, such as the energy, telecommunication, transport, or financial sectors. This first type of agency includes the UK communications regulator (Ofcom) and energy regulator (Ofgem), the Australian Energy Regulator (AER), the French rail regulator *Autorité de Régulation des Activités Ferroviaires* (ARAF), and the Federal Communications Commission (FCC), Postal Regulatory Commission (PRC), and Federal Energy Regulatory Commission (FERC) in the United States. Germany in turn has BNetzA, the Federal Network Agency for Electricity, Gas, Telecommunications, Post, and Railway.[1] These types of agencies are also referred to as market or sectoral regulators. Competition authorities, on the other hand, seek to protect the process of competition, rather than the market participants, by enforcing competition laws. Often, these authorities include consumer protection agencies, which have been set up in order to monitor organizations' conduct. Examples of this second type of independent agency include the French competition authority *Autorité de la Concurrence*, the Federal Trade Commission (FTC) of the United States, the UK Competition & Markets Authority (CMA), and the Authority for Consumers & Markets (ACM) in the Netherlands. These market regulators and competition authorities are the parties forming the central theme of this book, and their typology is discussed in detail in the chapter on the types of agencies.

Forging independent agencies into good independent agencies

Attention has recently shifted from the question of 'What is good regulation?' to the question of 'What are good regulators?' For many years, specifically between 1990 and 2005, the focus in research and literature was primarily on substantive rules and means to make better regulation. Since the financial crisis, however, focusing on improving independent agencies and their work has been found to have a major impact on the effectiveness of these substantive rules, with the agencies' architecture and practices being seen as particularly important in this respect. Attention has consequently shifted to a new central issue: which principles should independent agencies adhere to in order to become good agencies?

Independent authorities operate in a complex landscape, with many stakeholders—enterprises, consumers, politicians, ministers, and legislators—playing an important role in and seeking to influence their decision-making processes. Agencies, governments, and the people and organizations they seek to regulate and supervise within these relationships are closely intertwined and interdependent.[2]

All these stakeholders' interests need to be balanced against the background of the statutory remit, the social context, and the applicable rights in each area of regulation.[3] The agency has to find its way through this force

[1] In German: *Bundesnetzagentur für Elektrizität, Gas, Telekommunikation, Post und Eisenbahnen*.

[2] A Freiberg, *The Tools of Regulation* (Sydney: Federation Press 2010) 19.

[3] T Prosser, *The Regulatory Enterprise. Government, Regulation and Legitimacy* (Oxford: Oxford University Press 2010) 19.

field, using the powers and instruments it has been given. As Prosser states, 'The regulatory enterprise is one of collaboration in determining the correct balance of different principles in each social and political context'.[4] The regulatory ecosystem[5] comprises many rules, procedures, and principles, and agencies have to take all these into account, while also receiving directions from politicians that may contradict the message from the general public. This dilemma puts agencies in a vulnerable position as they have to manage a whole range of expectations. On the one hand, agencies are subject to budgetary constraints as their oversight is not allowed to incur too many costs (i.e. no regulatory burden) for society and industries, while, on the other hand, the political scene and society expect agencies to reduce risks to a minimum, in the belief that they are able to oversee everything and everybody. If an accident or incident occurs, the relevant agency is blamed for lack of control and enforcement, and society is quick to ask 'Where was the regulator?' But how do we establish whether agencies have failed?

The general public's readiness to find fault has been augmented by the financial crisis, with financial market authorities being blamed for lack of enforcement and for showing too much leniency towards the financial sector. In addition, the internet and social media mean that not only have society in general, and consumers in particular, become more alert and assertive, but so, too, have agencies become more visible. This puts more pressure on agencies to perform instantly and promptly. Moreover, we are living in a world where technological developments are following each other in quick succession. Legislators are finding it difficult to keep pace with the speed of these developments and to anticipate every single potential problem in legislation. Agencies consequently need to be given wide-ranging discretionary powers and tools to ensure they are able to cope with these developments and, where necessary, intervene.

Given, however, limited capacity and resources, it is obviously impossible for any party to oversee every risk and potential problem in society. Agencies have to prioritize if their work is to be efficient and effective, and the way they analyse risks and select cases has become an art in itself. Although there is a clear desire, especially among politicians, to restrict the number of independent agencies, the latter are in practice being charged with more and more

[4] ibid 235.

[5] This term is taken from Professor Kovacic, who referred to the 'regulatory ecosystem'. See D A Hyman and W E Kovacic, 'Enforcing Competition Law: Benefits and Costs of a Multi-Purpose Agency', draft date unknown, <https://www.law.upenn.edu/live/files/1140-dualpurposecompetitionagency.pdf> accessed 25 April 2014.

tasks, while simultaneously also having to respond to regular calls for more, and more stringent, oversight.

The major agencies' costs, however, are also being scrutinized more critically, and they are being instructed to do more with fewer resources. Politicians are demanding that resources be deployed effectively, and this has repercussions for how agencies perform their enforcement tasks. At the same time, evaluation committees and judges are subjecting decisions and interventions to critical review. There is therefore a risk of agencies being squeezed in a 'Bermuda triangle of supervision'; in other words, of shrinking budgets, critical judges, and ever higher societal expectations.[6]

For market and competition authorities to have more impact within these triangular boundaries, they need to have a clearer and limited set of principles to guide their behaviour. This book provides an in-depth analysis of the issues and dilemmas facing modern market and competition agencies and sets out a series of 'good agency principles'; in other words, key fundamental principles to guide them in their decisions and to establish whether they have failed in the performance of their tasks. This book identifies five fundamental principles that are key to good agency behaviour: legality, independence, transparency, effectiveness, and responsibility, together referred to as the good agency, or LITER, principles.

European dimension to regulatory space

The regulatory space[7] of national independent agencies is becoming more and more internationally oriented: markets are increasingly international, while many problems now extend beyond national borders. This tendency is forcing market and competition authorities to work together in European and international networks (of agencies, and institutions such as the European Commission). In many cases, the rules applying to these networks originate from international codes and standards, or EU legislation, and have to be applied in a harmonized way, while also taking account of the national context and interests. Although national agencies play a key role in implementing and enforcing the European rules, and their activities and how they operate are largely governed by EU law, their work is based on the principles

[6] Interview with C Fonteijn, former chairman of the Netherlands Competition Authority (NMa) in L Berentsen and G den Brinker, 'Supertoezichthouder: 'Eén hand uitsteken, de andere altijd gereed om hard uit te halen', Het Financieele Dagblad (Amsterdam, 12 October 2011) 3.

[7] This term comes from L Hancher and M Moran, 'Organizing Regulatory Space' in L Hancher and M Moran (eds), *Capitalism, Culture and Economic Regulation* (Oxford: Clarendon Press 1989) 271–99.

of institutional and procedural autonomy. Since the start of the twenty-first century, the member states of the European Union have seen many different market and competition authorities being set up under the influence of EU law.

This 'Europeanization' is multifaceted and does not always manifest itself in the same way in the various independent agencies. In addition to the influence of EU law at a national level ('level 1'), various European networks of national agencies ('level 2') have been set up over the years, and these are also playing a role in the further harmonization, implementation, and enforcement of EU law. A recent development has been the establishment, alongside the national agencies, of European Union bodies or market authorities ('level 3') with supranational powers stemming from EU legislation. These EU-wide entities are new on the agency front and can be seen as a tool created by the European Union to regulate national agencies.[8]

These three different levels make the European supervisory and regulatory landscape highly complex. The creation of an institutional structure for coordination has resulted in a mixed administration comprising both national and supranational EU elements. This book analyses this European dimension with regard to the various topics at hand and with a focus on the national agencies, while also examining the European influence on their activities.

Agency Dilemmas

Whatever their type and structure, all market and competition authorities face certain dilemmas. Resolving these dilemmas requires agencies to show how they balance the circumstances, stakeholders' interests, and ethical standards and considerations that govern their society. Agencies need in this respect to follow the five key fundamental principles of good agency behaviour. These are the principles of legality, independence, transparency, effectiveness, and responsibility, together referred to as the LITER principles. These good agency principles form the basis of this book and are discussed throughout in relation to the issues at hand. But first, we need to understand the dilemmas agencies face and the trade-offs they make to resolve them.

[8] Interview with C Fonteijn, formerly chairman of BEREC (Body of European regulators of Electronic Communications) in M Franklin, 'Regulating the Regulators' (2011) October-December M Lex Magazine 14.

Regulatory dilemma

The most notorious dilemma is the regulatory dilemma, where calls for greater supervision following a crisis or incident are accompanied by simultaneous claims of supervisory and regulatory overkill, and excess intervention. This dilemma means independent agencies are continually under pressure when deciding whether to intervene. They need to manage these opposing views, while also having to balance stakeholders' differing and sometimes conflicting rights and expectations, and weighing the public interest against the various private interests at stake. The agency is rather like a tightrope walker or, to put it differently, an agency's life is one long balancing act. And indeed there is a lot for agencies to balance, as the dilemmas summarized under the following four headings show.

Trust versus distrust

There is a common understanding that oversight must—to a certain extent—be based on trust in the organizations being supervised. The starting point in this respect is organizations' willingness to comply with the rules that have been set and to provide information to the appropriate agencies. However, independent agencies must not be naïve and must remain critical and able to differentiate between those organizations that will aim to comply and those that will not. Too much cooperation with sectors and individual organizations may result in an agency being captured by market forces seeking to influence its decisions and in rules being applied too leniently (i.e. a risk of capture). Agencies that are too accommodating are at risk of becoming too involved and of losing their objectivity. At the same time, however, agencies are highly dependent on the organizations they supervise for obtaining the relevant information (i.e. there is an information asymmetry) and need to cooperate with them to gain a better understanding of a market or the circumstances of a case. The need to receive information on the one hand, while keeping a distance on the other hand is a continual struggle and requires ongoing awareness of the need to maintain a balance between trust and distrust.

Cooperation versus repression

As well as contending with the trust/distrust dilemma, independent agencies also have to decide whether to apply a cooperative or more repressive style of enforcement in situations in which severe sanctions can be imposed. In practice, they have to balance different styles and use a mixture of instruments by, for example, observing, highlighting problems, and giving advice and feedback, while also intervening and imposing any sanctions that may be required. In practice, cooperation and repression commonly go hand in hand. It is not a matter of choosing one or the other, but rather of knowing when a specific approach, or combination of approaches, is required. In my experience, this requires a continual investment in developing the agency's skills and expertise so that it can make informed judgements, not only in the disciplines of law and economics, but also in disciplines such as sociology and psychology.

Transparency versus confidentiality

Society is increasingly demanding openness from public bodies and full transparency in their activities. This is also true for market and competition authorities accountable to the public, particularly if these agencies are independent of government ministries and the political scene, and take decisions for their own account. Their actions must be clear and predictable. This requirement for transparency can conflict with the need for confidentiality, however. The latter is vital if supervised organizations have to provide confidential information on their position; they will not be willing to do so if there is a danger of this information coming into the public domain. At the same time, independent agencies have to inform markets, competitors, and consumers of any intervention or non-compliance. This puts the agencies in a difficult position: to what extent do they need to protect the private interests of the supervised organizations, or should they allow the public interest to prevail?

Efficiency versus carefulness

Market and competition authorities need to act promptly and appropriately if they are to achieve their objectives. For reasons of efficiency they have to stick to their stated goals and to achieve results as soon as possible. However, this need for efficiency can conflict with the need for carefulness: all the various interests involved must be balanced against each other, the procedures followed (consultations, hearings, information procedures, and so on) must be fair, and any measures taken must be proportionate. Tools and remedies can, for example, be highly efficient, but at the same time unfair or disproportionate. The need for carefulness can slow down the decision-making process and influence the agency's efficiency. An agency needs to strike the right balance between acting efficiently and acting carefully in order to achieve its objectives effectively. And effectiveness is ultimately the more sustainable indicator of good agency behaviour.

These dilemmas and the way they are dealt with correlate with how market and competition authorities are designed and organized, how they behave, and the choices they make. In reality, an agency's design and organization tend to influence the dilemmas it most commonly encounters. Ideally, however, an agency should be designed and organized so as to be able to respond to the dilemmas it will inevitably face. A well-performing agency knows how to handle the dilemmas it has to deal with and how to apportion weight to the behavioural standards pertinent to the society it operates in. Those behavioural rules can be broken down into the five key fundamental principles of good agency behaviour that were introduced earlier as the good agency, or LITER, principles and that can apply across the world. Let us now have a closer look at these key fundamental principles of good agency behaviour that should guide market and competition authorities.

Good Agency Principles

This book analyses the general rules and principles with which market and competition authorities have to comply when taking action or intervening. These 'good agency principles', as I call them, will ultimately enable substantive rules to be applied in an appropriate manner. In his paper 'Rating the competition agencies: what constitutes good performance?', Professor Kovacic correctly emphasizes that by fulfilling their duties in a capable manner, agencies directly influence not only the outcome and effectiveness of substantive rules, but also contribute to the public's trust and confidence in public governance, and thereby strengthen the legitimacy of public administration.[9]

Rather than examining issues relating to measuring techniques or impact analysis, I take a step back and consider the underlying general principles to be complied with and the qualities required of the relevant market and competition authorities. The term 'principle' is used generically to refer to the whole set of standards other than rules; it can be embodied in a single word, or can be maximized and quantified as a concept.[10] Principles have an

[9] W E Kovacic, 'Rating the competition agencies: what constitutes good performance?' (2009) 16(4) George Mason Law Review 906.

[10] W van Gerven, 'Two Twin-Principles of EU Law: Democracy and Accountability, Consistency and Convergence' in U Bernitz, J Nergelius and C Cardner (eds), *General Principles of EC Law in a Process of Development* (Alphen aan den Rijn: Wolters Kluwer 2008) 25–46.

abstract nature and express moral values enjoying a degree of wide acceptance, i.e. they represent a 'conventional morality'.[11]

The inspiration for these good agency principles can be found in the Dutch doctrine of public economic law, which distinguishes between the instrumental and the guardian roles in this field of law.[12] The instrumental school of thought sees law as instrumental to policy objectives and as a tool for implementing government policy. Many forms of legislation on organizing the market can be described as instrumental. The guardian role, by contrast, focuses on the regulation of government activity through administrative law and seeks to safeguard the legal position of ordinary citizens vis-à-vis the state. In this role, the administrative body is bound by rules, both in the form of substantive law and procedure. A tension exists between these two functions of public economic law: combining these two elements therefore requires a continuous balancing between being effective on the one hand (i.e. achieving the goals that have been set) and being fair and careful (i.e. complying with the principles of legitimacy) on the other hand.

This tension forms the red thread running through public economic law and also, therefore (as a *lex specialis*), the rules regulating independent agencies. In many fields of sector-specific regulation, as well as in general public economic law, these rules are—at both a national and EU level—of a purpose-oriented nature. The goals that have been set for regulation form the basis for testing the outcomes and results. There is a tendency for independent agencies to focus on these goals and to evaluate results along these lines as agencies have to achieve their public tasks as efficiently and effectively as possible. However, a one-sided focus on achieving the goals (i.e. the instrumental vision) can result in the non-instrumental values and principles being overlooked. Independent agencies' decisions and interventions also have to adhere to the principle of justice (i.e. the guardian role of administrative law).

The general principles of administrative law, and particularly the rules on due process, are also of relevance here. Principles such as proportionality, fairness, carefulness, consistency, and predictability apply to the public entities examined in this book.

Compare the five criteria for good regulation of R Baldwin, M Cave, and M Lodge, *Understanding Regulation. Theory, Strategy, and Practice* (2nd edn, Oxford: Oxford University Press 2012) 26–34.

[11] T Tridimas, *The General Principles of EU Law* (Oxford: Oxford University Press 2006) 25–27.

[12] K Hellingman and K J M Mortelmans, *Economisch publiekrecht. Rechtswaarborgen en rechtsinstrumenten* (Deventer: Kluwer 1989); A T Ottow, *Mastering the Market? Exploring New Forms of Market Supervision* (inaugural lecture, 18 September 2008, University of Utrecht, The Hague: Boom Juridische Uitgevers 2009).

LITER, the good agency's acronym

These general principles of public economic law and administrative law can all be reduced and translated into general 'good agency principles' that combine the instrumental and guardian roles of public economic law. Brought up to their highest level, the five fundamental principles identified in this book, which are key to good agency behaviour, are the principles of legality (L), independence (I), transparency (T), effectiveness (E), and responsibility (R). Together these good agency principles are referred to as the LITER principles.

What 'good' agency principles are is inevitably a matter of subjective choice. Rather than claiming that these principles are fixed, this book classifies all the relevant aspects under five general headings. These headings, or principles, contain the most common benchmarks that independent agencies and their stakeholders can use as a general framework. These five key fundamental principles can be applied across a wide range of regulatory and supervisory bodies and agencies, including competition authorities, and are of paramount importance in assessing independent agencies' work and behaviour.[13] This section briefly explains these five principles, which are analysed at length in the rest of the book.

Legality principle

The constitutional principle of legality is of particular importance: it forms the basis of all key fundamental principles and for any action by an independent agency. Under this principle, unilateral administrative action impinging upon the rights and freedoms of citizens should be exercised on the basis of and in accordance with the legislative mandate authorized by parliament. At the same time the agency has to have discretionary powers to make policy choices and complex legal and economic assessments. In a rapidly changing environment that is being driven to a large extent by developments in technology, it is essential for powers, instruments, and procedures to be able to keep pace with these developments. An inadequate or delayed response to such changes will result in failure to meet the objectives of regulatory oversight. An independent agency therefore has to have flexibility in its decision-making powers; if its legislative mandate is too tight, it will be

[13] J Black, 'Constructing and Contesting Legitimacy and Accountability in Polycentric Regulatory Regimes' (2008) LSE Legal Studies Working Paper No. 2/2008 <http://ssrn.com/abstract=1091783> accessed 7 November 2013.

unable to intervene appropriately, and the purpose of the regulation will not be achieved.

Independence principle

Independence has long been considered an essential element of any market and competition supervision. Market and competition authorities, for example, are expected to apply rules and regulations impartially and independently of the interests of market parties and also of the political arena.[14] Independence from market parties is necessary in order to create a level playing field and to ensure market confidence in impartial decision-making. A sufficient degree of independence is seen as a key ingredient in allowing proper enforcement of policy in general, and also consequently of competition policy.[15] EU regulations contain an increasing number of requirements for independence and impose obligations for independence on market and competition authorities. The term 'independence' also implies regulatory expertise: in other words, agencies' professional judgement must be objective and based on valid, reliable information and justification.

Transparency principle

Market and competition authorities are bound by the need for transparency. Their procedures must therefore be fair, accessible, and open, while also making sufficient provision for consultation and stakeholder participation. Decisions and interventions must also be based on sufficiently reliable and sound justification, and legal and economic reasoning. These transparency requirements reflect the guardian role of this principle. However, this principle also has an instrumental aspect in that transparent oversight will help make supervision more effective (i.e. it will have preventive and legitimacy effects). Transparency can create certainty and better compliance, and thus prevent enterprises from committing infringements.

[14] See, for example, G Majone, *Regulating Europe* (London: Routledge 1996); F Gilardi, 'Policy Credibility and Delegation to Independent Regulatory Agencies; a Comparative Analysis' (2002) 6 Journal of European Public Policy 873; A Larsen, L H Pedersen, E M Sørensen, and O J Olsen, 'Independent Regulatory Authorities in European Electricity Markets' (2006) 34 Energy Policy 2858; F Gilardi, 'The Same, But Different: Central Banks, Regulatory Agencies and the Politics of Delegation to Independent Authorities' (2007) 5(3) Comparative European Politics 303, 306.

[15] International Competition Network, 'Advocacy and Competition Policy' (Report prepared by the Advocacy Working Group, presented at the first ICN's conference in Naples, Italy, 2002) 53–58 <http://www.internationalcompetitionnetwork.org/uploads/library/doc358.pdf> accessed 7 November 2013.

Effectiveness principle

Oversight must be effective: it must be able to meet the goals of regulation and allow the interventions needed to achieve these goals. The enforcement styles and the instruments and tools selected must be chosen in accordance with this principle, while procedures must also be fair and interventions proportionate (procedural fairness). Otherwise, intervention may conflict with administrative law principles and be void, in which case it cannot be considered effective. Effectiveness is linked to the need for efficiency: the burden of input in terms of effort and work force, and also the costs, must remain reasonable and affordable, while also not preventing institutional and instrumental innovation at the agency.

Responsibility principle

The principle of responsibility is evident in various aspects of public economic law. The state itself can accept responsibility for social issues by taking steps to protect specific interests, but it can also create rules to encourage social responsibility among other parties, including enterprises. Appealing to an organization's and consumers' own sense of social responsibility may be a better way of ensuring that certain objectives or interests are achieved than imposing unilateral public measures. This view is based on the premise currently being researched within the field of experimental governance that good results are possible through consultation and collaboration, irrespective of the fact that organizations and consumers also have interests of their own, such as a desire to avoid risks or to protect their reputation.[16]

The belief that organizations are willing to consider other stakeholders' interests, even if solely for the purpose of protecting their own reputation, explains some of the choices that states make when structuring market supervision. The principle of responsibility plays a role, either consciously or unconsciously, in the selection of enforcement and regulatory instruments. This is because market and competition authorities have to focus on the most effective way to persuade organizations to comply with rules. If the agency assumes it can achieve better results by appealing more to an organization's own sense of responsibility, it could choose to deploy more consultative instruments, while supervision based primarily on a distrust of supervisees will result in more stringent and repressive action.

[16] C F Sabel and J H Zeitlin, 'Experimentalist Governance' in C F Sabel and J H Zeitlin, *Experimentalist Governance in the European Union: Towards a New Architecture* (Oxford: Oxford University Press 2010).

These LITER principles are used throughout the book to analyse several key agency topics: institutional design, enforcement, and the evaluation of agencies and judicial review by the courts (as illustrated in annex 1). The weight attributed to the five criteria in specific cases may vary, according to the specific circumstances and context of a case, but also depending on individuals' personal, political, or philosophical views on society.[17] In addition, trade-offs will have to be made by weighing the different principles and interests at stake.

Institutional Design

There is currently a worldwide trend to restructure market and competition authorities, with several mergers of such organizations having taken place and new combinations being formed. Competition and market agencies are consequently now moving away from being single-function bodies and towards becoming multifunctional agencies, where antitrust and regulatory functions are housed under a single roof. In October 2013, for example, Spain established a 'super regulator' in the form of the National Commission on Markets and Competition (CNMC).[18] How should we view this trend from a design perspective?

Bringing separate institutions under one roof does not in itself create integration and innovation. As Hyman and Kovacic correctly comment, 'The coordination of functions and responsibilities will not happen merely because previously separate bureaus are combined into a single department'.[19] There remains a risk that no cohesion will take place and that the new design will simply create separate operating units for each function. Consequently, these units may once again become rivals and have to fight for prestige, headcount, and budgetary resources.[20]

The literature has so far devoted little attention to institutional design, the implementation of policy goals in the organizational fabric, governance aspects, and issues such as the optimal design of market and competition authorities. Institutional approaches believe, however, that institutional structures and arrangements significantly and fundamentally shape regulation, including its substantive rules.[21] The institutional architecture forms an important building block of agencies' working environment. The

17 R Baldwin, M Cave, and M Lodge (n10) 32–33.

18 In Spanish: *Comisión Nacional de los Mercados y la Competencia*

19 D A Hyman and W E Kovacic (n5) 18.

20 D A Hyman and W E Kovacic (n5).

21 R Baldwin, M Cave, and M Lodge (n10) 53.

way in which an agency is designed can have a major influence on its work and performance. Identifying the optimal design is, therefore, crucial for the agency's effectiveness. Institutional design and the institutional questions relating to governance and legitimacy are areas that have recently seen fundamental changes; they are therefore discussed in depth and will be analysed in the context of the LITER principles in the chapter on institutional design.

This book analyses some of the instruments used to prevent such separation and to promote integration. New combinations create opportunities for institutional innovation, while also preventing silos of regulatory and competition work, and preventing an agency from being captured by market forces seeking to influence its decisions, or at least reducing the risks of those phenomena. In addition, greater coordination of market and competition authorities' interpretations of legislation and interventions may promote cross-fertilization between the different fields of law. Improved integration of these different areas is possible.

Various different options are available, as I illustrate by analysing two cases of agency mergers. In my analysis I examine the different design elements and identify the pros and cons of each specific choice. The mergers in question took place in the Netherlands and the United Kingdom. The first was the merger on 1 April 2013 of the Netherlands Competition Authority (NMa), the Independent Post and Telecommunications Authority (OPTA), and the Consumer Authority (CA) into the newly created Netherlands Authority for Consumers & Markets (ACM), while the second was the merger on 1 April 2014 of the Office of Fair Trading (OFT) and the Competition Commission (CC) that created the new British Competition & Markets Authority (CMA). These cases are used to illustrate how a bundling of tasks can be translated into an institutional strategy and to examine the implementation issues arising. In this way, they show us how institutional structures and arrangements shape the substantive rules of regulation and competition law, and which factors matter when it is decided to combine a series of functions under one roof. Taking an inside look at these cases will enable us to learn lessons for other jurisdictions.

Enforcement Styles and Tools

An independent agency's enforcement task should represent the essence of its work, and general principles for enforcement and for the agency's qualities and actions should be developed accordingly. Which elements are relevant in relation to enforcement?

Theory broadly distinguishes between two enforcement styles: vertical and horizontal.[22] Vertical enforcement, or conduct that is dictated top-down, employs conventional regulatory instruments (such as orders, administrative fines, and punitive sanctions) to uphold the law and is a classic command-and-control model.[23] The force of law is used to prohibit certain types of conduct, to demand positive action, and to stipulate conditions for access to a certain industry. Infringement of the law is seen as the starting point for intervention.

This contrasts with horizontal enforcement, which focuses on collaborating with the supervised organization and is based on an assumption of trust between the agency and that organization. Horizontal enforcement demands a different approach, not only in enforcement practice, but also in enforcement law. It is designed to give supervised organizations more responsibility and uses instruments such as covenants or compliance agreements, while the independent agency maintains a greater distance than in vertical enforcement. Examples of horizontal enforcement include self-regulation, co-regulation, covenants, and voluntary compliance programmes. Other terms used to distinguish between these two practices include informal versus legalistic or formal supervision, and cooperative versus adversarial supervision, while another distinction made is between the sanction style and the accommodative style.[24]

Case law and legal literature on competition and regulatory enforcement focus mainly on sanctions. Formal sanctions, however, are just one aspect of the enforcement pyramid.[25] Indeed, assessing the enforcement practice of independent agencies is almost completely case-driven. Kovacic refers to this practice as the 'activity-oriented calculus'.[26] This approach, however, completely ignores what he refers to as 'non-litigation activities': in other words, enforcement activities that do not lead to formal decisions or sanctions and so are not taken into account when assessing an agency's work, even though they form an important part of the latter's activities and can produce effective results.

In practice, independent agencies regularly combine vertical and horizontal enforcement styles in their attempts to find the right mix of instruments.[27]

[22] A T Ottow, *Mastering the market? Exploring New Forms of Market Supervision* (n12).

[23] R Baldwin, M Cave, and M Lodge (n10).

[24] H de Bruijn, E ten Heuvelhof, and M Koopmans, *Law Enforcement. The Game Between Inspectors and Inspectees* (Boca Raton, Florida: Universal Publishers 2007).

[25] I Ayres and J Braithwaite, *Responsive Regulation: Transcending the Deregulation Debate* (New York: Oxford University Press 1992). The pyramid is discussed on pages 38–39.

[26] W E Kovacic, 'Rating the Competition Agencies: What Constitutes Good Performance?' (n9) 908.

[27] A. T. Ottow, *Mastering the Market? Exploring New Forms of Market Supervision* (n12).

In addition to the conventional administrative law instruments, market and competition agencies now seem to be seeking to identify new forms of oversight that place more responsibility on the supervised organization. Greater horizontalization is a response to an increasingly complex society, where continuing to adhere to top-down supervision is virtually impossible. If this new form of oversight is to work, societal stakeholders will need to cooperate, while still leaving independent agencies sufficient scope to respond effectively to new developments. The chapter on enforcement in this book focuses on these non-litigation enforcement activities of independent agencies.

Evaluation and Judicial Review

Although it is very important for market and competition authorities to be independent, the principle of independence also raises some questions about their accountability.[28] This accountability can be seen as the relationship between an actor and a forum, in which the actor has to explain and justify his conduct, while the forum can ask questions and pass judgement, and the actor may face consequences.[29] The questions commonly asked in respect of accountability concern who, to whom, how, why, based on what standards, and with what effects?[30] Since public resources are at stake, independence inevitably results in agencies being held accountable ('Are they effective and do they achieve their supervisory goals?') and made subject to evaluation and judicial review.

Evaluation committees

In the years after 2007—in other words, following the financial crisis—a multitude of evaluation committees were set up to assess and judge the behaviour of independent agencies. Critical reflections were undertaken to find out what went wrong, and what role was played by the agencies.[31] This

[28] J Black (n13).

[29] M Bovens, 'Analysing and Assessing Accountability: A Conceptual Framework' (2007) 13(4) European Law Journal 450.

[30] For an excellent iteration of these questions see J L Mashaw, 'Accountability and Institutional Design: Some Thoughts on the Grammar of Governance' (2007) Yale Law School Research Paper No 116 <http://ssrn.com/abstract=924879> accessed 7 November 2013.

[31] 'De Larosière Report' (High-Level Group on Financial Supervision in the EU, Brussels, 25 February 2009) <http://ec.europa.eu/internal_market/finances/docs/de_larosiere_report_en.pdf> accessed 7 November 2013; Financial Services Authority, 'The Turner Review: A Regulatory Response to the Global Banking Crisis' (2009) <http://www.fsa.gov.uk/pubs/other/turner_review.pdf> accessed 7 November 2013.

critical attitude also triggered a more sceptical approach towards independent agencies and authorities in general, thus resulting in yet more evaluation committees and reports. The roles played by internal supervisors (at educational institutions and medical centres, for example) were also subjected to scrutiny. Rather than being based on strict legal requirements, these assessments focused on vaguer grounds such as reasonableness and carefulness. These evaluation reports and internal assessments both contain useful lessons and guidance for market and competition authorities on how to avoid failure in the future and how to decide on which measures to take.

Review by the courts

Market and competition authorities' decisions can be challenged before national—and, in some cases, European—courts. Courts therefore play a crucial role in the debate on agencies' accountability by ensuring market parties' right to effective legal protection and by holding agencies legally accountable for their acts.[32] This aspect of the national courts' task is complex, mainly due to a more economic approach towards the application and interpretation of economic regulation and competition law.

This new approach has raised questions about the standards of judicial review. Should the courts respect the agencies' margin of appreciation, defer as much as possible to the choices made by the agencies, and merely subject the question of whether they have reasonably exercised their powers to marginal review? Or should they conduct an intense review of whether the market and competition authorities have correctly exercised their powers so as to protect market parties' right to effective legal protection? How should courts establish a balance between safeguarding the right to effective legal protection on the one hand and an effective and efficient functioning of national independent agencies in a multilevel governance setting on the other hand? How should we assess the degree of judicial scrutiny performed by national courts when reviewing decisions taken by independent agencies? The possible liability of independent agencies must also be considered in this context.

Standards of judicial review cannot be studied in isolation from the issues relating to evidence and the rules on the standard and burden of proof.[33] The

[32] S A C M Lavrijssen, 'More Intensive Judicial Review in Competition Law and Economic Regulation in the Netherlands: Vice or Virtue' in O Essens, A Gerbrandy, and S A C M Lavrijssen (eds), *National Courts and the Standard of Review in Competition Law and Economic Regulation* (Groningen: Europa Law Publishing 2009) 175–77.

[33] A T Ottow, 'Observations on Economic Proof in Economic Cases' in O Essens, A Gerbrandy, and S A C M Lavrijssen (n32) 48.

burden of proof refers to which party in the proceedings is required to prove the requisite facts or arguments of the case, whereas the standard of proof refers to how difficult it is to prove a point or case. There is a link between the standard of review and the standard and burden of proof.[34]

The focus on economic evidence in economic cases has resulted in more intense judicial review. The intensity of the review has immediate consequences for the evidence needed to substantiate allegations.[35] A more economic approach in competition law and regulatory cases also requires more economic-based evidence and results in a more critical approach by European and national courts when analysing independent agencies' decisions. Decisions based merely on form or this economic analysis will not be upheld as courts will review these decisions critically and demand more actual proof to justify intervention by the European Commission or national independent agencies.

Scope and Methodology of the Book

The rules regulating the behaviour of market and competition authorities are equally important for the work of these agencies as the substantive rules themselves. Rather than discussing the law (such as competition law or telecommunications regulation), this book focuses on behavioural elements: how should agencies behave? This question is answered with reference to five key fundamental principles of good agency behaviour: the LITER principles of legality, independence, transparency, effectiveness, and responsibility. These LITER principles provide a framework for agency design and actions, not only for the agencies themselves, but also for the actors reviewing the agencies' actions.

The book identifies the five LITER principles so as to enable market and competition authorities and practitioners worldwide to apply these lessons in their own specific environment. Theory and practice are combined throughout as a means of providing insight into market and competition authorities' organization and behaviour. These behavioural issues regarding market, competition, and consumer authorities are outlined and analysed in an 'eco-systemic' way by addressing questions such as how, and on the basis of which good agency principles, should these independent authorities be assessed and

[34] C Graham, 'Judicial Review of the Decisions of the Competition Authorities and the Economic Regulators in the UK' in O Essens, A Gerbrandy, and S A C M Lavrijssen (n32) 244.

[35] A T Ottow, 'Observations on Economic Proof in Economic Cases' (n33).

judged, and what we can expect from them. The focus is mainly on national agencies, but the European context and its agencies will also be discussed.

Chapter 2 provides an overview of the different agencies and their roles and functions, while also describing the three identified levels within the European context: national, networks, and European bodies and authorities. The LITER principles are introduced and analysed in chapter 3 and then linked to three key processes: institutional design (chapter 4), enforcement (chapter 5), and evaluation and judicial review (chapter 6). Each chapter takes an inside look from a public law perspective and draws on the work and experience of academics so as to identify key factors for the success and failure of these processes. Each chapter applies the LITER principles to the issues at stake, not only by building on theory and academic work, but also by using several cases in illustration, mainly from the Netherlands and the United Kingdom, and sometimes with a special focus on the EU context.

Although the LITER principles are applied mainly to market, competition, and consumer authorities, they may function as common denominators for all types of independent agencies. Market regulation has so far mainly been studied sector by sector and, in many cases, wheels have been re-invented. There has been little if any cross-fertilization between the different fields of market regulation, or between market regulation, competition, and consumer protection, and these areas have tended to be studied in an isolated and fragmented manner. This is the natural result of the specialization of law-making and the introduction of specialized independent agencies for oversight. As, however, the current worldwide trend is to merge different types of agencies, and since the basic characteristics of all these agencies are the same and they face the same problems in their day-to-day practice, there is every reason to study what these agencies have in common and how they can learn from each other. Cross-fertilization can lead to new insights and new approaches. Chapter 7 consequently sets out a series of conclusions and recommendations for independent agencies, legislators, governments and policymakers, and finally the courts.

2

Types of Agencies

Introduction

Agencification has been a clear trend, with the introduction of agencies becoming the dominant mode of governance—at least in the industrialized world (i.e. the 'regulatory state model').[1] By agencification I mean the trend of creating semi-autonomous organizations that operate at arm's length from government in order to carry out public tasks, implement policies, regulate markets and policy sectors, or deliver public services relatively autonomously.[2] Agencification has several aims: increased efficiency, strengthened and clarified responsibility and accountability lines, a more motivated and professional administration, and a more service-oriented administration that is closer to citizens.[3] Although the variety between the different types of agencies makes it hard to arrive at a precise definition,[4] agencies can generically be defined as public organizations that are legally subordinated to but structurally disaggregated from government and that enjoy considerable policy and managerial autonomy.[5]

[1] M Quintyn, 'Independent Agencies: More Than a Cheap Copy of Independent Central Banks?' (2009) 20 Constitutional Political Economy 267, 268. See T Christensen and P Lægreid (eds), *Autonomy and Regulation: Coping with Agencies in the Modern State* (Cheltenham: Edward Elgar 2006); J Jordana and D Levi-Faur, 'The Politics of Regulation in the Age of Governance' in J Jordana and D Levi-Faur (eds), *The Politics of Regulation* (Cheltenham: Edward Elgar 2004) 1–28.

[2] K Verhoest, S van Thiel, G Bouckaert, and P Laegreid (eds), *Government Agencies: Practices and Lessons from 30 Countries* (London: Palgrave MacMillan 2012) 3.

[3] OECD 2005. Modernizing Government. The Way Forward. OECD Publishing, 108–11.

[4] C Pollit, J Caulfield, A Smullen, and C Talbot, *Agencies: How Governments Do Things Through Semi-Autonomous Organizations* (Basingstoke: Palgrave MacMillan 2004); C Talbot, 'The Agency Idea: Sometimes Old, Sometimes New, Sometimes Borrowed, Sometimes Untrue' in C Pollitt and C Talbot (eds), *Unbundled Government: a Critical Analysis of the Global Trend to Agencies, Quangos and Contractualisation* (London and New York: Routledge 2004) 3–21.

[5] C Pollitt and G Bouckaert, *Public Management Reform: a Comparative Analysis* (2nd edn, Oxford: Oxford University Press 2004) 7–11; G Majone, 'The Credibility Crisis of Community Regulation' (2000) 2 Journal of Common Market Studies 273.

While the idea and practice of delegating specific policy or monitoring responsibilities to agencies is not new,[6] the rise of market and competition authorities is a phenomenon that first started being seen in the early 1990s.[7] Such agencies have increasingly populated the field of economic (as opposed to social) regulation (in competition policies, financial sector regulation, telecommunication, and utilities),[8] with liberalization, privatization, and competition all leaving their mark. Indeed, competition law has completely penetrated every market (at different levels), with all kinds of competition and market authorities existing, and each market having its own special features.[9]

This chapter provides a general overview of the different types of independent agencies existing around the world. It is descriptive in nature and sets the scene for identifying the good agency principles, the design of independent agencies, their enforcement styles and practices, and the evaluation and review of their behaviour and decisions. First, the very reason for agencies' existence is examined by taking a closer look at their different roles, functions, and tasks, then the different types of agencies and combinations of agency types are discussed, followed by an outline of the European landscape and a few words on the international context.

Independent Agencies: Why Do We Have Them?

How market liberalization created independent agencies

Prior to the 1980s it was generally accepted that only the state could oversee public services such as telephony and public utilities.[10] In the late 1980s and early 1990s, however, partly as a result of technological advances,

[6] G Majone, 'Controlling Regulatory Bureaucracies: Lessons from the American Experience' (1993) European University Institute Working Papers No. 93/3; G Majone, 'The Regulatory State and its Legitimacy Problems' (1999) 22(1) West European Politics 1; C Pollit, J Caulfield, A Smullen, and C Talbot (n4); R Wettenhall, 'Agencies and Non-Departmental Public Bodies. The Hard and Soft Lenses of Agencification Theory' (2005) 7(4) Public Management Review 615.

[7] M Quintyn (n1) 268; D Geradin and N Petit, 'The Development of Agencies at EU and National Levels: Conceptual Analysis and Proposals for Reform' (2004) Jean Monnet Working Paper 01-04, 4, 8.

[8] M Thatcher, 'Regulation after Delegation: Independent Regulatory Agencies in Europe' (2002) 9(6) Journal of European Public Policy 954; D Geradin, 'Institutional Aspects of EU Regulatory Reforms in the Telecommunications Sector: An Analysis of the Role of National Regulatory Authorities' (2000) 1 Journal of Network Industries 5.

[9] A T Ottow, *Mastering the Market? Exploring New Forms of Market Supervision* (inaugural lecture, 18 September 2008, University of Utrecht, The Hague: Boom Juridische Uitgevers 2009) 2.

[10] ibid 2.

people started believing that these public services could be safeguarded more effectively and efficiently by introducing competition into these markets. Keynesianism and nationally based industrial policies were rejected, and competition policy came instead to the fore.[11] Competition was seen as the instrument of choice for eliminating inefficiencies, for promoting technological advances, and for achieving greater prosperity.

The state responded by divesting itself of various tasks and leaving these to the market.[12] The conventional industrial policy instruments of nationalization, planning, selective intervention, and subsidy were replaced by a new portfolio of privatization, deregulation, and market-friendly re-regulation.[13] The 'free market' became the dominant concept. Competition is now broadly accepted as the best available mechanism for 'maximising the things that one can demand from an economic system in most circumstances'.[14]

But competition, too, comes at a price. And this price can be market failure, which occurs when a market left to its own devices fails to allocate resources efficiently.[15] There is then a potential role for government to correct these market failures, four types of which can be distinguished:

1. *Market power.* If one enterprise has the ability to raise the price of a good or service above its marginal costs, it has market power. In perfectly competitive markets, market participants have no market power. The ability of an incumbent enterprise to raise its price above competitive levels is limited by the existence or threat of competition. Examples of market power include a natural or actual monopoly, where there is a single supplier, and an oligopoly, where a small number of enterprises control the market.
2. *Information asymmetry.* Such an asymmetric situation occurs when one party (typically the seller) in a transaction has more or better information than the other party (typically the buyer). This can prevent consumers from making fully informed decisions.
3. *Externalities.* The concept of externalities refers to costs or benefits from a transaction that are incurred or received by a party not involved in the transaction. Externalities can be either positive (i.e. an external benefit) or

[11] S Wilks and I Bartle, 'The Unanticipated Consequences of Creating Independent Competition Agencies' (2002) 25(1) West European Politics 148.

[12] A T Ottow, *Mastering the Market? Exploring New Forms of Market Supervision* (n9) 3.

[13] S Wilks and I Bartle (n11) 149.

[14] P Crampton, Head Outreach Unit, Competition Division OECD, 'Competition and Efficiency as Organising Principles for All Economic and Regulatory Policymaking', Prepared for the First Meeting of the Latin American Competition Forum (7–8 April 2003) 2.

[15] The first known use of the term 'market failure' was by F M Bator, 'The Anatomy of Market Failure' (1958) 72(3) Quarterly Journal of Economics 351.

negative (i.e. an external cost). The existence of externalities can result in the production or consumption of too many or too few goods and services than is economically efficient.

4. *Public goods*. A public good is a good or service for which exclusion is prohibitively costly and for which the marginal cost of adding another consumer is zero. National defence, law enforcement, and generally available knowledge are all examples of public goods. Free-riding is a problem that may arise when marketing public goods as the fact that the good is non-excludable means everyone can use it once it has been provided. This makes it impossible to extract payment from users in order to recoup the costs of providing the good.

It did not always turn out to be easy, therefore, to create competition, especially in the case of newly liberalized industries, where incumbents usually wanted to retain considerable market power for as long as possible.[16] Most telecommunications incumbents, for example, continued to hold strong market positions, even though the sector had been fully liberalized for several years, and findings for the gas, electricity, postal, and transport sectors were also similar.[17]

Two factors clearly contributed to the difficulty of creating competition in these industries.[18] New entrants had to make a huge and difficult catch-up compared to established companies as the incumbents generally had an established brand name, considerable expertise, and sufficient financial resources. Another potential barrier to entry in these network industries is the fact that incumbents often own all or part of the network infrastructure and are not eager to give this up.

Opening up markets to more competition consequently did not automatically result in the expected levels of competitiveness and consumer benefits.[19] In order to offset the risk of market failure, states set up a range of different competition and market authorities to promote and oversee fair competition, and to monitor the liberalization process.[20] The state itself was unable

[16] D Geradin, 'The Opening of State Monopolies to Competition: Main Issues of the Liberalization Process' in D Geradin (ed), *The Liberalization of State Monopolies in the European Union and Beyond* (Deventer: Kluwer Law International 2000) 181.

[17] D Geradin, 'Enhancing Competition in the Postal Sector; Can We do Away with Sector-Specific Regulation', Paper prepared for the 14th Conference on Postal and Delivery Economics, Bern, 1–3 June 2006, 1–2.

[18] ibid 2.

[19] K J Cseres, 'Integrate or Separate—Institutional Design for the Enforcement of Competition Law and Consumer Law' (2013) Amsterdam Law School Legal Studies Research Paper No 2013-03, 13–14 <http://ssrn.com/abstract=2200908> accessed 25 November 2013.

[20] A T Ottow, 'Europeanization of the Supervision of Competitive Markets' (2002) 18(1) European Public Law 191, 191.

to assume this role, given that it had an interest in some of the market players needing to be overseen.[21]

Following the 2008 financial crisis, the question also arose as to whether competition should be the primary goal, and whether a more interventionist approach by governments should be introduced, or re-introduced, to protect public goods and interests.[22] It is commonly seen as the state's task to protect interests at risk of falling between two stools as a result of a free-market system. Prosser, for example, advocates a 'social solidarity-based' approach to protect universal or public services.[23]

On independent agencies' functions, tasks, and roles

In order to identify the principles to which independent agencies should adhere, the roles, functions, and tasks that have been entrusted to them must first be established. Only then can we determine how these authorities should behave and what we can expect from them. The question of whether an agency can be regarded as having committed regulatory failure, such as under-performance/under-inclusiveness or over-performance/over-inclusiveness, can be answered only if its tasks and functions are clearly defined. Expectations of what agencies can actually do and achieve are in many cases too high. Society should, therefore, remain realistic in its expectations and needs to recognize that there are limitations to agencies' capacity, resources, and expertise.

The question of how well market and competition authorities perform their tasks has to be answered with reference to the goals that have been set for them. Competition and market agencies may seek to achieve different goals. Most of these agencies are dealing with liberalized sectors; their main goal, therefore, is to promote competition in order to achieve competitive markets (thus creating a 'level playing field'). Promotion of consumer welfare is seen as an essential part of their duty to give consumers more and better choices.[24] A socio-economic approach, as advocated by Prosser, is based on

[21] A T Ottow, *Mastering the Market? Exploring New Forms of Market Supervision* (n9) 3.

[22] See for example T Prosser, *The Limits of Competition Law. Markets and Public Services* (Oxford: Oxford University Press 2004) and C Townley, *Article 81 EC and Public Policy* (Oxford/Portland: Hart Publishing 2009).

[23] T Prosser, *The Regulatory Enterprise. Government, Regulation and Legitimacy* (Oxford: Oxford University Press 2010) 15–17.

[24] See for example the objective of the ACCC: 'Enhance the Welfare of Australians Through the Promotion and Fair Trading and Provision of Consumer Protection' <http://accc.gov.au/about-us/australian-competition-consumer-commission/about-the-accc> accessed 8 April 2014, or the Strategy Document of ACM: 'Increasing consumer welfare is ACM's primary goal' Strategy Document Netherlands Authority for Consumers & Markets, 2 <https://www.acm.nl/en/about-acm/mission-vision-strategy/our-mission/> accessed 14 March 2014.

economic efficiency, and consumer welfare and protection. In this approach, competition and market agencies' tasks may also include non-economic interests, such as healthcare or the protection of the environment (i.e. 'sustainability goals').[25]

The independent agencies' tasks and functions can be derived from the legislation establishing the agencies and from the objectives underlying the applicable regulations. Their institutional design, and the powers and instruments assigned to them, also have to be seen in the light of their tasks and functions, and of their roles. Indeed, agencies' tasks and functions may involve them playing a range of roles, of which I distinguish five:

1. An advisory role that involves providing advice to the government, other agencies, the general public, or the enterprises they supervise. As agencies are seen as the 'authority' in the relevant field, their advice has to meet certain criteria for independence, fairness, and objectivity.
2. An advocacy role that also forms an important part of their day-to-day work. Advocacy means educating the general public and government, and communicating messages on good practices.
3. A reflective role, in which agencies are expected to identify risks and problems in markets and urge the adoption of any new legislation considered necessary to deal with these issues.[26]
4. A preventive role, which is key to ensuring that the goals of the rules are achieved (preventing harm and infringements is better than curing them).
5. A repressive role, in which agencies are required to ensure that rules are complied with and that any infringements of such rules are punished (i.e. the enforcement function).

These different roles may require adherence to different principles of the LITER set of principles for good agency behaviour. Some principles may be considered more essential to some of the roles than others. In the case, for example, of enforcement, the repressive role will self-evidently be regarded as key. The principle of effectiveness will then come more to the forefront. There is consequently a close relationship between the functions and roles on the one hand, and the principles to be considered on the other hand.

[25] WRR Report no. 89-2013 'Supervising Public Interests. Towards a Broader Perspective on Government Supervision' <http://www.wrr.nl/fileadmin/en/publicaties/PDF-samenvattingen/Supervising_public_interests.pdf> accessed 17 March 2014.

[26] ibid.

Types of Agencies

Agencies, discussed in this book, generally fall into one of three categories:

1. market authorities, also called sector or market regulators (i.e. those with a mandate pertaining to a specific sector);
2. competition authorities (i.e. established to enforce national competition laws covering all sectors of the economy); and
3. consumer protection agencies (i.e. established to enforce national consumer protection law).

These three types of agencies share common objectives, all in order to protect and enhance social and economic welfare:[27] they promote well-functioning markets, ensure well-organized and transparent market processes, and guarantee fair treatment of consumers. Market authorities, competition authorities, and consumer protection agencies tend to play a complementary role; it is no coincidence, therefore, that they have been extensively relied upon in liberalized industries.

Despite sharing common objectives, the three agency types—market authorities, competition authorities, and consumer protection agencies—have in most jurisdictions developed as separate fields of law and policy within their particular institutional framework and enforcement mechanism.[28] They have different legal mandates, while their perspectives on competition may also differ as each of them approaches the issue from a different angle.

Market authorities

The market regulator oversees one or a limited number of specific economic sectors, mostly in previously monopolistic markets, such as the energy, telecommunications, transport, or financial sectors. Market agencies co-exist alongside each other and provide specialized regulation for sectors that require in-depth knowledge of their domain. A typical feature of such agencies (which the EU liberalization directives refer to as 'National Regulatory Authorities', or 'NRAs') is that they have the power to regulate the behaviour of market parties *ex ante*, a power that other agencies usually do not have.

[27] K J Cseres, 'The Controversies of the Consumer Welfare Standard' (2007) 3(2) Competition Law Review 121.

[28] K J Cseres, 'Integrate or Separate—Institutional Design for the Enforcement of Competition Law and Consumer Law' (n19) 12.

Random examples of market regulators include the UK communications regulator (Ofcom) and the UK energy regulator (Ofgem), the Australian Energy Regulator (AER), the French rail regulator *Autorité de Régulation des Activités Ferroviaires* (ARAF), and the Federal Communications Commission (FCC), Postal Regulatory Commission (PRC), and Federal Energy Regulatory Commission (FERC) in the United States. Germany in turn has BNetzA, the Federal Network Agency for Electricity, Gas, Telecommunications, Post and Railway.[29]

Within this category of market regulators, a further distinction can be made between economic regulators set up to promote and protect competition (NRAs) and financial supervisory authorities.[30] Although the latter are also involved in overseeing and regulating enterprises, they can be distinguished from other economic regulators in that their main task is not to create competition in previously monopolistic markets. Instead, they have to ensure the stability, and focus on the transparency, of the financial markets and protect consumers against unfair competition by, for example, enforcing financial regulations.

The overall task of market authorities is to oversee and regulate the relevant markets in order to encourage and promote competition.[31] To this end, they must be entrusted with various powers to regulate certain matters, including tariffs and access rights, as well as the power to settle disputes. Extensive *ex ante* regulatory powers are considered necessary to ensure what is referred to as the introduction and promotion of 'controlled competition' in markets where national monopolists—also referred to as incumbents—traditionally enjoyed exclusive rights and privileges to supply goods and services, and to operate energy and communications networks.[32] Even now that these formal rights have long been abolished, many incumbents continue to enjoy significant market power, not least because they own essential infrastructure that cannot easily be duplicated. To ensure competition, market regulators must devise specific regulatory solutions and take action to promote consumer interests in the market so that consumers can enjoy the benefits of affordable tariffs and high-quality essential services.[33]

[29] In German: *Bundesnetzagentur für Elektrizität, Gas, Telekommunikation, Post und Eisenbahnen.*

[30] S A C M Lavrijssen and A T Ottow, 'Independent Supervisory Authorities: A Fragile Concept' (2012) 39(4) Legal Issues of Economic Integration 419, 423.

[31] A T Ottow, 'Europeanization of the Supervision of Competitive Markets' (n20) 192.

[32] A T Ottow, 'Europeanization of the Supervision of Competitive Markets' (n20) 192; S A C M Lavrijssen and A T Ottow, 'The Legality of Independent Regulatory Authorities' in L Besselink, F Pennings, and S Prechal, *The Eclipse of Legality in Europe* (Deventer: Kluwer International 2010) 73–96.

[33] A T Ottow, 'Europeanization of the Supervision of Competitive Markets' (n20) 192.

Market agencies have specific tasks in regulated industries. When it comes to their competitive positions, providers (both new and incumbent) in these industries are usually dependent on a small number of established parties (which often used to be the only providers). These established parties control the infrastructure (for example, telecommunications networks, grids, transmission towers, rail networks, or entire airports), which cannot be duplicated (partially or fully) because of the high costs involved. The regulator may set prices and conditions for access to certain infrastructure, so as to allow competitors to offer services themselves. In addition, the regulator also protects public interests relating to the affordability, quality, and availability of certain products and services on the basis of the regulations specifically covering transport, telecommunication, energy, and postal services. Examples of these include consumers' rights to be connected to the power and natural gas networks, and to have basic access to telephony services.[34] By fulfilling these tasks, regulators ensure that consumers have a choice in such markets.[35]

According to Geradin, one advantage of regulation is that it tends to provide some degree of certainty for market actors. Access to the network regime, for example, guarantees potential market players that they will be able to access the incumbent's network if they decide to penetrate the market. A disadvantage, however, is that regulatory regimes may be excessively rigid and thus impede innovation. Such regimes may also contain gaps, which tend to appear only once legislation has been adopted and is being implemented.[36]

Competition authorities

The second category of agencies comprises competition authorities. Competition agencies are entrusted with the general competition task of ensuring compliance with national (and EU) competition rules. National competition agencies have a regulatory mandate over competition issues covering all sectors of the economy. Random examples of such competition agencies include the French *Autorité de la Concurrence*, the Federal Trade Commission (FTC)

[34] Netherlands Authority for Consumers & Markets, 'Strategy Document', 7 <https://www.acm.nl/en/publications/publication/11993/Strategy-Netherlands-Authority-for-Consumers-and-Markets/> accessed 25 November 2013

[35] Netherlands Authority for Consumers & Markets, 'Strategy Document', 5 <https://www.acm.nl/en/publications/publication/11993/Strategy-Netherlands-Authority-for-Consumers-and-Markets/> accessed 25 November 2013

[36] D Geradin, 'Enhancing Competition in the Postal Sector; Can We Do Away With Sector-Specific Regulation' (n17) 3.

of the United States, and the UK Competition & Markets Authority (CMA), which became operational on 1 April 2014.

Competition agencies seek to protect the process of competition, rather than the participants in the market. Competition law focuses mainly on market failure caused by collusive or exclusionary practices.[37] In order to enhance the competitive structure of markets, competition law prohibits anticompetitive behaviour, such as price-fixing or abuse of a dominant position. As competition rules tend to apply *ex post*, competition authorities play a role only after anticompetitive action has occurred. The exception to this is the control over mergers and acquisitions, where the focus tends to be *ex ante*. Competition rules typically apply to all economic sectors as they seek to prevent certain general types of behaviour that can occur in any sector of the economy.[38]

Since they have a more general character, competition rules cannot provide the same degree of certainty as sector-specific rules. Competition law proceedings tend to be complex and to take a lot of time to complete, while their outcomes tend to be uncertain. Furthermore, since competition law applies *ex post*, the damage is often already done. On the other hand, competition rules are very flexible and can apply to a wide range of situations that the legislator could not necessarily have anticipated.[39] They also allow the deterring or challenging of various anticompetitive practices that cannot be addressed by *ex ante* regulations.[40]

Consumer protection agencies

The third agency type consists of consumer protection agencies. Their main task is to enforce national (and EU) consumer protection law and they have a duty to protect consumers' interests. Random examples of these consumer protection agencies are the Federal Attorney's Office for Consumers (Profeco)[41] of Mexico, the Swedish consumer agency *Konsumentverket*, the Hungarian Authority for Consumer Protection, and the Nigerian Consumer Protection Council (CPC).

[37] K J Cseres, 'Integrate or Separate—Institutional Design for the Enforcement of Competition Law and Consumer Law' (n19) 13–14.

[38] D Geradin, 'Enhancing Competition in the Postal Sector; Can We Do Away With Sector-Specific Regulation' (n17) 3.

[39] ibid 3.

[40] See for a discussion on *ex ante* and *ex post* for example: A Porat, 'Ex-Post Right, Ex-Ante Wrong' (2014) 89(3) Notre Dame Law Review 1209; S Hwang and S Satchell, 'Tracking Error: Ex-Ante versus Ex-Post Measures' (2001) Financial Econometrics Centre Working Papers Series WP01-15.

[41] In Spanish: *Procuraduría Federal del Consumidor*.

Consumer protection law denotes a body of law designed to protect consumers' interests at the level of individual transactions[42] and covers a broad and diffuse field. Unfair and deceptive advertising is prohibited, as are acts of outright fraud.[43] Consumer protection laws impose certain obligations on providers. These obligations are aimed at countering unfair commercial practices, and stipulate, for example, that information be provided clearly, applicable contractual terms be communicated unequivocably, sales methods be fair and transparent, and products and services offered be of good quality.[44]

Consumer problems of a serious nature may arise even in competitive markets.[45] Due to information failures, consumers are sometimes unable to take advantage of benefits made possible by effective competition. Consumers may have insufficient information about the choices they can make, or may face high search and switching costs, and consequently conclude bad deals or become disconnected from certain markets. Consumers are unable to activate competition in such situations, and this ultimately retards competition.[46]

Different Combinations of Agencies

Independent agencies can be designed in various ways, especially with regard to the scope of the responsibilities delegated to them (i.e. the 'agency scope'). It is possible, for example, for one country to have a single-purpose agency for competition, a single-purpose agency for consumer protection, and multiple single-sector regulators. On the other hand, it is also possible to have a single multifunctional agency responsible for competition, consumer protection, and multisector regulation. This means that the distinction made above is not always entirely clear-cut.

Many countries are in the process of restructuring their competition and market authorities.[47] Although several single-purpose agencies still

[42] M Huffman, 'Bridging the Divide Theories for Integrating Competition Law and Consumer Protection' (2010) 6(1) European Competition Journal 7.

[43] S Weber Waller, 'In Search of Economic Justice; Considering Competition and Consumer Protection Law' (2005) 36 Loyola University Chicago Law Journal 3.

[44] Netherlands Authority for Consumers & Markets, 'Strategy Document', 5 <https://www.acm.nl/en/publications/publication/11993/Strategy-Netherlands-Authority-for-Consumers-and-Markets/> accessed 25 November 2013.

[45] K J Cseres, 'Competition and Consumer Policies; Starting Points for Better Convergence' (2009) Amsterdam Center for Law & Economics Working Paper No. 2009-06, 1–2.

[46] K J Cseres, 'The Impact of Consumer Protection on Competition and Competition Law; The Case of Deregulated Markets' (2006) Amsterdam Center for Law & Economics Working Paper No. 2006-05.

[47] E M Fox and M J Trebilcock (eds), *The Design of Competition Law Institutions. Global Norms, Local Choices* (Oxford: Oxford University Press 2013). See also the World Competition Database

exist, the trend is towards creating multitask agencies that combine various functions.[48] In the UK, for example, the Office of Fair Trading (OFT) and the Competition Commission (CC) merged into the Competition & Markets Authority (CMA) on 1 January 2014,[49] while six industry-based regulators in Spain merged with the Spanish National Competition Commission in October 2013, to form the new National Commission for Markets and Competition (CNMC).[50] In Finland, meanwhile, the Competition Authority and the Consumer Agency merged to form a single agency (KKV) on 1 January 2013,[51] while the Danish Competition Authority and the Consumer Agency merged in August 2010 to create the Danish Competition and Consumer Authority (KFST).[52] Based on these examples and the types of agencies already identified, we can logically distinguish four different types of multiple agencies (for more examples, see table 2.1 in annex 3).

Multisector regulators

Germany: BNetzA (*Bundesnetzagentur für Elektrizität, Gas, Telekommunikation, Post und Eisenbahnen*), which regulates the electricity, gas, telecommunications, post, and railway markets;

Luxembourg: ILR (*Institut Luxembourgeois de Régulation*), which regulates the electricity, gas, telecommunications, post, and transport markets.

Competition and consumer protection agencies

Denmark: KFST (*Konkurrence- og Forbrugerstyrelsen*);

France: DGCCRF (*Direction Générale de la Concurrence, de la Consommation et de la Répression des Fraudes*);

of the Competition Law Center of George Washington University <http://www.gwclc.com/World-competition-database.html> accessed 27 September 2013.

48 A T Ottow, 'Erosion or Innovation?: The Institutional Design of Competition Agencies—A Dutch Case Study' (2014) 2(1) Journal of Antitrust Enforcement 25.

49 Enterprise and Regulatory Reform Act 2013, which received Royal Assent on 25 April 2013.

50 *Ley 3/2013, de 4 de junio, de creación de la Comisión Nacional de los Mercados y la Competencia* (Act 3/2013 on the creation of the National Commission on Markets and Competition), BOE-A-2013-5940, available in Spanish at <https://www.boe.es/boe/dias/2013/06/05/pdfs/BOE-A-2013-5940.pdf> accessed 25 September 2013.

51 HE 108/2012, Finnish Government Bill proposing Competition and Consumer Protection Office, as well as certain related Acts, published 17 September 2012, available in Finnish and Swedish at <http://www.finlex.fi/fi/esitykset/he/2012/?_offset=80> accessed 25 September 2013.

52 OECD, 'Annual Report on Competition Policy Developments in Denmark' (2012) DAF/COMP/AR3. See also 'Denmark: The Danish Competition Authority and the Danish Consumer Agency have Merged' (2010) 4 ECN Brief <http://ec.europa.eu/competition/ecn/brief/04_2010/dk_merger.pdf> accessed 27 September 2013.

Finland: KKV (*Kilpailu- ja kuluttajavirasto/Konkurrens- och konsument-verket*);
UK: CMA (Competition & Markets Authority);
USA: FTC (Federal Trade Commission).

Combinations of competition authorities and multisector regulators

Netherlands: the former NMa (*Nederlandse Mededingingsautoriteit*), which regulated the energy and transport markets;
Spain: the new CNMC (*Comisión Nacional de los Mercados y la Competencia*), which regulates the energy, telecommunications, post, audiovisual, and railway markets.

Combinations of competition authorities, consumer protection agencies, and multisector regulators

Netherlands: ACM (*Autoriteit Consument & Markt*), which regulates the energy, transport, postal services, and telecommunications markets;
Australia: ACCC (Australian Competition and Consumer Commission), which regulates the telecommunications, water, and postal markets.

International Context: Europeanization and Global Networks

The EU system for overseeing sectors, as laid down in regulations and directives, is based on the principle that execution of this EU legislation is primarily the responsibility of independent, national agencies.

These national agencies are entrusted with general competition tasks and, alongside ensuring compliance with national competition rules, also have the power to enforce European competition rules in all markets. The national consumer protection agencies have as their main task the duty to protect specific groups of consumers, while also being obliged to assist in the event of a cross-border infringement of the EU rules on protecting consumer interests. These national agencies play a key role in applying EU rules.

National implementation practices are to a large degree 'coloured' by the specific features of the various national systems and the enforcement practices of the national agencies. It is not only the powers assigned to the national agencies, but also the applicable rules on decision-making, the powers of enforcement, and the supervisory practices that have a critical influence on how they perform the tasks entrusted to them. National independent agencies have to ensure that the decisions they take as the parties responsible for overseeing the national markets result in correct application of EU legislation. Although there are certain similarities between national practices, there are also some major differences (some examples of these are given in chapter 5 on enforcement) which lead to disparities in the way the applicable EU rules are implemented. In the absence of minimum or maximum harmonization standards,[53] these disparities can result in a downwards spiral and distort competition in the internal market. From this perspective, the reliance on correct national implementation can be seen as a major shortcoming in the European Union's legislative system.[54]

The European legislator and the European Commission have introduced some innovative institutional tools aimed at harmonizing oversight and enforcement practices at a national level and EU regulations and directives now use various methods to shape Europe's influence on market supervision at member state level.[55] These methods can be categorized on a scale ranging from 'light' to 'heavy', depending on whether they involve little influence from Brussels (i.e. decentralization) or a high degree of influence (i.e. centralization).[56] The methods use instruments such as the jurisdiction rules applying between national competition authorities and the European Commission on the basis of Regulation 1/2003,[57] the obligation for national telecommunications regulators to submit draft decisions to the European Commission on the basis of Article 7 of the Framework Directive,[58] and the exclusive powers of the European Securities and Markets Authority (ESMA) to oversee credit rating agencies (thus setting aside the national financial authorities).[59]

[53] On the harmonization of financial regulation, see, for example: G Hertig, 'Regulatory Competition for EU Financial Services' (2000) 3(2) Journal of International Economic Law 349 <http://ssrn.com/abstract=228445> accessed 15 April 2014.

[54] R Baldwin and Martin Cave, *Understanding Regulation* (Oxford: Oxford University Press 1999) 159.

[55] The part of this section on European bodies and agencies is based on and partly taken from: A T Ottow, 'Europeanization of the Supervision of Competitive Markets' (n20).

[56] See for a complete overview of these instruments: A T Ottow, 'Europeanization of the Supervision of Competitive Markets' (n20).

[57] Council Regulation (EC) No 1/2003 of 16 December 2002 on the implementation of the rules on competition laid down in Articles 81 and 82 of the Treaty [2003] OJ 2002 L 001/1.

[58] Directive 2002/21/EC of the European Parliament and of the Council of 7 March 2002 on a common regulatory framework for electronic communications networks and services ('Framework Directive') [2010] <http://eur-lex.europa.eu/legal-content/EN/TXT/?qid=1411514708317&uri=URISERV:l24216a> accessed 23 September 2014.

[59] See for this exclusive task the website of ESMA <http://www.esma.europa.eu/page/Credit-Rating-Agencies> accessed 23 September 2014.

There is clearly a tension between the establishment of central control on the one hand and respect for the autonomy of the member states on the other. In the various liberalization directives the European legislator has consistently sought to find a middle way between these two extremes. The solutions opted for vary from sector to sector and have been arrived at within differing political contexts and differing market conditions. Indeed a whole range of hybrid forms has arisen, involving responsibilities being shared to varying degrees between the European Commission, the new European regulatory bodies, and the national independent agencies. This phenomenon, which Jans et al. refer to as a 'mixed administration',[60] results in a complex mix of European and national decision-making and enforcement procedures in the various fields of economic supervision. This book refers to it as 'Europeanization'; in other words, the process by which Europe achieves greater influence on the set-up and structure of oversight.[61]

This process of Europeanization can be perceived from a multilayer perspective, with three levels distinguished in the financial, energy, and telecommunications sectors and for the general regulatory agencies responsible for competition and consumer protection law: the national agencies operate at the first level, while the supranational networks that national independent agencies have formed constitute the second level, and the European bodies and authorities are at the third level.[62]

Level 1: National independent agencies

First of all, Europe's influence on economic supervision takes place at the national level, with EU norms having to be transposed into national legislation. Norms have to be interpreted in the light of the objectives of EU law and to comply with EU rules and regulations. This European influence at the national level applies not only to substantive law (i.e. legal norms), but also

[60] J H Jans, R de Lange, S Prechal, and R J G M Widdershoven, *Europeanisation of Public Law* (Groningen: Europa Law Publishing 2007) 53.

[61] The concept of Europeanization has been used on many occasions to indicate the influence of European law on national law. See, for example, J H Jans, R de Lange, S Prechal, and R J G M Widdershoven (n60); and J A E Vervaele (ed), *Compliance and Enforcement of European Community Law* (The Hague: Kluwer Law International 1999).

[62] Thatcher and Coen analyse this process from a European institutional perspective, seeing it as an evolutionary European design: M Thatcher and D Coen, 'Reshaping European Regulatory Space: An Evolutionary Analysis' (2008) 31(4) West European Politics 806. For a governance perspective, see C F Sabel and J Zeitlin, 'Learning from Difference: The New Architecture of Experimentalist Governance in the European Union' in CF Sabel and J Zeitlin (eds), *Experimentalist Governance in the European Union: Towards a New Architecture* (Oxford: Oxford University Press 2010) 1–28.

to the institutional structures of the national agencies. Although the principle of autonomy—EU member states carry out EU law through their own national law and national procedural rules[63]—is still the guiding principle and EU law respects member states' institutional and procedural structures, secondary European legislation and European Court of Justice (ECJ) case law have over the years imposed some considerable requirements on agencies' institutional design and enforcement practices. These requirements have had a substantial influence on and even restricted member states' national autonomy.[64]

Level 2: Networks of national agencies

The second level of Europeanization comprises the European networks of national agencies. Over the years, national agencies have established various forms of cooperation in sectors subject to economic supervision. This has mainly taken the form of networks, in which the national agencies participate and exchange information and experience. An evolutionary process has taken place, with the networks starting out as a rather informal form of cooperation, but developing over the years into more institutionalized structures, in which the national members actively participate. As a result, these networks have been transformed into institutions organized on an increasingly European scale.

An example of such a network is the European Competition Network (ECN), which comprises the competition authorities of the member states and the European Commission itself.[65] This network was established, following adoption of Regulation 1/2003, to assign responsibility for ensuring efficient application of Articles 101 and 102 of the Treaty on the Functioning of the European Union (TFEU) between the national competition authorities themselves, and between the national competition authorities and

[63] See S Prechal, *Directives in EC Law* (Oxford: EC Law Library 2005) 137–45 and 172–79 and A T Ottow, *Telecommunicatietoezicht. De invloed van het Europese en Nederlandse bestuurs(proces) recht* (dissertation, University of Amsterdam, The Hague: SDU 2006) 67–71.

[64] For the European influence on the Dutch legality principle in the context of the European autonomy principle, see S A C M Lavrijssen and A T Ottow (n32). For the consequences of the energy directives for the position of national regulators, see Commission Staff Working Paper, Interpretative note on Directive 2009/72/EC concerning common rules for the internal market in electricity and Directive 2009/73/EC concerning common rules for the internal market in natural gas, The regulatory authorities, Brussels, 22 January 2010.

[65] For a discussion of the network (also compared to the communications network), see M de Visser, *Network-based Governance in EC Law. The Example of EC Competition and EC Communications Law* (Oxford: Hart Publishing Ltd 2009).

the European Commission.[66] The cooperation within the network is also designed to ensure that EU competition rules are applied effectively and uniformly. Various powers are available to assist national competition authorities to achieve these aims. The agencies are required, for example, to inform each other of formal investigative measures,[67] while proceedings may be suspended or rejected if another competition authority is already dealing with the case.[68] Member states' competition authorities are also authorized to exchange information, whether such information is a matter of fact or of law, and including confidential information, and are also authorized to use such information as evidence.[69] In addition, national competition authorities can request each other to conduct certain inspections.[70] Although the ECN was originally set up for notification purposes, it has since evolved into a form of structural cooperation, where details of EU competition law, and indirectly also national competition law, are discussed and aligned.[71]

Another example can be found in the field of consumer protection, where Regulation 2006/2004[72] provides various mechanisms for cooperation and coordination between national consumer protection agencies. The regulation requires national agencies to grant each other mutual assistance in the event of an actual or potential cross-border infringement of the EU rules designed to protect consumer interests. In order to channel this mutual assistance properly, the regulation also establishes a network of national independent agencies. A secure IT tool—the Consumer Protection Cooperation System (CPCS)—has been created within this network to facilitate the exchange of information. The network members also exchange views on interpreting

[66] Commission Notice on cooperation within the Network of Competition Authorities, C 101, OJ 2004/43, and the Joint statement of the Council and the Commission on the functioning of the network of competition authorities, available at <http://ec.europa.eu/competition/ecn/joint_statement_en.pdf> accessed 23 September 2014 (document no. 15435/02 ADD 1). For further reading on ECN, see: R Smits, 'The European Competition Network: Selected Aspects' in *Legal Issues of Economic Integration* 32(2) (2005) 175, 184–88; and Y Svetiev, 'Networked Competition Governance in the EU: Delegation, Decentralization or Experimentalist Architecture?' in Sabel and Zeitlin (n62) 79–120.

[67] Article 11, paragraph 3, Regulation 1/2003 (n57).

[68] Article 13 Regulation 1/2003 (n57). For the procedures for allocating powers between the national competition authorities and the Commission, see section 2.1.3 of A T Ottow, 'Erosion or Innovation?: The Institutional Design of Competition Agencies—A Dutch Case Study' (n48).

[69] Article 12 Regulation 1/2003 (n57).

[70] Article 22 Regulation 1/2003 (n57).

[71] See for the evaluation by the Commission of the ECN: *Communication from the Commission to the European parliament and the Council. Ten years of Antitrust Enforcement under regulation 1/2003: achievements and future perspectives* (2014) 453 COM <http://ec.europa.eu/competition/antitrust/legislation/antitrust_enforcement_10_years_en.pdf> accessed 23 September 2014.

[72] Regulation (EC) No 2006/2004 of the European Parliament and of the Council of 27 October 2004 on cooperation between national authorities responsible for the enforcement of consumer protection laws, [2004] OJ L 364/1.

relevant legislation. However, the network needs to develop its activities further and to increase its profile.[73]

The year 2010 was a year of major Europeanization in the market supervision landscape of the European Union. Many existing European networks were replaced by new European bodies that took over the tasks and functions of the networks, as in the case of the communications, energy, and financial sectors (see table 2.2 in annex 3 for the situation as at 1 January 2011). Many existing networks were consequently abandoned, and this resulted in a significant shift towards level 3.

Level 3: European bodies and authorities

From 2010, the European Commission started to believe there was a need for regulatory agencies at a EU level, given the continuing existence of too many inconsistencies in national implementing practices, and that further coordination was necessary. At the time of writing, new EU regulatory authorities were being put in place in the communications market, the energy sector, and the financial sector. How can this acceleration in the establishment of new European bodies and authorities since 2009 be explained? In previous years the European Commission had been pushing for greater harmonization, in parallel with fine-tuning of the energy and communications legislative frameworks. In addition, various new EU agencies were created in response to crises,[74] including the new European financial bodies set up following the 2008 financial crisis. The concurrence of these factors consequently brought about a major change in the European landscape of market supervision. These new institutions are analysed in this section.

Communications regulator: BEREC

At the time of the telecommunications market being liberalized, the European Commission's ambition had been to set up an EU regulator for centralized supervision of the market. This ambition, however, came up against strong opposition from the Council and the member states, and this ultimately led to the Commission abandoning its ambition.[75] After years of the national regulators working together within the European Regulators

[73] See Commission Report on ECN (n71) 8.

[74] D Curtin, 'Delegation to EU Non-Majoritarian Agencies and Emerging Practices of Public Accountability' in D Geradin et al, *Regulation Through Agencies in the EU. A New Paradigm of European Governance* (Cheltenham, UK: Edward Elgar 2005) 88–119.

[75] For a discussion of this process, see P Larouche, *Competition Law and Regulation in European Telecommunications* (Oxford: Hart Publishing Ltd 2000) 415–23.

Group (ERG), ERG has since been converted into the Body of European Regulators for Electronic Communications (BEREC)[76] so as to achieve greater Europeanization of oversight in this market. BEREC has been set up to advise the European Commission on and help promote development of the communications market, as well as to serve as an interface between national regulators and the Commission.

BEREC's aim is to ensure consistent application of the EU telecommunications regulatory framework by promoting cooperation between national regulators, and between national regulators and the European Commission.[77] The communications directives contain various procedures for BEREC to deliver opinions to national regulators and the European Commission.[78] BEREC's tasks in the communications sector are solely of an advisory nature, and the agency has no authorization to issue binding decisions. The advice it gives, however, is not wholly without obligation as the European Commission 'shall take the utmost account' of any advice, recommendation, and guidelines.[79]

Energy regulator: ACER

The Agency for the Cooperation of Energy Regulators (ACER) has been set up to help national energy regulators perform their regulatory tasks and to coordinate their action at EU level.[80] These were previously the objectives of the European Regulators Group for Electricity and Gas (ERGEG), which was an independent advisory body set up to structure advice, coordination, and cooperation between national energy regulators, and between those regulators and the European Commission.[81] As a result, however, of the increasing internationalization of the energy markets, the member states and national regulators perceived a need for more structured EU cooperation. It was widely recognized within the sector that the original form of cooperation between regulators should be replaced by an EU structure with clear powers.[82] This difference in approach in the energy and communications markets is

[76] Regulation (EC) No 1211/2009 of the European Parliament and of the Council of 25 November 2009 establishing the Body of European Regulators for Electronic Communications (BEREC) and the Office [2009] OJ L 337/1.

[77] Preamble to Regulation 1211/2009 (n76) paragraph 8.

[78] Article 3, paragraph 1, Regulation 1211/2009 (n76).

[79] Article 3, paragraph 3, Regulation 1211/2009 (n76).

[80] Regulation (EC) No 713/2009 of the European Parliament and of the Council of 13 July 2009 establishing an Agency for the Cooperation of Energy Regulators [2009] OJ L 211/1. ACER's objective is described in Article 1 of the Regulation.

[81] Commission Decision 2003/796/EC of 11 November 2003 on establishing the European Regulators Group for Electricity and Gas [2003] OJ L 296/34. In addition, there is the informal Council of European Energy Regulators (CEER), which had strong links with the ERGEG.

[82] Preamble to Regulation 713/2009 (n80) paragraph 3.

attributable to differences between these markets, with the energy market having a greater need for closer cooperation at EU level.

ACER issues opinions and recommendations to transmission system operators, regulators, and the European Parliament, the Council, and the Commission.[83] It can also issue binding decisions on certain technical issues[84] and issues in which the competent national agencies have been unable to reach agreement,[85] as well as on cross-border infrastructure[86] and certain exemptions and derogations.[87] ACER consequently has considerably more powers than BEREC.

Financial authorities: EBA, ESMA, and EIOPA

According to the European Commission, the 2008 financial crisis demonstrated serious failings in cooperation, coordination, consistency, and trust between national supervisory authorities. The Commission therefore asked Jacques de Larosière to write a report on the scope for regulatory and supervisory reform in the EU. It responded to De Larosière's report by taking the steps in its Communication of 27 May 2009[88] that were needed to amend European financial supervision. The European Council President and the European Parliament reached provisional agreement on these proposals on 2 September 2010,[89] and consequently created a new supervisory framework, the European System of Financial Supervision (ESFS), to remedy these failings. It was decided not to set up a centralized European regulator, but instead to continue having financial supervision performed by national regulators at a national level, overseen by European Supervisory Authorities (ESAs).[90] The three ESAs are the European Banking Authority (EBA), the European Insurance and Occupational Pensions Authority (EIOPA), and the European Securities and Markets Authority (ESMA) These three new European authorities are operational as from 1 January 2011, all three having the power to issue certain binding decisions.[91] The difference compared with the institutional

[83] Article 4 Regulation 713/2009 (n80). [84] ibid Article 7. [85] ibid Article 8.

[86] ibid Article 7, paragraph 7. [87] ibid Article 9.

[88] Communication from the Commission, European financial supervision, Brussels, 27 May 2009, COM(2009) 252. For a discussion of these new regulations, see for example E Ferran, 'Understanding the New Institutional Architecture of EU Financial Market Supervision' in G Ferrarini, K J Hopt, and E Wymeersch (eds) *Rethinking Financial Regulation and Supervision in Times of Crisis* (Oxford: Oxford University Press 2012).

[89] Brussels, 6 September 2010, 13179/10, EF 92, ECOFIN 499, SURE 39, CODEC 772.

[90] For a discussion of the system, see N Moloney, 'EU Financial Market Regulation after the Global Financial Crisis: "More Europe" or More Risks?' (2010) 47 Common Market Law Review 1317 and E Ferran (n88).

[91] See for an overview of their powers: A T Ottow, 'The New European Supervisory Architecture of the Financial Markets' in M Everson, C Monda, and E Vos (eds), *EU Agencies in and the External*

structure operating before 2011 is that the European networks (the 'level 3 committees') have been converted into European Supervisory Authorities.

Alongside the ESAs, it was also decided to establish the European Systemic Risk Board (ESRB) to oversee macroprudential supervision within the European Union. Instead of being assigned binding powers, this Board can only issue warnings and recommendations.

Monetary policy and prudential supervision: European Central Bank

The European Central Bank (ECB), which was created on 1 June 1998 and gained official status as an EU institution on 1 December 2009 when the Treaty of Lisbon[92] entered into force, is the central bank for the euro, and is responsible for defining and implementing monetary policy in order to maintain price stability within the euro zone.[93]

It became increasingly evident during the financial and monetary crisis of 2008-14 that further restructuring of the banking sector at a European level was necessary. More steps needed to be taken to achieve integrated management of the banking crisis and control at a European level.[94] It was consequently decided to create a single European supervisory system in the form of a Single Supervisory Mechanism (SSM) for the European banking sector, with responsibility for direct and central supervisory control of all banks in the euro zone being assigned to the ECB, which means the ECB effectively has taken over almost all supervisory tasks of the national agencies.[95] As the ECB also is fully responsible for prudential supervision of credit institutions (banking supervision)[96] as from November 2014, the primary responsibility

Relations of the EU (The Hague: Wolters Kluwer Law & Business 2014) 123–43; and M Andenas and I H-Y Chiu, *The Foundations and Future of Financial Regulation: Governance for Responsibility* (London and New York: Routledge 2013) 48–50.

[92] Treaty of Lisbon Volume 50 2007/C 306/01 <http://eur-lex.europa.eu/legal-content/EN/TXT/HTML/?uri=OJ:C:2007:306:FULL&from=EN> accessed 22 September

[93] Article 127(1) of the Treaty on the Functioning of the European Union, see: Consolidated versions of the Treaty on European Union and the Treaty on the Functioning of the European Union—Consolidated version of the Treaty on the Functioning of the European Union—Protocols—Annexes—Declarations annexed to the Final Act of the Intergovernmental Conference which adopted the Treaty of Lisbon, signed on 13 December 2007—Tables of equivalences [2012] OJ C 326/1.

[94] Report by the presidents for the European Council, the Commission, the Eurogroup and the ECB of 26 June 2012 <www.consilium.europa.eu/uedocs/cms_data/docs/pressdata/en/ec/131359.pdf> accessed 23 September 2014.

[95] For further details on the scope of the powers of the ECB and the banks involvend, see: M Andenas and I H-Y Chiu (n91).

[96] Council Regulation (EU) No 1024/2013 of 15 October 2013 conferring specific tasks on the European Central Bank concerning policies relating to the prudential supervision of credit institutions [2013] OJ L 287/63.

for overseeing a significant part of the banking activities in the euro zone is now in the hands of the ECB. Although the national banking authorities remain actively involved in day-to-day practice, a real transfer of powers from the national to the EU level has taken place. This represents a fundamental change in the way the member states supervise the banking sector, as well as the best example of centralization of the supervisory system.

International context

Although less well-developed than their European counterparts, some more internationally oriented networks exist in some areas. The most important international network for the purposes of this book is the International Competition Network (ICN), to which around 117 national competition authorities from 103 jurisdictions belong.[97] This network was founded in 2001 by 15 competition authorities and has since grown steadily. It was created with the aim of addressing the antitrust enforcement and policy issues of common interest and of formulating proposals for procedural and substantive convergence through a results-oriented agenda and structure.[98] The ICN members have worked together to develop a series of best practices, manuals, reports, and templates that are used around the world.[99]

Another internationally oriented network worth mentioning operates in the field of consumer protection. The International Consumer Protection and Enforcement Network (ICPEN) encourages global cooperation among law enforcement agencies and shares information on cross-border commercial activities that may affect consumer welfare.[100]

Conclusion

Supervisory bodies in the form of market regulators, competition authorities, and consumer protection agencies exist in many different forms and combinations within a national, European Union, and international context. Although the national context in which they operate differs, they have certain characteristics in common and generally have similar roles, functions,

[97] <www.internationalcompetitionnetwork.org> accessed 1 May 2014.

[98] The ICN's Vision for its second decade, presented at the 10th annual conference of the ICN, The Hague, 17–20 May 2011.

[99] See on the work of ICN: P Lugard (ed), *The International Competition Network at Ten. Origins, Accomplishments and Aspirations* (Antwerpen: Intersentia 2011).

[100] <www.icpen.org> accessed 23 September 2014.

and tasks. Their primary task is to apply and enforce substantive laws on sector regulation, competition, and consumer law. The dilemmas they face, their regulatory space, and their enforcement toolkit are also comparable. These agencies consequently can be seen as belonging to the same family, and this makes them an interesting example for study and for learning from each other's choices, experiences, and problems. The focus of study in this book revolves around the good agency or LITER principles identified in the following chapter.

3

Good Agency Principles

Introduction

Although the focus in the period 1990-2000 was mainly on substantive rules and means to make regulat*ion* better,[1] since the global financial crisis started in 2007 it has become evident that making regulat*ors* work better has a major impact on the effectiveness of these substantive rules. The quality and performance of independent agencies' architecture and supervisory and regulatory practices are particularly important in this respect. In many areas, therefore, principles of good regulat*ion* have been translated into principles of good regulat*ors*.

Take the situation in the United Kingdom, for example. In 2000 the Cabinet Office's Better Regulation Task Force issued its famous *Principles of Good Regulation*.[2] Although this report did not deal directly with competition and market authorities, it had a significant impact on the development of regulation and regulators, while also forming the basis for a further analysis of independent agencies' practices. The report lays down five principles of good regulation: transparency, accountability, proportionality, consistency, and targeting. It was followed in 2003 by the Better Regulation Task Force's *Independent regulators* report,[3] which concentrated on issues relating to competition and market authorities, including independence, accountability, better regulation tools, governance, enforcement, and appeal mechanisms.[4] This second report stated that all independent agencies should adhere to principles of good regulation. The third report, *Regulation—Less is*

[1] See, for example, the OECD Guiding principles for regulatory quality and performance (2005) drawing on the 1995 OECD Recommendation on improving the quality of government regulation.

[2] Better Regulation Task Force, *Principles of Good Regulation* (2000) UK Cabinet Office, London.

[3] Better Regulation Task Force, *Independent Regulators* (2003) UK Cabinet Office, London.

[4] T Prosser, *The Regulatory Enterprise: Government, Regulation and Legitimacy* (Oxford: Oxford University Press 2010) 210–14.

More: Reducing Burdens, Improving Outcomes,[5] which was published in 2005, focused on reducing costs and used a cost model to assess the administrative costs of regulation. This report, too, had an impact on competition and market authorities as it presented them with a series of impact assessment criteria and challenged them to reduce administrative burdens. In brief, whereas earlier studies focused on regulat*ions*, the primary focus more recently has been on developing principles for the regulat*ors* so as to ensure that rules are implemented effectively.

This chapter puts these agency principles centre stage. Firstly, it identifies the sources for such agency principles and then goes on to analyse the individual principles identified. It discusses which principles should be at the heart of the roles, functions, and tasks of competition and market authorities, and what such principles should entail.

The hypothesis of this book is that principles of good agency behaviour enable substantive rules to be applied appropriately; in other words, they govern the proper application of substantive rules. To have such effect, the principles have to be embedded in the agency's design and philosophy and subsequently in concrete actions relating both to internal and external organizational and procedural elements, such as the appointment of the agency's board members, the consultation procedures put in place, and the styles of enforcing the rules and intervening in the market place. Such good agency principles and characteristics also have consequences for the indicators and factors used to measure and assess agencies.

This chapter analyses the general rules underlying the agencies' actions and interventions. Firstly, the roles and functions of agency principles need clarification: why do we have them, and why do we need them? These agency principles provide the agencies with guidance on their behaviour (internal perspective), while those who need to assess the agencies' behaviour, such as evaluation committees and courts, are provided with a framework for evaluating this behaviour (external perspective). Ultimately, agencies that comply with principles of good agency behaviour will gain legitimacy for their interventions.

This is followed by an inventory of the values and principles that governments, governmental organizations, and market and competition authorities themselves consider important in the work of independent agencies. By looking at where these values and principles overlap and where they cluster, a more fundamental level emerges for each common value or principle. I have opted for five umbrella concepts, which comprise several different values.

[5] Better Regulation Task Force, *Regulation—Less is More: Reducing Burdens, Improving Outcomes* (2005) UK Cabinet Office, London.

Others may classify these values as separate principles, thus creating more principles. There are also values that can be found within several principles, and this leads to a certain overlap. Every reduction and categorization holds its own arbitrary choices. What matters is that common values and principles are assigned to one of these more fundamental levels and that it becomes clear why the categorized values and principles belong to the more fundamental principle they are assigned to. Ultimately, I will arrive at the five key fundamental principles which constitute the LITER principles of good agency behaviour: legality, independence, transparency, effectiveness, and responsibility.

Having identified these good agency or LITER principles, I set out in the following chapters to examine how these fundamental principles influence agencies' institutional design, their enforcement practices, and the assessment of their behaviour and the judicial review of their decisions.

In Search of Key Fundamental Principles

The critical question is where to find such key fundamental principles of good agency behaviour for market and competition authorities. There is a variety of sources we can consult for this purpose. Firstly, this chapter examines the legal framework relevant for market and competition authorities. Secondly, it discusses a selection of the governmental reports on core principles for oversight and agencies. And finally, it analyses the core values, characteristics, and principles identified by the independent agencies and their national and international organizations. However, before examining these sources in more detail, the search for key fundamental principles is introduced by discussing the roles, functions, and definition of these principles, and the academic work in four scholarly publications, which will help gain insight in which principles are considered to be key to good agency behaviour.

Roles and functions of key fundamental principles

Providing legitimacy and authority

Independent agencies need legitimacy and authority in order to get the persons and enterprises they supervise to behave in the way the agencies want. For that purpose they have the five different roles at their disposal discussed in chapter 2, which are all equally important: they may advise, advocate, reflect, prevent, and repress in order to motivate supervisees to comply with the rules. A legal basis for agencies' interventions is not enough in itself;

more is needed, including a general level of acceptance and respect for obeying the rules and standards set by the agency. Legitimacy therefore means social credibility and acceptability: 'In a governance or regulatory context, a statement that a regulator is "legitimate" means that it is perceived as having a right to govern both by those it seeks to govern and those on behalf it purports to govern'.[6] Compliance with the five key fundamental principles of good agency behaviour, which will emerge in this chapter, will ensure the agency not only has a legal basis for its interventions, but also social credibility and acceptability. Or, in other words, it will provide the agency with authority.

The key fundamental principles serve as guidance for competition and market authorities and provide a framework for their behaviour, actions, and interventions. Or, as Black states, 'General rules or principles on their own will result in standards of compliance'.[7] Independent agencies adhering to these principles will enjoy greater authority and legitimacy. At the same time, these principles are also of relevance to agencies' stakeholders (i.e. the legislator, ministries, parliament, enterprises, consumers, and the judiciary) because the way in which these principles are applied influences the relationship between the agencies and their stakeholders, as well as providing stakeholders with a frame of reference for assessing the agencies.

Internal and external perspectives

There are two perspectives to the key fundamental principles of good agency behaviour: an internal and an external perspective.[8] The principles will be used by independent agencies as guidance for their own behaviour (internal perspective), whereby the principles dictate how the agencies should structure their organization, how they should take decisions, and how they should develop their enforcement styles and practices. The agencies meanwhile will adhere to these principles and use them as a framework.

The outside world—evaluation committees, the courts, parliament, ministers, and stakeholders—will use the key fundamental principles to evaluate and control the behaviour, interventions, and decisions of these independent agencies (external perspective). Can these actions be considered appropriate, or have the agencies made mistakes? In practice, this is not only a legal

[6] J Black, 'Constructing and Contesting Legitimacy and Accountability in Polycentric Regulatory Regimes' (2008) LSE Law, Society and Economy Working Papers 2/2008, 16.

[7] J Black, 'Managing Discretion' (2001) ARLC Conference Paper on Penalties: Policy, Principles and Practice in Government Regulation <http://www.lse.ac.uk/collections/law/staff%20publications%20full%20text/black/alrc%20managing%20discretion.pdf> accessed 15 April 2014, p. 28.

[8] These two perspectives are taken from: H Addink, *Goed Bestuur* (Den Haag: Boom Juridische Uitgevers 2010) paragraph 3.2.

question, but also a societal one: the actions, or in many cases non-actions (i.e. the agency did not intervene), may be considered 'wrong' or 'inappropriate', and this may mean something different than 'against the law'.

Different dimensions of the principles

There is another aspect that needs attention when considering the individual principles. Many of the key fundamental principles combine two dimensions: a safeguard dimension and an instrumental dimension. These dimensions may appear to be opposites, but in fact are just weights in the scales of a balance.

The safeguard dimension relates to the administrative standardization of government action, which safeguards and protects citizens' legal position against that of the government. National administrative law, including its procedural component, is very much focused on creating safeguards for citizens vis-à-vis the government. The governing body is bound not only procedurally, but also substantively by legal rules. European Union law, competition law, and much of the sector-specific regulation, on the other hand, is characterized by a highly instrumental dimension. The goals of regulation form an essential part of the rules and powers, and the applicable instruments are tailored around these goals. However, an approach that is too instrumental is at risk of placing too much emphasis on the effectiveness of regulation and oversight. The safeguard dimension of law may then become neglected, thus creating a tension between the instrumental-oriented (regulatory) rules on the one hand and the safeguard-oriented (administrative law) rules on the other.

Substantive legal principles form a counterweight to an interpretation that is all too instrumental.[9] Strictly formulating this opposition would imply that EU law (and its implementation at a national level) focuses mainly on achieving the objectives underlying the supervision and regulation as effectively as possible without building in any safeguards or legal protection mechanisms. This picture, however, is too black-and-white, given that although many EU directives concentrate on effective competences and procedures, they also provide mechanisms prescribing transparency, consultation (public enquiry), safeguards for confidential information, proportionality of measures, and effective legal protection. It should be noted that the EU legislator has sought

[9] A T Ottow, *Telecommunicatietoezicht. De invloed van het Europese en Nederlandse bestuurs (proces)recht* (dissertation, University of Amsterdam, The Hague: SDU 2006) 20–27; A T Ottow, *Mastering the Market? Exploring New Forms of Market Supervision* (inaugural lecture, 18 September 2008, University of Utrecht, The Hague: Boom Juridische Uitgevers 2009) 3.

to find a certain balance in these directives between effective oversight on the one hand and legal safeguards on the other.[10]

From an administrative and procedural law perspective, it can be stated that attention has generally concentrated on the safeguard dimension of law and that more attention now is paid to the instrumental side of these rules; in other words, to their effectiveness in the concrete circumstances of the case. It has been acknowledged, on a more fundamental level, that the general principles underpinning proper administrative and procedural rules should also contain instrumental features.[11]

Establishing the right balance between effectiveness and legality has proved to be a major challenge for supervisory practice. In their daily practice, independent agencies make trade-offs between achieving regulatory objectives as quickly as possible on the one hand and the need to take account of principles of legality, proportionality, and carefulness, as well as a sufficient degree of legal and procedural protection, on the other hand. Although effectiveness and carefulness may go hand in hand, they always require careful weighing and balancing.

Following the key fundamental principles of good agency behaviour can increase the effectiveness of oversight, as well as the legitimacy of action taken by an independent agency. In this way the instrumental and safeguard dimensions blend together in the key fundamental principles, thus optimizing the supervisory process.[12] Key fundamental principles of good agency behaviour should therefore contain aspects of both the instrumental and the safeguard dimensions. The different values of a principle just combine the two.

Definition of principles

Although ethical, socio-economic, political, and cultural principles, for example, may not yet form part of the law, they may nevertheless help to define it from the outside.[13] Principles can refer to some 'purpose, goal, entitlement,

[10] A T Ottow, *Telecommunicatietoezicht* (n9) 385–96 (English summary).

[11] A T Ottow, *Telecommunicatietoezicht* (n9) 385–96 (English summary). See also: H Addink, 'Principles of Good Governance, Lessons from Administrative Law' in D M Curtin and R Wessel (eds), *Good Governance and the European Union. Reflections on Concepts, Institutions and Substance* (Antwerp—Oxford—New York: Intersentia 2005) 21–48; H Addink, *Goed Bestuur* (n8).

[12] A T Ottow, *Telecommunicatietoezicht* (n9) 2020.

[13] W van Gerven, 'Two Twin-Principles of EU Law: Democracy and Accountability, Consistency and Convergence' in U Bernitz, J Nergelius, and C Cardner (eds), *General Principles of EC Law in a Process of Development* (Alphen aan den Rijn: Wolters Kluwer 2008) 27. See also: M Aelen, *Beginselen van goed markttoezicht. Gedefinieerd, verklaard en uitgewerkt voor het toezicht op de financiële markten* (dissertation, Utrecht University, Boom Juridische Uitgevers 2014).

or value, [and] are [therefore] regarded from some point of view as desirable to maintain, or to adhere to, so not only as providing an explanation or rationale of the rules which exemplify them, but as at least contributing to their justification'.[14] Other principles may already have been incorporated into legislation and so form part of the legal principles and laws. One possibility of finding principles of good agency behaviour, therefore, is to develop principles on the basis of social and ethical norms that are generally accepted in society as a whole, or—as in this case—in the independent agencies' environment. What behaviour is generally accepted or criticized? Which values are considered to be key for the acceptance and legitimacy of competition and market authorities? Are there any core values they have to adhere to?

Once we have identified the core values and characteristics, we can translate them into key fundamental principles. These principles can have a legal status—legal norms that form part of the national, European, or international legal order and are incorporated into the law—or may be moral or social principles that provide guidance to independent agencies on how to behave and on how society will assess and judge them. These societal views and perceptions play an important role in developing principles.[15] This book discusses principles that are generally accepted in law and society, given that both types of principles form part of the general framework to which good agencies have to adhere.

Academic work

The work of Das and Quintyn[16] on institutional economics can be mentioned as a useful model and source for further study and for developing general principles of good oversight. Although these authors clearly take a governance approach (and view the agencies in relation to their stakeholders), their model can be used as a building block for developing these principles. The authors identify four fundamental pillars of good supervisory governance: independence, accountability, transparency, and integrity. They see

[14] H L A Hart, *The Concept of Law* (2nd edn, Oxford: Clarendon Press 1994) 260.

[15] G Callies and M Renner, 'Between Law and Social Norms: the Evolution of Global Governance' (2009) 22 Ratio Juris 260.

[16] U S Das and M Quintyn, 'Financial Crisis Prevention and Crisis Management—the Role of Regulatory Governance' in R E Litan, M Pomerleano, and V Sundararajan (eds), *Financial Sector Governance: The Roles of the Public and Private Sectors* (Washington, D.C.: Brookings Institution Press 2002) 163. See also M Quintyn, 'Independent Agencies: More Than a Cheap Copy of Independent Central Banks?' (2009) 20 Constitutional Political Economy 267. Their work is mainly based on the model of O E Williamson, 'The New Institutional Economics: Taking Stock, Looking Ahead' (2000) 38(3) Journal of Economic Literature 595.

these four principles as underpinning most of the key elements of internal and external governance arrangements for independent agencies. A major feature of their model is that the four pillars are interdependent and so reinforce each other; in other words, weakening one undermines the effectiveness of the others.

Das and Quintyn make it clear that good supervisory governance forms a critical component for an independent agency seeking to perform its tasks adequately and to attain the goals that have been set for oversight. They claim that good governance of financial regulators, for example, is essential to ensure financial stability, which is one of the main goals of financial regulation. If, for instance, a financial authority is insufficiently independent, this may ultimately also undermine financial stability in the market.

The work of Das and Quintyn is relevant here in that it links the quality of governance to the agency's performance: the four pillars of independence, accountability, transparency, and integrity have to be in place to ensure that an agency functions well. Good governance will enable agencies to gain acceptance and legitimacy for their work and will create the right conditions for enforcement. As the authors say, 'By failing to apply good governance principles, regulatory agencies lose the credibility and moral authority to promulgate good practices in the institutions under their oversight. This could create a moral hazard problem, contribute to unsound practices in the markets, and, ultimately, accentuate crises in the financial system'.[17] Or, to put it differently, the agencies themselves have to set the right example and demonstrate good practices.

Baldwin, Cave, and Lodge identify what they refer to as five criteria for good supervision.[18] They list (i) the legislative mandate—does a legislative authority support the action or regime?; (ii) accountability—is there an appropriate scheme of accountability?; (iii) due process—are procedures fair, accessible, and open?; (iv) expertise—is the agency acting with sufficient expertise?; and (v) efficiency—is the action or regime efficient? They consider these criteria to be 'benchmarks' for assessing supervisory regimes and state that 'More plausible than wealth maximization is an approach to regulatory evaluation that involves looking at those arguments that have general currency when regulatory arrangements and performance are discussed in the public domain. Certain arguments have force in debating whether this or that regulatory action or regime is worthy of support (is "legitimate")'.[19]

[17] U S Das and M Quintyn (n16) 5.

[18] R Baldwin, M Cave, and M Lodge, *Understanding Regulation. Theory, Strategy, and Practice* (2nd edn, Oxford: Oxford University Press 2012) 25–34.

[19] ibid 26–27.

In *The Tools of Regulation* Freiberg[20] identifies what he calls 'evaluating criteria' for public agencies. In his view these are effectiveness and efficiency, compliance, the general principles of administrative law, clarity, understandability, transparency, predictability and consistency, flexibility, accountability, correctability, proportionality and parsimony, and compatibility with fundamental rights. While Freiberg specifically refers to fundamental rights as an essential evaluating criterion, Barkhuyzen and Prosser also mention this aspect. It has therefore become generally accepted that these rights form an integral part of supervisory principles and the law stemming from these principles.[21]

The paper by Hancher, Larouche, and Lavrijssen also identifies 'principles of good market governance'.[22] These authors analyse the principles that they consider should form the basis of market legislation and oversight. They identify the following principles: transparency, independence, a clear legal mandate, flexible powers, proportionality, consistency, predictability, accountability, respect of general principles of competition policy and EU law, and effective cooperation with and within the EU. In their view the legislator should take these principles into account and agencies should adopt and comply with a code of good market governance in all administrative processes.

Reference is finally made to the comparative study of Fox and Trebilcock, in which the global convergence of process norms is described from an institutional design perspective. The authors identify the key issues of institutional design and provide an overview of selected countries around the world.[23]

Relevant Legal Framework

National administrative law and good governance

Core values and principles for market and competition authorities are in fact a further specification of national administrative laws and the principles of

[20] A Freiberg, *The Tools of Regulation* (Sydney: Federation Press 2010) 258–68.

[21] A Freiberg (n20) and T Prosser (n4) 33–4.

[22] L Hancher, P Larouche, and S A C M Lavrijssen, 'Principles of Good Market Governance' (2004) 49(2) Tijdschrift voor Economie en Management 339. See also S A C M Lavrijssen, *Onafhankelijke mededingingstoezichthouders, regulerende bevoegdheden en de waarborgen voor good governance* (dissertation, Tilburg University, Boom Juridische Uitgevers 2006); and M Aelen, *Beginselen van goed markttoezicht* (n13).

[23] E M Fox and M J Trebilcock (eds), *The Design of Competition Law Institutions. Global Norms, Local Choices* (Oxford: Oxford University Press 2013).

good governance. Most countries' national administrative laws provide a general framework of principles that govern the behaviour of and interventions by governmental bodies. These include the principles of proportionality, fairness, carefulness, predictability, and sufficient justification. The national rules derived from such principles also apply to national supervisory bodies such as market and competition authorities. These national administrative law principles play an important role in case law on decisions of such agencies and influence their day-to-day practices.

Related to these rules on administrative laws are the principles of good governance that have been identified by national[24] and EU governments and broadly discussed in literature.[25] These elaborate further on the general administrative rules and provide a general framework for administrative behaviour.

National constitutional law is also of major importance as it may limit agencies' regulatory space and influence their institutional design, as well as the role that ministers and parliament can play. The latter is an important aspect as relationships with ministries and parliament are a key issue for independent agencies. In many countries, the minister remains responsible for the agencies' activities, although it can only influence its behaviour in a limited way. This causes a tension between the democratic principles and an agency that must be able to intervene in an independent way.[26]

[24] See, for example, in the Netherlands: *Nederlandse code voor goed openbaar bestuur*, which identifies the following principles: openness and integrity, participation, fairness and decency, effectiveness, sufficient reasoning, legitimacy, the ability to learn and self-correct, accountability. Also the European Commission published a code: Code of Good Administrative Behaviour [2000] OJ L 267. The Commission identifies the following general principles: lawfulness, non-discrimination, proportionality, consistency, objectivity and impartiality, right of information. This code has been criticised, for example: D M Curtin and I Dekker, 'Good Governance: The Concept and its Application by the European Union' in D M Curtin and A R Wessel (eds), *Good Governance and the European Union: Reflections on Concepts, Institutions and Substance* (Antwerp: Intersentia 2005) 3–19.

[25] See for example H Addink, *Goed Bestuur* (n8). Addink identifies the following principles of good governance: proper administration, transparency, participation, effectiveness, accountability, human rights. For more on the subject of good governance see: M Bovens, 'Two Concepts of Accountability: Accountability as a Virtue and as a Mechanism' (2010) 33 (5) West European Politics 946; M Bovens, 'Analysing and Assessing Public Accountability. A Conceptual Framework' (2006) European Governance Papers C-06-01 <http://www.uu.nl/SiteCollectionDocuments/REBO/REBO_USBO/REBO_USBO_OZZ/Analysing%20and%20Assessing%20Public%20Accountability1.pdf> accessed 21 September 2014; and D M Curtin, 'Positioning Accountability in European Governance: An Introduction' (2010) 33 (5) West European Politics 929.

[26] S A C M Lavrijssen and A T Ottow, 'The Legality of Independent Regulatory Authorities' in L F M Besselink, F Pennings, and S Prechal, *The Eclipse of the Legality Principle in the European Union* (The Hague: Kluwer Law International 2010) 73–96.

European law

Since oversight in EU member states is often based on EU regulations or directives, the regulatory framework of EU member states' independent agencies is influenced to a large extent by European rules and principles (chapter 2 discusses the Europeanization process of agencies).[27] The European Union has multiple sources of EU law. EU treaties form the primary source of EU law, while regulations, directives, and decisions are other important sources of codified law. Whereas decisions are generally administrative acts aimed at individual organizations, and regulations have direct effect (they do not have to be implemented into national laws to be binding for the member states), directives are EU laws that must be transposed into national law by the member states.[28]

Besides these sources of codified law, the European rules and principles include the general principles of EU law, which are unwritten sources of law deduced by the European Court of Justice (ECJ) when ruling on a case.[29] The ECJ uses the general principles of EU law in order to 'close off lacunae' in primary sources of EU law, such as EU treaties and other primary and secondary legislation.[30] Besides being a 'gap-filler' for primary and secondary legislation, general principles serve two more functions, namely as an aid for interpreting European and national law, and as a judicial ground for reviewing these laws.[31] There is general agreement on the existence of five general principles: fundamental rights, proportionality, legal certainty, equality (before the law), and the principle of subsidiarity.

Fundamental rights

As we have seen, fundamental rights are one of the established general principles of EU law. Given that the importance of fundamental and human rights is codified in the United Nations' Universal Declaration of Human Rights, the European Convention of Human Rights, and the Charter of Fundamental Rights of the European Union (EU Charter), this general

[27] See for the European dimension: A T Ottow, 'Europeanization of the Supervision of Competitive Markets' (2012) 18(1) European Public Law 191.

[28] F Duina, 'Explaining Legal Implementation in the European Union' (1997) 25 International Journal of the Sociology of Law 155.

[29] K Lenaerts and J A Gutiérrez-Fons, 'The Constitutional Allocation of Powers and General Principles of EU Law' (2010) 47 Common Market Law Review 1629.

[30] J Donnelly, 'Publication Review "The General Principles of EU Law" by Tridimas' (2010) 32 Dublin University Law Journal 401.

[31] K Lenaerts and J A Gutiérrez-Fons (n29).

principle is sometimes seen as a source of primary EU law. Apart from national and EU rules on administrative law, fundamental rights aspects are also of particular importance in the context of oversight. On a global level, and especially in the European Union, the protection of fundamental rights is increasingly relevant in relation to supervision of market regulation and competition law.[32]

Fundamental or human rights are commonly understood to be 'fundamental rights to which a person is inherently entitled simply because she or he is a human being'.[33] Fundamental rights can generally be divided into procedural rights (such as the right to access to justice and a fair trial) and substantive rights (such as the right to property and privacy). The purpose of fundamental rights is primarily to provide a guarantee against disproportionate government intervention by regulating the relationship between the state (including public authorities and public bodies) and individuals. At the same time, and under certain circumstances, fundamental rights create a positive obligation for the state to provide protection against infringements of rights by third parties. This means that fundamental rights can play two different roles in respect to supervision of economic regulation and competition law. Firstly, some competition and market authorities may have the task of protecting fundamental rights—such as privacy, independent media, or public health—as their core business. Secondly, fundamental rights rules impose severe restrictions on interventions and possible sanctions.

An important source of law for European countries is the aforementioned European Convention of Human Rights (ECHR), which entered into force on 3 September 1953. It is mandatory for all Council of Europe members to be party to the Convention, which is legally binding and, therefore, legally enforceable.[34] Actions by competition and market authorities are consequently bound by the ECHR. In addition to ECHR requirements relating to fairness, carefulness, proportionality, and legality, which are similar to the correlating requirements in the UN Universal Declaration on Human

[32] Tony Prosser (n4) 13–15; A Freiberg, *The Tools of Regulation* (Sydney: Federation Press 2010) 268.

[33] M M Sepúlveda et al, *Human Rights Reference Handbook* (5th edn, Reykjavik: Icelandic Human Rights Centre 2010) 4.

[34] Anyone believing that a state party has violated his or her rights under the Convention can take the case to court. National courts then have to assess whether the supervisory authorities have acted within the limits of the Convention. After exhausting the domestic remedies (i.e. a ruling by the country's highest court), the appellant can go to the European Court of Human Rights (ECtHR) in Strasbourg.

Rights,[35] the ECHR contains an additional requirement that is of relevance in this context. This is the legality principle of Article 7, which states that no person may be punished for an act that was not an offence at the time of its being committed, and that no heavier penalty may be imposed than was applicable at the time the act was committed.

On 7 December 2000, the European Parliament, the Council of Ministers, and the European Commission solemnly proclaimed the EU Charter, which is a second significant source of law in the field of fundamental rights. Until the Treaty of Lisbon,[36] the status of the EU Charter was uncertain and it did not have full legal effect. With the entry into force of the Treaty of Lisbon, however, the Charter became legally binding and so applies when national authorities implement EU law (when, for example, they apply a directive or regulation), and when they operate within the scope of EU law. Since many rules in the field of market supervision are of European origin, the EU Charter applies to most areas of regulatory law. Yet even though the EU Charter is the most prominent legal source of fundamental rights for EU member states, the ECHR is also important, given that the EU Charter makes an explicit link to this Convention.

The external perspective of fundamental rights is their interpretation by national courts and non-judicial human rights bodies. Some requirements arising from fundamental rights have been implemented in national law, with national governing bodies, including national courts, then being obliged to interpret these laws in conformity with the EU Charter and, if necessary, to refrain from applying national law. It is important to emphasize that such an obligation also rests on independent agencies, given that conflicts with the ECHR or the EU Charter also constitute grounds for annulling a decision.

Fundamental rights, and specifically the EU Charter, should be embedded within the work of all entities and at all levels of government that provide and support access to justice. Independent agencies are therefore required to act fairly, carefully, and proportionately in order to ensure these fundamental rights are respected.

35 The UN Universal Declaration on Human Rights contains some articles relevant to fairness, carefulness, proportionality, and legality. These are Article 8 (the right to an effective remedy), Articles 10 and 11 (the right to a fair trial within a reasonable time, the right to remain silent, the right against self-incrimination, and the presumption of innocence), Article 12 (the right to respect for one's privacy, family, home, and correspondence), and Article 20 (the freedom of assembly and association).

36 Treaty of Lisbon Volume 50 2007/C 306/01 <http://eur-lex.europa.eu/legal-content/EN/TXT/HTML/?uri=OJ:C:2007:306:FULL&from=EN> accessed 22 September 2014.

Governmental Reports Identifying Core Agency Principles

Apart from this general legal framework for governments, the question of whether special characteristics and values are relevant for independent agencies needs to be examined. Several national and international reports have sought over the years to identify key elements of good oversight.[37] These reports have certain aspects in common, even though their terminology and categorizations differ, and the agencies examined were studied from different backgrounds and perspectives. What they have in common is that they illustrate the agencies' current views on market and competition authorities and provide a general outline of what is considered to be a 'good' agency. Mostly, however, these reports refer only to specific characteristics and values that are considered to be essential for good behaviour, rather than discussing underlying principles. Although these reports were written from a pragmatic perspective, they can be used to gain a better understanding of the standards that agencies should aim for and the factors that are relevant for assessing their performance.

High-level general principles regarding good agency behaviour have also been identified in agency assessment studies, as well as in national and international policy documents concerning market and competition authorities. These principles can therefore be applied across a wide range of regulatory bodies and agencies, including market and competition authorities.[38]

[37] Reference can also made to the conducted self-study by the FTC in 2008, where a number of useful insights are given to set standards for good agencies performance: 'The FTC at 100', discussed in W E Kovacic, 'Rating the Competition Agencies: What Constitutes Good Performance?' (2009) 16(4) George Mason Law Review 923. These standards include elements such as: defining goals and purposes, defining a process for setting a strategy and selecting programs, problem solving orientation, adequate investments, and internal quality control mechanisms. Other examples are the UK reports on better regulation and better regulations, see notes 2, 3 and 5; the Dutch reports *Minder last, meer effect ('Less burden, more effect'): Kaderstellende Visie op Toezicht—2005*, Tweede Kamer 2005-2006, 27 831 no. 15, Ministry of the Interior and Kingdom Relations; *De bevoegdheden van de Nederlandsche Bank inzake Icesave*, report by A J C de Moor-Van Vugt and C E du Perron commissioned by the Ministry of Finance, 11 June 2009, Kamerstukken II 2008/09, 31 371, no. 205; and the OECD reports *Recommendation of the Council on Regulatory and Policy Governance* (2012) <http://www.oecd.org/gov/regulatory-policy/49990817.pdf> accessed 17 March 2014 and *Principles for the Governance of Regulators*, draft paper for public consultation, June 2013, <http://www.oecd.org/gov/regulatory-policy/Governance%20of%20Regulators%20FN%202.docx> accessed 17 March 2014.

[38] A T Ottow, 'Developing a Common Framework for Good Performances by Agencies' in P Lugard (ed), *The International Competition Network at Ten. Origins, Accomplishments and Aspirations* (Cambridge-Antwerp-Portland: Intersentia 2011) 251–65.

The following section discusses a selection of governmental reports that have been published over the years as a means of identifying some key elements of good oversight that are useful in seeking to establish key fundamental principles of good agency behaviour.

IMF paper on the making of good supervision (2010)

In May 2010 the International Monetary Fund (IMF) published a staff position paper on *The Making of Good Supervision: Learning to Say 'No'*.[39] This document identifies some key principles for effective oversight of the banking sector against the background of the financial crisis. The authors stated that the response of banking supervisory agencies to the crisis had focused solely on the need for more and better regulation, but that more discussion was needed on how to strengthen supervision, i.e. supervisory oversight by the agency itself. Although this report was written for financial market regulators, the observations made are of a general nature and can also be applied to other agencies, including competition authorities.

The authors list five supervisory standards, claiming that good supervision should be intrusive, sceptical but proactive, comprehensive, adaptive, and conclusive. Intrusive oversight should be based on an intimate knowledge of the supervised entity. The independent agency should not act as a distant observer. It should take a sceptical attitude while acting proactively: it cannot wait until after operations start to derail. Agencies should be comprehensive in their actions, constantly vigilant to ensure they can identify any emerging risks that may have systemic portents, and draw the proper conclusions for changing their supervisory practices. They should adapt continually to changes at the perimeter of regulation, with an eye to new or unregulated areas, and must constantly be in a learning mode. And, lastly, they should follow through conclusively on all matters progressing through the supervisory process. The challenge is not only to comply with the defined elements in practice, but also to institutionalize these principles in national organizational structures, legislation, and behaviour.

OECD principles for the governance of regulators (2013)

Good regulatory outcomes depend on more than well-designed rules and regulations. This was recognized in the Recommendation of the Council

[39] J Viñals and J Fiechter, 'The Making of Good Supervision: Learning to Say 'No'' (2010) IMF Staff Position Note, SPN/10/08 <https://www.imf.org/external/pubs/ft/spn/2010/spn1008.pdf> accessed 15 April 2014.

on Regulatory and Policy Governance published by the Organisation for Economic Co-operation and Development (OECD) in 2012, which recommended that member countries should '[develop] a consistent policy covering the role and functions of regulatory agencies in order to provide greater confidence that regulatory decisions are made on an objective, impartial and consistent basis, without conflict of interest, bias or improper influence'.[40]

In June 2013 the OECD published its draft *Principles for the Governance of Regulators*[41] for public consultation purposes. In this draft the OECD aimed to devise a framework for good governance by outlining general principles that may apply to all supervisory authorities, thus assisting member states to develop such a consistent policy. This framework provides[42] principles for assessing existing governance arrangements and for reviewing market and competition authorities and their administration, while it is at the same time intended as a guide to develop governance arrangements for any proposed new independent agencies. The document sets out seven principles to be considered in support of good governance by agencies. These seven principles mesh with the principles of good regulation and comprise role clarity, preventing undue influence and maintaining trust, decision-making and governing-body structures for independent agencies, accountability and transparency, engagement, funding, and performance evaluation.

A Dutch vision on oversight (2005)

In 2005 the Dutch Ministry of the Interior and Kingdom Relations published a report in Dutch entitled (translated) *Less burden, more effect.* Governmental oversight had been the subject of political debate in that year, following a rapid increase in the number of independent agencies, and also in their costs. This led to conflicting expectations in Dutch society and politics: on the one hand a demand for more and better oversight after certain shocking incidents, and on the other hand a call for less oversight (i.e. fewer burdens and lower costs) when things are going well. The report sets out the Dutch

[40] OECD, 'Recommendation of the Council on Regulatory and Policy Governance' (2012) 4 <http://www.oecd.org/gov/regulatory-policy/49990817.pdf> accessed 17 March 2014.

[41] OECD, 'Principles for the Governance of Regulators' (2013), draft paper for public consultation <http://www.oecd.org/gov/regulatory-policy/Governance%20of%20Regulators%20FN%202.docx> accessed 17 March 2014.

[42] OECD, 'Principles for the Governance of Regulators' (2013), draft paper for public consultation <http://www.oecd.org/gov/regulatory-policy/Governance%20of%20Regulators%20FN%202.docx> accessed 17 March 2014, p. 5.

government's view on supervision at that time and states that good oversight must meet six criteria: it must be selective, decisive, cooperative, independent, transparent, and professional.

As well as requiring independent agencies to weigh costs and benefits against each other, the criterion of selectiveness illustrates the government's aim of reducing the burdens of supervision, while also seeking to shift responsibilities from government to society. Being selective means accepting that responsibility for overseeing the functioning of society does not automatically lie with the government, but is instead to be shared between citizens, enterprises, institutions, and government.

BIS principles for economic regulation (2011)

In April 2011 the UK Department for Business, Innovation & Skills (BIS) published the *Principles for Economic Regulation*,[43] in which it emphasizes that competitive markets are, in the long run, the best way to deliver services on which all businesses and citizens depend. According to the BIS, independent market regulation is needed to provide consumers with protection and to ensure their interests are respected.

By establishing various principles for market regulation, the BIS has sought not only to reaffirm the importance of stable and predictable regulatory frameworks, but also to provide greater clarity on the roles of the government, the supervising agencies, and the supervisees. The principles are also intended to guide policymakers in assessing future developments. However, special emphasis is put on the government's actions: guiding the institutional design of the regulatory framework, and thus leaving agencies to carry out their regulatory duties independently. The principles are intended solely to articulate the key factors (i.e. 'principles')—for example, accountability, focus, and predictability—in the design of market regulation, while also setting out the government's commitments with regard to the high-level application of the commitments associated with the principles.[44]

[43] Department for Business, Innovation & Skills, 'Principles for Economic Regulation', published 12 April 2011 <https://www.gov.uk/government/publications/principles-for-economic-regulation> accessed 28 June 2014.

[44] These commitments include, but are not limited to, the Government preserving the independence of market regulators and the Government putting into place strategy and policy statements for the individual regulators to provide context, guidance, and desired outcomes.

Supervision report by the Netherlands Scientific Council for Government Policy (2013)

The Netherlands Scientific Council for Government Policy (WRR), an independent think tank for the Dutch government, published a report entitled *Supervising Public Interests* in September 2013.[45] This report makes recommendations for increasing the added value of government oversight performed by a wide range of inspectorates and independent agencies.

The WRR stated there to be a disproportionate emphasis on the administrative and financial burdens of oversight, and on its political–administrative role, while also too great a focus on compliance and enforcement. The issue of how oversight can best serve public interests had thus become side-lined in the process.[46] This statement is as comprehensible as it is problematic. The WRR therefore advises approaching oversight from a broader perspective, and specifically from a perspective focusing on supervision's role in society. The key, once again, is to put public interests and societal challenges first, both in policymaking and practice. Approaching oversight in this way makes it possible to weigh its intended and actual benefits against the administrative and financial burdens it creates.

The WRR argues that this approach involves taking a closer look at three core values of supervision: impartiality, independence, and public accountability. According to the WRR, it is only when these three values are guaranteed that an independent agency can exercise its oversight legitimately and authoritatively, and deliver the intended value.[47]

Core Values of Market and Competition Authorities

Another important source for identifying appropriate values and principles, specifically with regard to market and competition authorities, can be found in the statements that agencies themselves have made on core values. The start of the financial crisis in 2007 induced these agencies to publish various strategy documents setting out the core values that they consider to be key

[45] *Toezien op publieke belangen. Naar een verruimd perspectief op rijkstoezicht* (Report no. 89-2013 of the WRR (Wetenschappelijke Raad voor het Regeringsbeleid) (Amsterdam, Amsterdam University Press 2013). English synopsis '*Supervising Public Interests. Towards a Broader Perspective on Government Supervision*' available at <http://www.wrr.nl/fileadmin/en/publicaties/PDF-samenvattingen/Supervising_public_interests.pdf> accessed 17 March 2014.

[46] Synopsis of WRR Report no. 89-2013 (n45) 15.

[47] ibid 15.

for their work and that influence the choices they make and how they perform their allotted tasks.

Independent agencies from various countries around the world have published details of their core values. In the following section I analyse a selection of these documents and outline the core values that certain agencies, with varying degrees of prominence, have published in order to identify any common values and principles that can be derived from the elements that these agencies consider to be key in enabling them to perform their tasks well.

Competition authorities

ICN seminar on competition agency effectiveness

In January 2009 the Agency Effectiveness Working Group of the International Competition Network (ICN) organized a seminar to examine agencies' effectiveness. The working group adopted a pragmatic approach.[48] Although recognizing that there is no 'one size fits all' model, its report referred to the following universal characteristics of a good competition authority. Such a competition authority should have a clearly articulated, long-term strategy, and a plan for implementing that strategy. It should constantly review and assess its activity, and feed the results back into the planning process. It adapts its internal structure and processes to its environment and objectives, and ensures its internal organization remains flexible. A good competition authority has a range of policy tools at its disposal (notably including case investigations and different forms of advocacy and communication), it understands what these tools are, and it has a problem-solving approach that tries to identify the right tool to remedy each problem. It uses clear criteria to select which projects to undertake, choosing from among the many actions it can launch, and it keeps ongoing activities and projects under review, while terminating projects that do not meet its objectives. A good agency understands that its staff are its main resource and tries to provide them with a stimulating, pleasant, and rewarding working environment. According to the ICN report, a good agency understands that communication is an essential part of its task, and devotes adequate resources to communication adapted to various stakeholders. It is fully aware that it cannot work alone and so forms alliances with other public and non-public bodies (market agencies and other competition authorities,

[48] International Competition Network Competition Policy Implementation Working Group, 'Seminar on Competition Agency Effectiveness Summary Report' (2009) Brussels <http://ec.europa.eu/competition/information/icn_seminar_2009/report_final_version.pdf> accessed 15 April 2014.

non-governmental organizations, academia etc.). It also benchmarks itself against and exchanges best practices with other agencies worldwide.[49]

Competition & Markets Authority (UK)

The *Vision, Values and Strategy* document[50] published in January 2014 by the British Competition & Markets Authority (CMA) contains a statement of this agency's values. As well as the UK government-wide 'Civil Service Values' (i.e. honesty, integrity, impartiality, and objectivity), this statement specifies five 'CMA values': ambition, excellence, commitment, fairness, and teamwork. It is striking that the statement explicitly mentions that these CMA values (as well as the Civil Service Values) are demonstrated both externally (in relation to enterprises, consumers, the public, and so on) and internally (in relation to colleagues). Let us take a closer look at some of these five values to illustrate how internal features of each value correlate both with another value and with their external counterparts.[51] The CMA is committed to the outside world in that it undertakes to pursue its cases vigorously and professionally (external aspect of the value of commitment), while working effectively with other partners (external aspect of the value of teamwork), allowing all parties to have their say and avoiding unnecessary burdens on business (external aspect of the value of fairness). The CMA is also committed to its own organization in that its staff undertake to do what it takes to deliver (internal commitment), while working together flexibly and as good colleagues (internal aspect of the value of teamwork).

Federal Trade Commission (USA)

Although the US Federal Trade Commission (FTC) has not published any information on its core values, it has joined the Open Government Initiative, which 'lays out the Obama Administration plan to usher in a new era of open and accountable government that will bridge the gap between the American people and their government'. The core values of this initiative are transparency, participation, and collaboration. On transparency, the Open Government Initiative states that the government 'should provide citizens with information about what their government is doing so that government can be held accountable'. As regards participation, the initiative lies

[49] ICN Competition Policy Implementation Working Group (n48).

[50] Competition & Markets Authority, 'Vision, Values and Strategy for the CMA'(2014) <https://www.gov.uk/government/uploads/system/uploads/attachment_data/file/274059/CMA13_Vision_and_Values_Strategy_document.pdf> accessed 14 March 2014.

[51] For an illustrative table on all five CMA values, see: 'Vision, Values and Strategy for the CMA' (n50) 17. These five CMA values are Ambition, Excellence, Commitment, Fairness and Teamwork.

primarily with the government, in that it 'should actively solicit expertise from outside Washington so that it makes policies with the benefit of the best information'. Collaboration is to be understood both internally and externally: '[g]overnment officials should work together with one another and with citizens as part of doing their job of solving national problems'.[52]

Authority for Consumers & Markets (Netherlands)

The Netherlands Authority for Consumers & Markets (ACM) acts in accordance with three core values: independence, openness, and professionalism. Its *Strategy Document* explicitly states that 'these core values form the basis of all of ACM's actions. If these core values are compromised in any way by anyone from ACM, they can be held accountable for their actions, both by other ACM employees and by others'.[53] The independent position of ACM is formally enshrined in its legal status as an autonomous administrative authority under Dutch law. ACM fulfils its tasks independently of legislators and enterprises, in line with the requirements set by EU regulations. As ACM states in its Strategy Document, 'In practice, the independent position of ACM as an organization means, on the one hand, taking a critical attitude and exercising independent judgement, and, on the other, maintaining open and constructive relationships with ministries, other regulators, and stakeholders'. It goes on to say in the Strategy Document that it 'wishes to be engaged in a permanent and constructive dialog with its stakeholders. Through our activities, we aim to be sensitive to broader social trends that affect the areas of our oversight. Communicating clearly and in a timely manner about what ACM does, why and for whom are all elements that are critical to that aim'. ACM's professionalism is 'reflected in the expertise, commitment, and flexibility of its staff. Further professionalization is a permanent task at every level within the organization'. This requires investments in staff training and development. Being professional also means—according to ACM—that 'employees know what is happening in the market'.

Consultation Forum of Regulatory Bodies (Netherlands)

In February 2014 the Dutch Consultation Forum of Regulatory Bodies (MTB),[54] an informal network of independent market and competition

[52] For all quotations, see <http://www.ftc.gov/site-information/open-government> accessed 29 April 2014.

[53] ACM 'Strategy Document Netherlands Authority for Consumers & Markets' 3. <https://www.acm.nl/en/about-acm/mission-vision-strategy/our-mission/> accessed 14 March 2014.

[54] The Consultation Forum of Regulatory Bodies (*Markttoezichthoudersberaad*) is a collaboration between the Netherlands Authority for Consumers & Markets (ACM), the Netherlands

authorities, published a memo setting out its overall vision on the criteria for good oversight.[55] This memo states the three core values of good supervision to be effectiveness, efficiency, and professionalism, with effectiveness being the central concept. In other words, efficiency and professionalism are necessary conditions for achieving the primary goal of effectiveness. These three core values are fleshed out into several more detailed principles. For an agency to be professional, it has to have professional staff acting independently and transparently. If an agency is to be efficient, it has to be well-organized, taking a collaborative and empowering approach to its work. These aspects of professionalism and efficiency combine with the effectiveness aspects of an agency that is mission-driven, impact-focused, accountable, and willing to adapt to changing circumstances.

Australian Competition & Consumer Commission and Australian Energy Regulator

Since the financial year 2011–12 the Australian Competition & Consumer Commission (ACCC) and the Australian Energy Regulator (AER) have stated in their joint annual reports that they appreciate and uphold the ICARE values of the Australian Public Service. Alongside these ICARE values (I for impartial, C for committed to service, A for accountable, R for respectful, and E for ethical), they regard four additional complementary values as unique and meaningful to their work: they wish to act independently in that they objectively and transparently pursue the interests of the Australian community; they act as experts by making timely decisions based on evidence and rigorous analysis; they go about their jobs strategically, making the best use of the resources available by taking considered and targeted action; and they seek to remain trustworthy by communicating honestly and directly and acting respectfully.[56]

Other national competition authorities

Other authorities at a national level that have published core values include the Swedish Competition Authority,[57] the Media Development Authority

Authority for the Financial Markets (AFM), the Dutch Data Protection Authority (CBP), the Dutch central bank DNB, the Netherlands Gaming Authority (KSA), and the Dutch Healthcare Authority (NZa). The CBP oversees compliance with basic rights by public authorities and therefore occupies a somewhat special position in this regard.

[55] Consultation Forum of Regulatory Bodies (MTB), 'Criteria for Good Oversight' (2014) <https://www.acm.nl/en/download/publication/?id=12624> accessed 17 March 2014.

[56] 'ACCC and AER Annual Report 2011-12, part 2: Overview of the ACCC and AER paragraph Role and Functions' (2014) <http://registers.accc.gov.au/static_content/annual_reports/annual_report_2012/part2_02_role.html>.

[57] Swedish Competition Authority Annual Report 2012 <http://www.kkv.se/globalassets/omoss/annual-report-on-competition-policy-developments-in-sweden.pdf> accessed 14 March 2014.

of Singapore,[58] the Energy Market Authority of Singapore,[59] the Singapore Competition Commission,[60] the Competition Authority of Botswana,[61] and the Competition Bureau of Canada.[62] While the Swedes value a competent, respectful, and results-oriented way of acting in their Competition Authority, the Competition Authority of Botswana puts transparency, professionalism, integrity, and teamwork at the forefront. In Singapore, innovation, integrity, care, and professionalism are valued by two out of three agencies, while teamwork and passion both are mentioned by only one of the three agencies. The Competition Bureau of Canada is the odd one out, at least in this group of six agencies: it puts confidentiality, fairness, predictability, timeliness, and transparency at the heart of its activities.

Financial authorities

Autorité des marchés financiers (France)

In its *Strategy Document* the French financial authority, the *Autorité des marchés financiers* (AMF), gives three principles a prominent place in defining its identity: independent ('an authority that acts in the general interest'), open ('an authority in touch with its environment and with Europe'), and committed ('engaged and capable staff').[63] Its website elaborates on these three principles by stating, with regard to independence, that 'Independence is fundamental to our mission and is evidenced on a daily basis in our analysis and decision-making processes. Irrespective of their position, all our staff members strive to ensure that individual interests are subordinate to the general interest'. On openness it states that 'Open mindedness is a crucial quality for the modern-day regulator. We work in direct contact with our professional environment and value skills such as adaptability, responsiveness and teaching ability. These qualities are useful in our external relations, but they also form the basis of our team spirit'. On commitment it states that 'The AMF is defined by its staff members, their professionalism, their skills and

[58] See <http://www.mda.gov.sg/AboutMDA/MissionVisionCoreValues/Pages/MissionVisionCoreValues.aspx> accessed 14 March 2014.

[59] See <https://www.ema.gov.sg> accessed 14 March 2014.

[60] See <http://www.ccs.gov.sg> accessed 14 March 2014.

[61] See <http://www.proudlyafrican.info/Proudly-African/African-Growth-Development-Initiative/CLEAN-Botswana/Chapters/Corporate-Governance/Competition-Authority.aspx> accessed 14 March 2014.

[62] See <http://www.competitionbureau.gc.ca/eic/site/cb-bc.nsf/eng/h_00126.html> accessed 14 March 2014.

[63] AMF Strategy 2013-2016, 'Making Finance Meaningful Again' English Summary of the Consultation Document 'AMF Strategy 2013-2016', 4. <http://www.amf-france.org/en_US/Publications/Rapports-etudes-et-analyses/Divers.html?> accessed 29 April 2014.

their permanent commitment. Interest in their work is a powerful motivator. Coming from a wide variety of professional backgrounds, applicants join the AMF in order to give new meaning to their career and to perform a public service'.[64]

Authority for Financial Markets (Netherlands)

The Netherlands Authority for Financial Markets (AFM) states in its *Mission and Core Values 2014* that its oversight is based on the following five core values: AFM acts resolutely; AFM acts carefully; AFM acts appropriately; it seeks to be an orientation point for consumers, investors, and organizations; and AFM reasons from the own responsibility of consumers and the industry.

European Union bodies

European Securities and Markets Authority

The European Securities and Markets Authority (ESMA) states in its *2013-2015 multi-annual work programme* that its intention is to 'further build the external and internal communication of ESMA to ensure consistency between the external and internal perception of ESMA, and a clear communication of the objectives, key-characteristics and achievements of ESMA'.[65] The *2014 work programme* puts this intention more concretely, with the opening table setting out ESMA's mission, objectives, activities, priorities, and characteristics.[66] According to this table, ESMA's characteristics are European, independent, cooperative, accountable, professional, and effective. No further explanation is provided on how these characteristics are put into practice.

European Systemic Risk Board

The European Systemic Risk Board (ESRB) has adopted a code of conduct that states *inter alia* that the members of ESRB advisory committees 'are expected to act honestly, independently, impartially and solely in the interest of the Union as a whole, with discretion and without regard to self-interest and to avoid any situation liable to give rise to a personal conflict of interests'.[67]

[64] AMF Website <http://www.amf-france.org/en_US/L-AMF-recrute/Presentation.html>.

[65] ESMA, 2013-2015 multi-annual work programme, ref. 2012/632, 11. <http://www.esma.europa.eu/page/Corporate-information> accessed 17 March 2014.

[66] ESMA, 2014 work programme, ref. 2013/1355, 1. <http://www.esma.europa.eu/page/Corporate-information> accessed 17 March 2014.

[67] Decision of the ESRB of 25 March 2011 adopting the Code of Conduct of the European Systemic Risk Board (ESRB/2011/3).

Eurosystem

The Eurosystem, which is the central banking system of the euro zone and comprises the European Central Bank (ECB) and the national central banks (NCBs) of the 18 EU member states whose common currency is the euro, states on its website that the Eurosystem seeks guidance from nine different organizational principles in performing its activities:[68] participation; cooperation; exchange of resources; cohesion and unity; taking advantage of synergies and avoiding duplication; effective and efficient decision-making; cost efficiency, measurement, and methodology; transparency and accountability, and distinguishing Eurosystem activities.

LITER Principles of Good Agency Behaviour

Having considered the different sources, we can conclude that the various authors use different names to refer to the same sorts of principles, or list many qualities that can be brought under the same umbrella. By categorizing and reducing them to their fundamental meanings I have been able to identify five key fundamental good agency principles. These encompass the issues discussed in the reports, strategy documents, and literature, as well as the elements occurring most commonly in agencies' day-to-day practice. What these principles have in common is that they function as a central focal point for competition and market authorities and their stakeholders.

These five key fundamental principles are: legality (L), independence (I), transparency (T), effectiveness (E), and responsibility (R), together referred to as the LITER principles or good agency principles. Annex 2 gives an overview of the LITER principles and the subvalues contained in each of them. The LITER principles may have different functions and may contain elements of the instrumental and safeguard dimensions. They are also interdependent and reinforce each other, while some of them contain overlapping elements.

For pragmatic reasons, I have limited the total number of principles, and gathered related values and principles under the same umbrella. Accountability, for example, could be seen as a separate principle, while also being closely related to the principle of transparency. The element of participation, too, has been identified by some authors as a separate principle. In both cases I have chosen to classify these as subvalues under the concept of transparency. In the

[68] ECB Website <http://www.ecb.europa.eu/ecb/orga/escb/html/mission_eurosys.en.html> accessed 17 March 2014.

categorization used in this book, the LITER principles are seen as the overriding principles, comprising these various different elements that contain aspects other authors may have identified as separate principles and, moreover, have been referred to in the various sources using different terminology, thus complicating categorization. The key is that, together, they constitute the core framework to consider. Indeed, the principles conflict in practice, with the independent agency then having to balance them against each other and make justified choices. Trade-offs will be needed in any event.[69]

In this section I analyse the main elements of these LITER principles of legality, independence, transparency, effectiveness, and responsibility, while also explaining why these principles are key and encompass most of the other previously identified principles.

Legality principle

The legality principle encompasses the subvalues of legal mandate, fairness, carefulness, proportionality, sufficient reasoning, and fundamental rights. It is the container principle for all substantive legal rules and procedures. Independent agencies are bound by the rule of law, and the principles that this rule implies. The elements of a legal basis, discretionary powers, and the administrative rules of law (which includes principles such as legal certainty, procedural fairness, proportionality, and sufficient reasoning) are particularly significant and need special attention in the context of oversight.

Legal mandate

It is generally recognized that competition and market authorities should have the legal powers and tools needed to intervene, i.e. legal authority to carry out their mandates. The legality principle therefore forms the starting point of all their activities: without legal powers, authorities are toothless. National constitutional principles of legality are of particular importance here.[70] In many countries, the legality principle means that unilateral administrative action impinging on citizens' rights and freedoms has to be exercised on the basis of (and in accordance with) a legal base. Although it is not entirely clear what is meant by 'a legal base', it is suggested that the principles of legality and representative democracy in any event require the legislator to regulate at least the most essential elements of a law.[71]

[69] R Baldwin, M Cave, and M Lodge (n18) 33.

[70] Parts of this legality principle are discussed and taken from S A C M Lavrijssen and A T Ottow (n26).

[71] ibid.

Regarding the scope and interpretation of the legality principle, opinions are divided between the 'flexible' on the one hand and the 'rigid' on the other. In the Netherlands, for example, the legality principle is further delineated by means of the principle of 'the primacy of the legislator'. According to this principle, it is not enough merely to provide a legal base for administrative action by the legislator. The democratically elected legislator should also provide adequate regulation of powers delegated to administrative authorities, including independent administrative bodies, for the legislator cannot delegate powers to adopt generally binding rules to independent administrative authorities, or indeed any other powers entailing a significant degree of discretion. In the light of this interpretation of the principle of legality, where the legislator holds primacy, the Dutch legislator and some Dutch authors have claimed that independent national competition and market authorities cannot be attributed powers that involve policy choices; their responsibility is solely to implement (applying the rules) policy decisions taken by the legislator and the minister (making the rules).[72]

Discretionary powers

Some argue that, by virtue of the legality principle, the powers of the independent agencies should be interpreted as strictly as possible. They say that discretionary powers should be as limited as possible. Research shows, however, that the distinction between policymaking and policy implementation is difficult to make in practice and may result in independent agencies having too limited legal mandates to take proper action. This in turn creates a risk of independent agencies being unable to exercise their powers adequately and to contribute effectively to the attainment of the goals of regulation.[73]

There are, however, several reasons why independent competition and market authorities should be given discretionary powers. Firstly, rapid technological developments in most of the fields subject to market regulation (such as the telecommunications market) mean these markets are very dynamic. In a rapidly changing environment driven by technological developments, it is essential to have the competences, instruments, and procedures needed to keep up with these changes. If its response is inadequate or delayed, regulatory supervision will fail to meet its objectives. Both substantive and procedural law should concentrate on this important characteristic of these markets. Flexibility of competences and reasonable yet strict periods

[72] See for a discussion on the legality principle in economic supervision: A T Ottow, *Telecommunicatietoezicht* (n9) 86–102.

[73] See for a discussion: S A C M Lavrijssen (n22) 77; A T Ottow, *Telecommunicatietoezicht* (n9) 86; and L Hancher, P Larouche, and S Lavrijssen (n22).

for decision-making by the market regulator and for court judgements are important preconditions for this.[74] Secondly, these regulatory fields are complex and require technical expertise and experience, which are often lacking on the part of the legislator. It should be left to the market regulator to make an expert judgement because the agency was established specifically for that purpose. A certain degree of flexibility is also required to allow scope for taking new developments into account and for adapting the interpretation of the rules accordingly. This requires open legal norms.

This can be illustrated by the example of internet telephony in the Netherlands, when the question arose as to whether the former Dutch independent post and telecommunications authority, OPTA, was legally permitted to regulate this activity. The legislation used the term 'voice over fixed infrastructure'; there was no mention of the internet as this had not been in existence at the time the Dutch Telecommunications Act was introduced. On the basis of the legality principle, the highest administrative court ruled that this term could not be taken to include internet telephony, and that OPTA therefore lacked the powers to intervene, with the result that competition was distorted. It was only several years later, after the legislation had been redrafted, that these new powers became available.[75]

Granting sufficient discretionary powers to independent competition and market authorities consequently requires trust in these agencies and a creative, purpose-oriented approach towards rule-making in the economic context: powers have to be delegated in order to enable agencies to perform the tasks and goals envisaged by the applicable rules. An overly legalistic approach will kill regulation and make it impossible for the agency to perform its work properly. This could also lead to societal disappointment, for which the agency will be held accountable. If an agency is too constrained by the legal mandate, this may result in a lack of powers and in failure to live up to the expectations of regulation. In new areas, the agency will need to be courageous enough to interpret and apply competencies and norms in an innovative way, while the legislator and politicians will also have to be willing to leave the details of oversight to the skilled agency created specifically for that purpose.

Competition and market authorities must be given the powers and tools they need to become effective. This requires intelligent rule-making and avoidance of black-and-white approaches. As Black states, 'So whether we

[74] A T Ottow, *Telecommunicatietoezicht* (n9).

[75] This internet example is discussed in A T Ottow, *Telecommunicatietoezicht* (n9) 107–11. See CBb 16 April 2004, *OPTA en Tiscali v KPN Telecom*, 2004 (7/8) *Mediaforum*, Jur. nr. 28, m.nt. D. Schipper, p. 262–66, LJN AO8356.

like it or not, discretion is here to stay—what is important is how it is used'.[76] It is a matter of 'managing discretion',[77] through open legal norms, laid down in the legislation.

Administrative law aspects

Obviously, an agency cannot simply be given *carte blanche* to achieve the objectives of oversight; it needs to be bound by administrative law safeguards. The challenge for the legislator, the independent agency, and the court assessing the behaviour of the agency lies in finding a balance between applying a functional approach—as said previously, the instrumental dimension of all the principles is an important consideration—and simultaneously satisfying requirements for legality and safeguards. Establishing the right balance is no easy task. It should explicitly be recognized that implementing instrumental, purpose-oriented rules and complying with legality and safeguard principles are not always compatible, given that the objectives of regulation and the dynamic characteristics of markets mean that wide powers, independence, speed, and effectiveness are also important ingredients. These ingredients consequently have to be reconciled with the common administrative principles such as legal certainty, carefulness, and proportionality.

Conclusion

The legality principle contains the administrative law principles, such as legal certainty, procedural fairness, proportionality, and sufficient reasoning, while the protection of fundamental rights also forms an integral part of the legality principle in the context of market and competition authorities. Moreover, independent agencies cannot function properly without a sufficient legal basis, comprising flexible and sufficient discretionary powers.

Independence principle

The independence principle encompasses the subvalues of objectivity, impartiality, integrity, expertise, and professionalism. These subvalues together adhere to the concept of overall independence and ensure that the independent agency can do its work effectively and efficiently. This principle therefore overlaps to some extent with the principle of effectiveness, and so do its subvalues of professionalism and expertise, since these also constitute elements contributing to the effectiveness of the agency. I have

[76] J Black, 'Managing Discretion' (n7) 3. [77] ibid 22–23.

chosen to discuss them under the heading of the key principle of independence. The effectiveness principle elaborates further on the independence principle.[78]

In the case of market regulators it has been widely accepted that independence is one of the fundamental principles for good oversight. For competition agencies, too, a sufficient degree of independence is seen as a key ingredient in allowing agencies to enforce competition policy satisfactorily.[79] By delegating competition law powers to an independent body, the legislature tries to ensure that the application and interpretation of sector-regulation and competition rules are based primarily on economic and legal arguments, rather than being shaped by political pressure. Being independent allows the agency to take impartial decisions on its own account, without undue influence from political or party interests. This does not mean, however, that the agency takes its decisions in an ivory tower. These decisions have to be made on a well-informed basis, to which stakeholders have been able to contribute the necessary information and submit their observations. In addition, the level of independence cannot be absolute, and the independent agency must clearly operate within the boundaries of its legal mandate.[80]

The elements of impartiality, integrity, the distinction between *de jure* and *de facto* independence, and the different degrees and EU levels in relation to the independence principle merit special attention.

Impartiality

In general, independent agencies must take decisions without undue influence, based on the available information, and giving appropriate weight to the different interests at stake. The Netherlands Scientific Council for

[78] Parts of this paragraph on independence are taken from: C A Fonteijn and A T Ottow, 'Independence of Competition Authorities—Independence in Heart, Mind and Law' in D Arts et al (eds), *Mundi et Europae Civis: Liber Amicorum Jacques Steenbergen* (Brussels, Larcier 2014) 405; and A T Ottow, 'The Different Levels of Protection of National Supervisors' Independence in the European Landscape' in S Comtois and K. de Graaf (eds), *On Judicial and Quasi-Judicial Independence* (Netherlands Institute for Law and Governance, Series 7 Den Haag: Boom Juridische Uitgevers 2013) 139.

[79] See ICN (International Competition Network) Advocacy Working Group, 'Advocacy and Competition Policy' (2002) report presented at the first ICN's conference in Naples, Italy 53–55 <http://www.internationalcompetitionnetwork.org/uploads/library/doc358.pdf> accessed 17 April 2014. See also G Monti, 'Independence, Interdependence and Legitimacy: the EU Commission, National Authorities and the European Competition Network' (2014) EUI Department of Law Research Paper No. 2014/01, Fiesole and the references to literature in footnote 6 <http://papers.ssrn.com/sol3/papers.cfm?abstract_id=2379320> accessed 22 September 2014.

[80] Monti even speaks of 'an authority's appropriate degree of dependence': Monti (n79) 3.

Government Policy also recognized this element of impartiality as a fundamental aspect of good oversight when it stated that:

> Government supervision is essentially a policy instrument that should operate within politically defined frameworks. But the value for society is closely bound up with the impartiality of that role and the associated independence from politics and public administration. Impartiality and independence from those operating 'in the field' are likewise absolute requirements. As core values, they must be firmly entrenched before the public can place its trust in supervision, but also before supervisory bodies can play a vital role in identifying and addressing problems and risks and amending policy and legislation.[81]

Integrity

Integrity constitutes an important building block of independence. As Das and Quintyn rightly point out, integrity should be regarded as the 'forgotten pillar'. Although these authors treat independence and integrity as two distinct pillars in their four-pillar model, the independence principle functions in my categorization as an umbrella for the subvalue of integrity. According to their definition, integrity refers to the set of mechanisms that ensure that agencies' staff can pursue institutional goals without having to compromise their own behaviour or self-interest.[82] Appointment procedures, along with internal integrity standards and procedures, must be designed to avoid regulatory capture; in other words, to ensure that staff are not 'captured' by self-interest,[83] or by the interests of the enterprises they supervise. The term 'regulatory capture' is generally used to refer to the possibility of the agency being influenced by external interest groups ('captured') and reflecting these interests in its decisions.[84] It must make its own judgement on the basis of all the information available and having impartially weighed all the different interests against each other. Organizational measures have to be in place to ensure safeguards preventing capture. Integrity can be strengthened through the acceptance and implementation of the agency's core values. Greater professionalism can also form a buffer against capture and self-interest, although here, too, trust in the agency and in its willingness and ability to apply these core values is also vital.

[81] 'Supervising Public Interests. Towards a Broader Perspective on Government Supervision' (n45).

[82] See for further reading: T E Becker, 'Integrity in Organizations: Beyond Honesty and Conscientiousness' (1998) 23(1) Academy of Management Review 154.

[83] U S Das and M Quintyn (n16).

[84] See R Baldwin, M Cave, and M Lodge (n18) 40–49 for an overview of the economic literature on regulatory capture.

De jure *and* de facto *independence*

A distinction has to be made between *de jure* and *de facto* independence. The initial requirement is for *de jure* (or formal) independence: the legislation must contain safeguards to ensure that independence is legally protected. However, this does not guarantee *de facto* independence; an agency's behaviour and decisions also need to be independent.[85] As the 2013 OECD Report states, 'A culture of independence, strong leadership and an appropriate working relationship with government and other stakeholders are essential to independent regulatory behaviour'.[86] Leadership by the board of an agency is key to ensuring that an agency produces the intended results. Setting a clear mission and priorities, built around a transparent strategy, will create credibility, both within and outside the agency, and give the organization a strong drive to succeed. Independent agencies should keep up their independence themselves, and more or less earn it as a self-confident, professional organization that listens and knows there is not just one truth, and who can be trusted by all parties.[87]

However, if an agency is influenced, be it politically or otherwise, that influence can be both indirect and subtle. How budgets are allocated (and influence capacity and priorities) and how board appointments are made are important elements in this respect,[88] which are discussed in more detail in chapter 4 on institutional design.

Degrees of independence: independence is not absolute

What degree of independence should be regarded as acceptable? This varies across sectors and countries, depending on the exact institutional design of the agencies, and on their relationships with delegators and other actors.[89] Although there is no 'one size fits all' model,[90] empirical research shows that

[85] M Thatcher, 'Regulation after Delegation: Independent Regulatory Agencies in Europe' (2002) 9(6) Journal of European Public Policy 954; M Thatcher, 'The Third Force? Independent Regulatory Agencies and Elected Politicians in Europe' (2005) 18(3) Governance 347.

[86] OECD, 'Principles for the Governance of Regulators' (2013) Draft paper for public consultation 32 <http://www.oecd.org/gov/regulatory-policy/Governance%20of%20Regulators%20FN%202.docx> accessed 17 March 2014.

[87] C A Fonteijn and A T Ottow (n78) 414.

[88] See Advocacy Working Group, Advocacy and Competition Policy (n79).

[89] M Quintyn (n16) 268.

[90] F Gilardi, 'Policy Credibility and Delegation to Independent Regulatory Agencies: A Comparative Empirical Analysis' (2002) 9(6) Journal of European Public Policy 873; F Gilardi, 'The Formal Independence of Regulators: A Comparison of 17 Countries and 7 Sectors' (2005) 11(4) Swiss Political Science Review 139; F Gilardi, 'The Same, but Different: Central Banks, Regulatory Agencies, and the Politics of Delegation to Independent Authorities' (2007) 5(3) Comparative European Politics 303; M Thatcher 'Regulation after Delegation: Independent Regulatory Agencies in Europe' (n85).

independent agencies have some characteristics in common. After conducting a worldwide survey among 175 market and competition authorities from 88 countries (in fields such as competition, financial markets, food safety, and telecoms), Hanretty and Koop concluded that 'a picture emerges of an autonomously operating organization, which has nevertheless fairly strong links to government as a consequence of political appointments and nominations, reporting obligations towards politicians and political instructions and inquiries',[91] all of which are institutional design aspects of the independence principle and discussed in more detail in chapter 4.

Das and Quintyn stress that independence can never be absolute and is not an end in itself. Oversight cannot take place in an ivory tower: the independent agency is to a large extent dependent on the information it receives from those market parties, or other stakeholders, who in turn will have their own interests and agendas. Although the agency will need to consult and discuss the relevant issues with them, this input must not result in capture.

Political independence, too, is not absolute, although the exact extent of it is unclear.[92] It is generally accepted that policy guidelines can be given, but that they should not interfere with agencies' individual decisions.[93] How much influence ministers or ministries can have on an agency remains unclear in practice (this issue is discussed in more detail in chapter 4). Jenny points out that structural independence can have ambiguous effects on competition advocacy because an agency that is too separated from other parts of the government may lack access to decision-makers within the ministries or other areas of government.[94] Although this is certainly a risk, it cannot be allowed to form an obstacle to independence. Independent agencies should consequently be alert to this possible consequence and invest in their relationships with governmental bodies.

[91] C Hanretty and C Koop, 'Comparing Regulatory Agencies: Report on the Results of a Worldwide Survey' (2009) European University Institute Working Paper RSCAS 2009/63. On the basis of the answers of 175 regulatory agencies from 88 countries, we conclude that although their design shows huge variation, a picture of the model regulator can be drawn, further discussed in chapter 4 of this book.

[92] See chapter 2, 'Preventing Undue Influence and Maintaining Trust. Principles of the Degree of Independence', of OECD, 'Principles for the Governance of Regulators' (2013) Draft paper for public consultation 31-42 <http://www.oecd.org/gov/regulatory-policy/Governance%20of%20Regulators%20FN%202.docx> accessed 17 March 2014.

[93] L Hancher, P Larouche, and S A C M Lavrijssen (n22). CBb 29 June 2010 *Gas Transport Services Case* NJB 1499 ECLI:NL:CBB:2010:BM9470.

[94] F Jenny, 'Competition Authorities: Independence and Advocacy' in I Lianos and D D Sokol, *The Global Limits of Competition Law* (Stanford, Stanford University Press 2012) 166.

Different EU levels of protecting independence

From a *de jure* perspective four different levels of protection provided for the principle of independence can be distinguished at the EU level. There are, in fact, four categories of agencies, each enjoying a different level of legal protection, ranging from high-level protection, over medium-level and low-level protection, to no formal independence requirements at all.

First a high level of protection is given to central banks and data protection agencies. The independence of the ECB is safeguarded in the Treaty on the Functioning of the European Union (TFEU)[95] itself, while independence requirements for central banks with regard to monetary policy are also laid down in Article 130 TFEU, which states that 'When exercising the powers and carrying out the tasks and duties conferred upon them [...], neither the European Central Bank, nor a national central bank, nor any member of their decision-making bodies shall seek or take instructions from Union institutions, bodies, offices or agencies, from any government of a Member State or from any other body'.[96]

In the important judgement in the *European Commission v Germany*, the ECJ gives a very wide interpretation to the legal concept of independence. It ruled that the agencies responsible for monitoring the processing of personal data[97] were expected to perform their tasks 'with complete independence'.[98] The ECJ concluded from this that the independent agency should be able to fulfil its obligations objectively and impartially; in other words, without being exposed to any direct or indirect influence. Rejecting Germany's claim that this broad interpretation represented an infringement of the principle of democracy in Europe, the court ruled that a broad interpretation of the term 'complete independence' did not violate the principle of democracy as the legislator was permitted to define the powers available to the independent agency and could also require it to report on its activities to parliament.

[95] Treaty on the Functioning of the European Union (TFEU) [2010] OJ C083/01 <http://eur-lex.europa.eu/legal-content/EN/TXT/HTML/?uri=OJ:C:2010:083:FULL&from=EN> accessed 22 September 2014.

[96] M Quintyn, 'Independent Agencies: More Than a Cheap Copy of Independent Central Banks?' (n16).

[97] Directive 95/46/EC of the European Parliament and of the Council of 24 October 1995 on the protection of individuals with regard to the processing of personal data and on the free movement of such data [1995] OJ L 281/31.

[98] ECJ 9 March 2010, case C-518/07 *Commission v Federal Republic of Germany* 2010 I-01885. It must be noted that in this case the text of the Directive used this language and must be seen in the context of the protection of a fundamental right. It remains to be seen whether such a broad interpretation will also be used in other cases. A T Ottow and M Aelen, 'Commission v. Federal Republic of Germany' (2010) 11(6) European Human Rights Cases 679; A T Ottow, 'The Different Levels of Protection of National Supervisors' Independence in the European Landscape' (n78).

Similarly, parliament or the government may appoint the agency's board members.[99] Therefore, although consensus exists on the need for market and competition authorities to be independent, there is far less agreement on how this should be accomplished organizationally (i.e. on the formats for independent agencies).[100] Such institutional design aspects of independence are discussed in more detail in chapter 4.

Medium-level protection of independence can be found with the energy and telecommunications regulators. When market regulators were first established during the market liberalization processes, they had to be put at a distance from government. Many of the incumbents were still owned, or at least partly owned, by central or local governments. To ensure a level playing field and to avoid any conflict of interest, governments could not combine their supervisory function with market activities. Indeed, such 'double headedness' would have given rise to a direct conflict of interest. The liberalization directives consequently imposed requirements for these new market regulators to be independent of market parties, thus ensuring a legal and functional separation between the two sides.[101] These requirements have since been further clarified and specified in ECJ case law.[102] This independence principle has been expanded, since the end of the 1990s, to include independence from the political arena. Although regarded as more controversial, given that it directly interferes with member states' constitutional autonomy, this element has slowly been incorporated into the principle.[103]

Media regulators only enjoy a low level of protection for their independence. The only requirements for independence and efficient functioning of national regulatory bodies in the audiovisual media sector are found in Article 30 of Chapter XI ('Cooperation between regulatory bodies of the Member States') in the Audiovisual Media Services Directive.[104] The current text of Article 30 reflects a difficult compromise between the visions of the

[99] This judgement is recently confirmed in the case of ECJ 16 October 2012, *Commission v Austria*, case C-614/10, ECLI:EU:C:2012:631.

[100] International Competition Network Competition Policy Implementation Working Group (n48) 26.

[101] A T Ottow, *Telecommunicatietoezicht* (n9); A T Ottow in S Comtois and K de Graaf (n78); and S A C M Lavrijssen and A T Ottow, 'Independent Supervisory Authorities; A Fragile Concept' (2012) 39(4) Legal Issues of Economic Integration 419.

[102] See, for example, case C-202/88 *France v Commission*, [1991] ECR I-01223; case C-69/91 *Decoster* [1993] ECR I-05335; case C-18/88 *GB-Inno* [1991] ECR I-0594; and case C-82/07 *Comisión del Mercado de las Telecomunicaciones* [2008] ECR I-1265.

[103] A T Ottow, *Telecommunicatietoezicht* (n9); A T Ottow in S Comtois and K de Graaf (n78); and S A C M Lavrijssen and A T Ottow 2012 (n101). See, for example, the requirements of Directive 2009/140/EC (telecom directive), recital 13.

[104] Directive 2010/13/EU of the European Parliament and of the Council of 10 March 2010 on the coordination of certain provisions laid down by law, regulation or administrative action

European Parliament, the European Commission, and the Council. Recital 94 and Article 30 do not impose a formal legal obligation on member states to create an independent regulator where such an agency does not yet exist.[105] If, however, a new agency is created, this regulator should be independent. But what does that mean? In contrast to the Energy and Communications Directives, the Media Services Directive does not state any specific legal requirements. As media pluralism and freedom of expression must be considered to be fundamental rights, it is at least remarkable that the Media Services Directive does not provide any stricter provisions and safeguards to ensure the 'depolitization' of media regulation and independent oversight. Lessons need to be learned from other sectors, such as the communications sector, on amending the legal requirements in the Media Services Directive in that respect.[106]

For competition authorities, too, the formal EU rules on independence are underdeveloped; as a matter of fact, so far no formal requirements have been laid down in EU legislation, nor does Regulation 1/2003, for example, specify any formal requirements for independence. However, a sufficient degree of independence is seen as a key ingredient that allows agencies to enforce regulatory and competition policy satisfactorily.[107] This fourth level of protection for independence differs from the third one in that competition authorities' independence appears to gain protection from ECJ case law. The ECJ's recent ruling in the *Vebic* case[108] seems to suggest that the court is further curtailing member states' national autonomy to shape their national competition authorities in a certain direction. The ECJ observed in this case that Belgian law was in conflict with EU law, given that the

in Member States concerning the provision of audiovisual media services (Audiovisual Media Services Directive) [2010] OJ L 95/1.

[105] See the reports: Hans Bredow Institute for Media Research et al, 'INDIREG Final Report: Indicators for Independence and Efficient Functioning of Audiovisual Media Services Regulatory Bodies for the Purpose of Enforcing the Rules in the AVMS Directive' (2011) <http://cac.ceu.hu/node/26176> accessed 29 September 2014; and Hans Bredow Institute for Media Research et al, 'Indicators for Independence and Efficient Functioning of Audiovisual Media Services Regulatory Bodies for the Purpose of Enforcing the Rules in the AVMS Directive (INDIREG study)' (2012) <http://cac.ceu.hu/node/27383> accessed 29 September 2014. See further on the independence of media regulators: Wolfgang Schultz, Peggy Valcke, and Kristina Irion, *The Independence of the Media and its Regulatory Agencies* (Bristol/Chicago: Intellect 2013).

[106] A T Ottow, 'The Different Levels of Protection of National Supervisors' Independence in the European Landscape' (n78).

[107] See Advocacy Working Group, Advocacy and Competition Policy. Report presented at the first ICN's conference in Naples, Italy (2002) 53–55 <http://www.internationalcompetitionnetwork.org/uploads/library/doc358.pdf> accessed 17 April 2014.

[108] ECJ 7 December 2010, *Vebic v Raad voor de Mededinging and Minister van Economie*, case C-439/08.

Belgian competition authority was not afforded rights as a party to proceedings and was thus prevented from defending its own decision before the Belgian court. The ECJ reasoned, on the basis of the EU effectiveness principle and the text of Regulation 1/2003, that the member states were required to designate the competition authorities so that EU competition law could be complied with effectively. Is independence not one of the requirements for the effective application of competition law? If so, it can be argued—following the *Vebic* judgement—that independence of the national competition authorities forms an essential ingredient for the effective application of EU competition law.[109] In the ten years evaluation of the Commission of Regulation 1/2003, the Commission stresses the need of independent national competition authorities and that further guarantees need to be introduced.[110]

In summary, four levels of protection can be distinguished in the European landscape of the areas discussed. Firstly, there is the monetary policy and data protection area, where the EU legislator and court have recognized the importance of independence and have secured a high level of protection of independence. A mid-category is the energy and communications area, with legal requirements that can be qualified as a medium level of independence. Then there is the media sector, where the level of protection is low. This is also the case in the area of competition law, where there is no formal requirement in the legislation, although this can arguably be construed from the *Vebic* case.

Conclusion

The independence principle contains the subvalues of integrity, impartiality, objectivity, professionalism, and expertise. There is clearly a difference between the *de jure* protection of independence and independence in the daily life of an agency. In order to gain trust and authority, agencies have to earn their independence through their behaviour.

[109] C A Fonteijn and A T Ottow (n78). See also on the institutional consequences of the *Vebic* case: P van Cleynenbreugel, 'From Shared Competences to Constitutional Heteronomy. The Institutional Architecture of Supranationally Structured Market Supervision' (dissertation, KU Leuven 2013).

[110] *Communication from the Commission to the European Parliament and the Council. Ten Years of Antitrust Enforcement under Regulation 1/2003: Achievements and Future Perspectives* (2014) 453 COM, 9, 12 <http://ec.europa.eu/competition/antitrust/legislation/antitrust_enforcement_10_years_en.pdf> accessed 23 September 2014. See also the Commission Staff, 'Enhancing competition enforcement by the member States'competition authorities: institutional and procedural issues, Working Document SWD (2014) 231/2, 6–8.

Transparency principle

The transparency principle is a broad principle regarded as a fundamental basis, both for good regulat*ion*[111] and supervis*ion*, and for good regulat*ors* and supervis*ors*.[112] In the categorization used here, the transparency principle encompasses the subvalues of openness and accessibility, participation and consultation, and predictability. The transparency principle also comprises the value of accountability as these concepts are closely related. Some subvalues categorized in another LITER principle have overlap with the transparency principle, and vice versa.

The transparency principle clearly combines various distinct functions, all related to the instrumental and safeguard dimensions of the LITER principles identified. Competition and market authorities are bound by the need for transparency. Their procedures must therefore be fair, accessible, and open, while also making sufficient provision for consultation and stakeholder participation. Decisions and interventions must also be based on sufficiently reliable and sound justification, as well as on legal and economic reasoning. These transparency requirements reflect the guardian role of this principle. However, this principle also has an instrumental dimension in that transparent supervision will help make oversight more effective (i.e. preventive and legitimacy effects). Transparency can create certainty and better compliance, thus preventing enterprises from committing infringements.

The elements of openness and sufficient reasoning, confidentiality, accountability, and participation and consultation require special attention when discussing the transparency principle.

Openness and sufficient reasoning

Transparency relates to the agency's activities, interventions, and decision-making. It refers to an environment in which agencies' objectives, frameworks, decisions and their rationale, data, and other information are provided to stakeholders in a comprehensive, accessible, and timely manner.[113] Prechal and De Leeuw define the principle of transparency as follows:

> Transparency means that the process through which public authorities make decisions should be understandable and open, the decisions themselves should be

[111] L Hancher, P Larouche, and S A C M Lavrijssen (n22).

[112] See also E M Fox and M J Trebilcock (eds) (n23) 367–76. See also M Aelen, *Beginselen van goed markttoezicht* (n13) chapter 'Transparantie en accountability als beginselen van goed markttoezicht'.

[113] M Quintyn (n16) 280, with reference to the IMF Supporting Document of the Code of Good Practices on Transparency in Monetary and Financial Policies (2000) <http://www.imf.org/external/np/mae/mft/code/index.htm> accessed 24 April 2014.

reasoned and, as far as possible, the information on which the decisions are based should be available to the public.[114]

Transparency in the form of legal reasoning in decisions provides the grounds and justification for interventions and makes it possible to verify decisions.

Transparency clearly also has an instrumental aspect. Competition and market authorities themselves seek publicity and make efforts to increase their transparency so as to become more visible and to show what they stand for in what can be referred to as 'branding of the agency'. A modern agency is open, has its own website, mission statement, communications department, brochures, consultations, round table meetings, press conferences, press releases, and so on. Silent supervision is outdated. This increased visibility has also caused market and competition authorities to come in for more critical scrutiny. Paradoxically, therefore, increased visibility (i.e. increased transparency) also results in more concerns being raised about these agencies' behaviour. Distrust in agencies is high, with constant questions about whether they are doing their job properly. 'Where was the regulator?' has been a frequently heard question since the start of the financial crisis in 2007. Society is demanding more openness about agencies' measures and their effectiveness. The media are playing an increasingly important role in this respect, particularly when things go wrong ('no news is good news'). Competition and market authorities are expected to be transparent and to justify the assessment of how they perform their tasks and the effects of their interventions.

Transparency can also be used as an enforcement instrument: the publication of decisions, and of infringements by companies, constitutes a form of 'naming and shaming', and one which has certain deterrent effects. The instrumental dimension of this transparency instrument will need to be weighed against the impact on the enterprises involved; indeed it may give rise to privacy concerns relating to the counterpart of openness: confidentiality.

Confidentiality

The transparency principle can conflict with the confidentiality principle, i.e. with the need to protect confidential information or individual interests. However, overprotecting individual interests is also a risk. Although there may be sound arguments for secrecy (business secrets, price-sensitive information, or the wish to prevent a bank run), individual interests have

[114] S Prechal and M E De Leeuw, 'Transparency: a General Principle of EU Law?' in U Bernitz et al, *General Principles of EC Law in a Process of Development* (Alphen aan den Rijn: Kluwer Law International 2008) 201–41, 202.

to be balanced against the public interests involved, including the public's right to information and the goals of the supervision. Protecting information can make oversight less transparent and thus hinder the public interest. Competition and market authorities provide consumers with information, thus using communication as an enforcement tool to empower them to take informed decisions on, for example, switching energy providers.[115] In other cases they may seek to achieve a deterrent effect by publishing data, decisions, details of fines imposed, and so on (on dedicated websites or otherwise) as a means of improving compliance. A ban on publication of a fined offence (and the research associated with it), or other observed infringements or findings, hinders transparency in that the agency is then unable to be held accountable for its proceedings and to inform the public about infringements. Consumers should be able to obtain correct and complete information about supervised businesses and their products. Denying them this information can damage society. At the same time, however, publication can cause substantial reputational damage by the 'naming and shaming' of the enterprises concerned.

The tension between openness and confidentiality is admittedly a difficult issue, and one with which independent agencies have to deal in their daily practice. However, *not* providing openness, and thus setting aside the principle of transparency, can lead to ineffective oversight and enforcement. Openness and transparency should, therefore, be the basic starting points, given the clear link between the principle of transparency and the principle of effectiveness.

Accountability

The value of accountability, which is regarded here as forming part of the transparency principle, must be distinguished from accountability as a mechanism.[116] Being accountable, as a virtue, is used in a very broad (positive) sense to mean 'a willingness to act in a transparent, fair, and equitable way'.[117] Market and competition authorities are expected to be accountable: accountable to the minister, to the political arena, to the legislator, to the enterprises they supervise, and to citizens. This gives them legitimacy and authority.[118] There is therefore a clear relationship between transparency

[115] For example ACM in the Netherlands introduced the 'energy coach' stimulating the consumer to switch energy providers, encouraging more competition in the energy markets: see <http://www.consuwijzer.nl/thema/overstapcoach-energie> accessed 22 September 2014.

[116] M Bovens 'Two Concepts of Accountability: Accountability as a Virtue and as a Mechanism' (n25).

[117] ibid 949.

[118] J Black, 'Constructing and Contesting Legitimacy and Accountability in Polycentric Regulatory Regimes' (2008) 2 Law, Society and Economy Working Papers.

(including accountability) and legitimacy. These elements require more than just communication (and a strategy for this), which, albeit forming an important activity of an independent agency, is only one element for complying with the principle of transparency.

Quintyn and Taylor argue that accountability fulfils at least four functions in that it (i) provides public oversight (cf. LITER principle of responsibility); (ii) maintains and enhances legitimacy (cf. LITER principle of legality); (iii) enhances the integrity of both the institution and the individual staff member (cf. LITER principle of independence); and (iv) improves agency performance (cf. LITER principle of effectiveness).[119] Ogus[120] distinguishes three forms of accountability in the context of oversight: financial accountability, procedural accountability, and substantive accountability. He points out that independent agencies not only have to give financial account of their activities, but also have to ensure that they comply with procedural standards (procedures must be fair, transparent, and impartial) and that their decisions are in line with the goals of the regulations. Both Ogus' procedural and substantive accountability firmly overlap with the LITER principle of legality.

The way in which the independent agency can be held accountable relates to the instruments, or the mechanisms, used to inform stakeholders. Clearly, accountability and independence are two sides of the same coin. If effective accountability mechanisms are in place, the delegating government and other stakeholders will feel more confident in believing that the independent agencies will exercise their tasks and powers in compliance with the original intention of the delegating government.[121] A requirement for independence needs, therefore, to be matched by requirements for sufficient accountability[122] so as

[119] M Quintyn and M W Taylor, 'Robust Regulators and Their Political Masters: Independence and Accountability in Theory' in D Masciandaro and M Quintyn (eds), *Designing Financial Supervision Institutions: Independence, Accountability and Governance* (Cheltenham, UK: Edward Elgar 2007) 3.

[120] A I Ogus, *Regulation: Legal Form and Economic Theory* (Clarendon Press Clarendon Law Series 1994) 111.

[121] See in the same sense, International Competition Network Competition Policy Implementation Working Group (n48) 26 <http://ec.europa.eu/competition/information/icn_seminar_2009/report_final_version.pdf> accessed 15 April 2014: 'Accountability is in fact necessary to maintain independence in the longer term.'

[122] See, for example, D Curtin, 'Delegation to EU Non-Majoritarian Agencies and Emerging Practices of Public Accountability' in D Geradin et al, *Regulation Through Agencies in the EU. A New Paradigm of European Governance* (Cheltenham, UK: Edward Elgar 2005) 88–119; M Groenleer, *The Autonomy of European Union Agencies. A Comparative Study of Institutional Development* (Delft: Uitgeverij Eburon 2009); M Busuioc, *The Accountability of European Agencies. Legal Provisions and Ongoing Practices* (dissertation Utrecht University, Delft: Uitgeverij Eburon 2010); and M Scholten, *The Political Accountability of EU Agencies: Learning from the US Experience*, (dissertation Maastricht: Datawyse/Universitaire Pers Maastricht 2014).

to ensure the various bodies are subject to proper control. The mechanism of accountability is, therefore, a linking pin between the different components of the LITER principles, and the way in which they are linked is discussed in the next few chapters.

Participation and consultation

Some authors see participation as forming part of the subvalue of accountability (the virtue, as opposed to the mechanism),[123] whereas others see it as a separate principle.[124] The EU has granted citizens' right to participate in the Union's actions by means of consultations, dialogues, and petitions a specific article in the Treaty on European Union, i.e. Article 11 TEU. Many independent agencies use participation and consultation as tools for gathering information and for providing stakeholders with the opportunity to deliver input to the decision-making process in order to underpin the justification for the choices they make and to balance different interests against each other fairly and proportionally. In this respect, the safeguard and instrumental dimensions combine to reinforce each other: transparency during the decision-making process gives the agency greater legitimacy for its interventions, thus providing more legal certainty, preventing capture, and at the same time demonstrating the agency's openness. It obliges the agency to reflect on its own position by taking account of its critics, and thus possibly also preventing mismanagement or misuse of powers.[125] At the same time, trade-offs and potential conflicts are involved in pursuing the aims of participation on the one hand, and expert and efficient decision-making on the other.[126] There is a risk of overkill in accountability mechanisms or participation, and this risk is not always recognized. Oversight must remain effective, as discussed with regard to the effectiveness principle.

Conclusion

The transparency principle has a broad scope, including subvalues such as openness, accessibility, accountability, participation, and consultation. Transparency will create greater certainty and predictability, and ultimately improve the supervisor's legitimacy.

[123] M Bovens, 'Two Concepts of Accountability: Accountability as a Virtue and as a Mechanism' (n25) 959.

[124] H Addink, *Goed Bestuur* (Den Haag: Boom Juridische Uitgevers 2010).

[125] M Bovens, T Schillemans, and P 't Hart, 'Does Public Accountability Work? An Assessment Tool' (2008) 86(1) Public Administration 225, 231.

[126] R. Baldwin, M. Cave, and M. Lodge (n20) 339.

Effectiveness principle

This leads us to the fourth good agency principle: supervision must be effective. In my categorization, the effectiveness principle encompasses enforcement with its tools and instruments, and comprises the subvalues of speed, efficiency, flexibility, and prioritization. In order to be effective, oversight must be able to meet the goals of regulation and allow the interventions needed to achieve these goals. The way the supervisory space is structured has a major influence on the overall effectiveness of oversight. This requires a sufficiently clear mandate, optimal agency design, clear and efficient decision-making and appeal procedures, and lastly effective tools and instruments. The whole supervisory framework must also fit together well. Ogus summarized this in his standard work *Regulation*:

> All regulatory systems require a number of tasks: as an exercise of policy-making, the goals of a regime must be established; those goals must then be translated into the principles and rules which control behavior; and there must be procedures for explicating and enforcing the principles and rules and for the adjudication of disputes arising from them.[127]

To this end, an authority must have the legal powers and instruments it needs for this purpose. There is a clear link in that respect between the legality and effectiveness principles. Not only do the enforcement styles, and the selected instruments and tools, need to be chosen in accordance with these principles, but so, too, must procedures be fair, and interventions proportionate. Otherwise, intervention may conflict with administrative law principles and be void, in which case it cannot be considered effective.

With regard to the effectiveness principle, we will have a closer look into the elements of enforcement and its styles and tools and instruments, prioritization, and efficiency and speed. Additionally, special attention will be paid to the EU principle of effectiveness.

Enforcement

There is an important link between effectiveness and enforcement as enforcement forms a major building block in the overall effectiveness of an agency. A greater focus on enforcement can increase the effectiveness of regulatory supervision as the objectives of the regulation will then be met more effectively, although an emphasis on enforcement can also be at the expense of other activities, such as advocacy. Emphasis on enforcing the applicable rules and regulations, on complying with legal obligations, and on resolving

[127] A I Ogus (n120) 99.

problems in markets will ensure that the agency both correctly and sufficiently performs the tasks assigned to it by the legislator. The agency must use the means available to it in legislation, which can be applied either through formal or informal enforcement, whereby the agency seeks to ensure compliance through more informal instruments. Enforcement must in any event be proportionate: the agency should choose the tools and means that are proportionate to its aims and should restrict its interventions to those necessary in order to achieve the aims of the regulation or legislation. Proportionality forms an important element of enforcement and, therefore, also of the effectiveness principle, as discussed in more detail in chapter 5.

Styles and tools and instruments

One of the biggest challenges facing public enforcement authorities is in identifying the problems and selecting the right cases. How can they determine the appropriate risks and problems? Independent agencies are continually searching for the appropriate techniques, and many enforcement strategies have been developed around the world in an attempt to answer this question. In the event of under-enforcement, they will be blamed for not doing enough, while in the event of over-enforcement they will be blamed for being too stringent and forming an impediment to innovation and economic growth. It must be acknowledged that the optimal level of enforcement is hard to establish.

Prioritization

Although it has been argued that there should be an in-principle obligation to enforce (which is in some countries an established obligation), it is also recognized that independent agencies cannot do everything. Given the limited capacity and resources of the national competition and market authorities, the enforcement obligation (conferred upon them by EU law and ECJ case law) does not prevent them from setting their own priorities. This is an important issue in the area of enforcement. Agencies have to take their obligatory enforcement activities into account, while at the same time giving consideration to their capacity and budget restrictions. Which criteria can and should agencies select for their enforcement priorities? I will elaborate on the answer to that question in chapter 5 on enforcement.

Efficiency and speed

Effectiveness is linked to the need for efficiency: the burden of input in terms of effort and work force, and also the costs, must remain reasonable and affordable—both for the independent agencies and for the parties concerned.

The burdens on the agencies must not prevent them from institutional and instrumental innovation, nor from taking decisions efficiently. At the same time, a one-sided focus on budgets and costs may undermine the agency and conflict not only with the principle of independence, but also with the principle of effectiveness: the agency will then no longer be able to perform its tasks properly.

Speed and efficiency are also required for court appeals against decisions of the independent agency. A balance has to be found between access to justice (i.e. the agency's decisions must be reviewed by courts) and the effectiveness of the system. An example in which this problem cropped up, and which Dutch legislation promptly recognized when it revised the Telecommunications Act in 2004, relates to the legal protection procedures available for appeals against decisions issued by OPTA, the former independent Dutch postal and telecommunications authority. In keeping with the system provided for in the Dutch General Administrative Law Act, all OPTA decisions were open to both objection and appeal at two instances under the old Telecommunications Act. This multiple legal protection, and the long periods of time involved in the various procedures, had an adverse impact on the effectiveness of regulatory supervision in the telecommunications market. Indeed, the multiplicity of procedures created great legal uncertainty, and judgements frequently came too late or with far-reaching, and sometimes retroactive, effects for the relevant market(s), which had already implemented significant changes in response to new technological or other developments. Judgements on objections and court decisions were overtaken, as it were, by the new developments, or the solutions came too late. The new Telecommunications Act of 2004 dramatically changed this system as it did away with the possibility of objection for most OPTA decisions. In addition, appeals are now possible at one instance only: with the Dutch Trade and Industry Appeals Tribunal (CBb). Practice has shown meanwhile that this system correlates better to the specific regulation of this market.[128]

The EU principle of effectiveness

In the EU context effectiveness is clearly related to effective enforcement of EU law. EU law requires active enforcement by national agencies in the member states. ECJ case law makes it clear that member states have a duty

[128] See A T Ottow, *Telecommunicatietoezicht* (n9). Please note that OPTA has now merged with the Dutch competition authority and the Dutch consumer authority into the new authority Authority Consumer & Markets (ACM): see chapter 4 of this book.

to ensure effective enforcement. According to the ECJ, enforcement by the member states needs to be of an 'equal, effective, dissuasive and proportionate' nature.[129] In order to comply with these requirements, it is not sufficient simply to introduce legislation containing sanctions in the event of infringements. This duty to ensure effective enforcement rests partially on the national agency, which has to take action to ensure the rules of EU law are applied effectively (in, for example, banking or telecommunications law). In principle, the national agency is free to decide which sanctions it wishes to apply, providing they are effective and have a deterrent effect. Owing to different styles and cultures, divergent national oversight systems thus still exist in many sectors across the EU, and these differences may stand in the way of an EU-wide market. In secondary EU legislation this autonomy is now increasingly being curtailed by specific requirements of the EU legislator.

The carryover of EU law also comes up in the area of legal protection, both as a result of ECJ case law, which places additional requirements on access to justice, and the ability to invoke EU rights and duties.[130]

Conclusion

An effective framework for oversight must be in place for the independent agency to perform its tasks in accordance with the goals of the legislation. To this end, the agency needs a clear mandate (there is a clear link here with the legality principle), and the appropriate tools and instruments, as well as being able to choose the optimal enforcement style and having efficient procedures in place. At the same time, the legislator, the agencies, and the courts have to strike a delicate balance between efficiency on the one hand and building in sufficient safeguards to protect the interests of the supervisees and third parties concerned on the other hand.

Responsibility Principle

The responsibility principle is the principle according to which the agency is expected to make its choices based on the public needs of society, and the companies concerned are expected to accept their responsibility to comply with the rules. In my categorization, the responsibility principle encompasses trust, cooperation, and compliance. There is some overlap in subvalues between the responsibility principle and other LITER principles.

[129] A T Ottow, *Telecommunicatietoezicht. De invloed van het Europese en Nederlandse bestuurs(proces)recht* (n9); M Accetto and S Zleptnig, 'The Principle of Effectiveness: Rethinking its Role in Community Law' (2005) 11(3) European Public Law 375.

[130] A T Ottow, *Telecommunicatietoezicht* (n9) 336–59.

Participation, for example, is a subvalue of the transparency principle in this book's categorization, while it is also clearly linked to the principle of responsibility. And while the subvalue of compliance is categorized under the responsibility principle, it is obviously also linked to the effectiveness principle.

With regard to the responsibility principle elements discussed in more detail include the belief in market forces (or the limits to that belief), public interest, the modern-day concept of responsibility as in 'social responsibility', and aspects of trust.

Belief in market forces

The concept of responsibility calls the work of VerLoren van Themaat to mind, who singled out the principles of liberty, equality, and solidarity (*liberté, égalité, fraternité*) as the three fundamental principles of economic law (referred to here as 'VerLoren's trinity of principles').[131] He believed that economic law decisions should be made on the basis of these three principles and that these legitimized the rule of economic law. He proceeded on the basis of the principle of liberty—giving citizens the freedom to participate in the economy as they see fit. This principle is supported by the principle of equality, whereby the state has to ensure that all players are able to participate in the market on an equal competitive footing. However, the supply and demand mechanism in the market place does not necessarily protect general interests, and this is where his principle of solidarity comes in. Absolute reliance on the supply and demand mechanism—in the years of full liberalization of markets—has resulted in the principle of solidarity, as formulated by VerLoren van Themaat, disappearing further and further into the background. If the spotlight is strongly focused on commercialism, which is based on a more individualistic view of society and which means that the state maintains a greater distance leaving various issues up to market forces, there is a clear emphasis on the principles of liberty and equality, but less on solidarity. It is the state's task to protect those interests that are at risk of falling between two stools as a result of a free-market system.

Public interest

Views on state interventions have changed, however, in the years since the outbreak of the financial crisis in 2007. Against the background of societal change, mainly in Europe, where market competition is now being looked at

[131] '*Kenmerkende drieslag*' in Dutch. This paragraph is based on my inaugural lecture: A T Ottow, *Mastering the Market? Exploring New Forms of Market Supervision* (n9).

more critically, attention has been redirected towards issues of public interest. Introducing competition as such is no longer accepted as the sole remedy for market failures; instead, additional remedies are seen as being required in order to protect societal needs.[132] This also puts pressure on competition and market authorities to take these concerns into account when considering market interventions and formulating remedies.[133] Translating these developments into principles of public economic law means demanding attention, once again, for solidarity. This has several consequences. Firstly, more interventions are expected from the state, and consequently also from market and competition authorities, in order to protect public interests. Market and competition agencies will have to take these aspects into account when developing their strategic choices and enforcement cases. Secondly, if more attention is devoted to the principle of solidarity, state measures will also have to be designed to take more account of the need to encourage enterprises to accept their own responsibilities.

Responsibility

The solidarity principle is essentially the forerunner of what is now commonly referred to as 'social responsibility', and in that respect can be considered equivalent to what I call the modern-day principle of responsibility. It is increasingly accepted, for example, that enterprises have social responsibilities to respect fundamental rights and the environment, and this is reflected more and more often in corporate governance codes.[134]

The responsibility principle affects various aspects of public economic law. The state itself can accept responsibility for social issues by taking steps to protect certain interests, but it can also create rules to encourage corporate social responsibility. By appealing to an enterprise's own sense of social responsibility, we can ensure that certain objectives or interests are achieved more effectively than through unilateral state measures, assuming we believe that good results are possible through consultation and collaboration. This does not alter the fact that the enterprises concerned also have their own interests, such as a desire to avoid risks or to protect their reputation.

[132] K Cseres, 'The Controversies of the Consumer Welfare Standard' (2007) 3(2) Competition Law Review, 133

[133] T Prosser, *The Limits of Competition Law. Markets and Public Services* (Oxford: Oxford University Press 2004).

[134] See, for example, S Deva, 'Guiding Principles on Business and Human Rights: Implications for Companies' (2012) 9 (2) European Company Law 101; A Johnston, 'ISO 26000: Guiding Companies to Sustainability Through Social Responsibility?' (2012) 8 (2) European Company Law 110.

The responsibility principle places responsibility on the shoulders of the independent agency (What is expected from the agency in the specific circumstances of the case? Which public interest, for example, must be protected?) and on the shoulders of the enterprises concerned (What measures do they themselves need to take to ensure compliance with the rules?) and the consumers (What can they do themselves to prevent harm to happen?). Relying solely on the state to resolve societal problems will clearly create a moral hazard.

Trust

But what does this mean for oversight? The application of the responsibility principle could result in different choices being made for oversight. In my opinion, the belief that enterprises are willing to consider the interests of others explains some of the choices that have been made when designing market supervision. The responsibility principle, either consciously or unconsciously, plays a role in the selection of regulatory instruments. After all, an independent agency has to focus on how enterprises can be persuaded most effectively to comply with the rules. Oversight based on distrust of the supervisees will lead to more stringent and repressive action. If, however, an independent agency assumes it can achieve better results by appealing more to an enterprise's own sense of responsibility, it could deploy instruments based more on participation and cooperation than otherwise.[135]

Compliance strategies of market and competition authorities are therefore related to trust: if there is no belief that enterprises will comply with the rules on a voluntary basis, the enforcement style will switch to a more deterrent-based enforcement strategy and different enforcement instruments will be used.

Conclusion

The responsibility principle reflects the views on society and the role that the state, market and competition authorities, and enterprises have to play if the goals of regulation are to be achieved. Differing views will result in different choices for the design, not only of the substantive rules, but also of institutional governance, and of the enforcement strategies at stake. Trust or distrust in market parties' compliance may also result in different choices. At the same time, every problem will need a tailor-made solution, depending on the circumstances and characteristics of the market and parties involved.

[135] This paragraph is based on A T Ottow, *Mastering the Market? Exploring New Forms of Market Supervision* (n9).

Conclusion

This chapter identifies and discusses the good agency or LITER principles, which are legality, independence, transparency, effectiveness, and responsibility. These key fundamental principles all form essential ingredients for the choices to be made in the supervisory environment and how we view market and competition authorities. Trade-offs will have to be made as there is no single, overriding principle, and applying one principle may conflict with another in practice. This makes the life of an independent agency one great balancing act, in which difficult choices have to be made. It is of key importance, however, for the agency to operate within its legal mandate, in an independent way, based on sound legal and economic grounds, and in a transparent, efficient, and responsible way.

The following chapters examine how these LITER principles of good agency behaviour influence the institutional design of agencies (chapter 4), their enforcement practices (chapter 5), and the assessment of their behaviour and the judicial review of their decisions (chapter 6).

4

Institutional Design

Introduction

This chapter's central theme is the institutional design of market and competition authorities.[1] On the basis of the LITER principles of good agency behaviour, the institutional aspects of independent agencies are analysed in order to formulate an answer to this chapter's key questions: how do these principles influence the choices made with respect to institutional design and what is the optimal design for adhering to the LITER principles?

The extent to which design choices influence the functioning of an agency has so far been underestimated. Research on institutional design in organizational and political science has to date sought mainly to explain the chosen design; in other words, why public organizations are structured as they are. Various models of institutional design have been presented, with most of these aligning either with the contingency theory[2] or with the theory of structural change.[3] Organizational science looks at the task environment of organizations and seeks to identify the functions that explain the outcome of the institutional design and change, while the theory of structural change in political science claims that organizational forms are merely the result of political considerations.

The areas of competition law and sector regulation focus mainly on substantive law, on the decisions of these agencies, and on measuring the

[1] Parts of this chapter are based on A T Ottow, 'Erosion or Innovation?: The Institutional Design of Competition Agencies—A Dutch Case Study' (2014) 2 (1) Journal of Antitrust Enforcement 25; C A Fonteijn and A T Ottow, 'Independence of Competition Authorities—Independence in Heart, Mind and Law' in D Arts et al (eds), *Mundi et Europae Civis: Liber Amicorum Jacques Steenbergen* (Brussels: Larcier 2014).

[2] L Donaldson, *The Contingency Theory of Organizations* (Thousand Oaks CA, London, New Delhi: Sage 2001).

[3] F Gilardi, 'Policy Credibility and Delegation to Independent Regulatory Agencies: A Comparative Empirical Analysis' (2002) 9 Journal of European Public Policy 873; K Yesilkagit and J Christensen, 'Institutional Design and Formal Autonomy: Political versus Historical and Cultural Explanations' (2010) 20 Journal of Public Administration Research and Theory 53.

outcome of these decisions. The fact that the design itself of the agencies may also have a major impact on the outcome of the cases has been overlooked.[4] The way in which the independence requirement is implemented in the governance structure of an agency, for example, may influence the agency's decisions. Even though no formal requirements have so far been laid down in EU legislation for competition authorities, in contrast to market authorities in regulated sectors such as energy and telecommunications, a sufficient degree of independence is seen as a key ingredient if agencies are to be able to enforce regulatory and competition policy satisfactorily.[5] By delegating competition law and regulatory powers to an independent body, the legislature tries to ensure that the application and interpretation of competition rules and regulations are based primarily on economic and legal arguments, rather than being shaped by political pressure. The chosen design can be the appropriate response to the institutional forces and constraints under which agencies operate on a day-to-day basis.[6] How these organizations are structured can therefore strengthen the outcome of their decisions and improve their effectiveness.

This chapter provides insight into the practice of institution building by drawing on academic work[7] and experience and using this to identify key factors for design in the light of the LITER or good agency principles. Its

[4] Examples of materials on institutional design include: D Chisholm, 'Problem-Solving and Institutional Design' (1995) 5 Journal of Public Administration Research and Theory: T-Part 451; D Carpenter, *Reputation and Power: Organizational Image and Pharmaceutical Regulation at the FDA* (Princeton: Princeton UP, 2010); E Fox, 'Antitrust and Institutions: Design and Change' (2010) 41 Loyola University of Chicago Law Journal 473; H First, E Fox, and D Hemli, 'Procedural and Institutional Norms in Antitrust Enforcement: The US System' (2012) NYU Law and Economics Research Paper No 12-18 <http://ssrn.com/abstract=2115886> accessed 27 September 2013; E Fox and M Trebilcock, 'The Design of Competition Law Institutions and the Global Convergence of Process Norms: The GAL Competition' (2012) NYU Law and Economics Research Paper No 12-20 <http://ssrn.com/abstract=2128913> accessed 27 September 2013; W Kovacic and D Hyman, 'Competition Agency Design: What's on the Menu?' (2013) 8 European Competition Journal 527 <http://ssrn.com/abstract=2179279> accessed 7 November 2013; D Hyman and W Kovacic, 'Competition Agencies with Complex Policy Portfolios; Divide or Conquer?' (2013) George Washington University Law Faculty Publications & Other Works, Paper 631; K Cseres, 'Integrate or Separate—Institutional Design for the Enforcement of Competition Law and Consumer Law' (2013) Amsterdam Law School Legal Studies Research Paper No 2013-03 <http://ssrn.com/abstract=2200908> accessed 27 September 2013.

[5] See International Competition Network Advocacy Working Group, Advocacy and Competition Policy, Report presented at the first ICN's conference in Naples, Italy (2002) 53–55 <http://www.internationalcompetitionnetwork.org/uploads/library/doc358.pdf> accessed 17 April 2014 and Fonteijn and Ottow (n1).

[6] D Hyman and W Kovacic, 'Institutional Design, Agency Life Cycle, and the Goals of Competition Law' (2013) 81 Fordham Law Review 2163.

[7] Inspiration has been found in: D Hyman and W Kovacic, 'Competition Agency Design: What's on the Menu?' (n4); OECD, 'Principles for the Governance of Regulators' (2013) Public consultation

perspective is both internal and external: internal, in that it looks at the internal design of the organization; external, in that it examines the relationship between the agency and its stakeholders. These issues are discussed primarily in relation to the LITER principles of legality, independence, transparency, effectiveness, and responsibility, with the key question being how these principles influence agency design.

To examine institution building I have chosen to study two cases of mergers in the field of competition law, sector-specific regulation, and consumer protection rules: one in the Netherlands and the other in the United Kingdom. In my research and thinking about the LITER principles in the context of institutional design these two cases have proven to be the starting point for a more conceptual consideration of this chapter's subject matter. Agency creators may like to examine these cases in order to identify the issues they need to consider. Many design choices have to be made. This analysis centres around issues such as governance structures, budgets, personnel, relationships with ministries, parliament, and other stakeholders, and importantly the institutional culture. These questions, too, are illustrated, taking the two case studies as examples. Although other aspects play also a role in institution building,[8] these issues have been picked for this chapter because of their relevance to the discussion on the way in which the LITER principles not only influence agency design, but are also fundamental to their outcomes.

After introducing the cases, this chapter examines them in their governance structure, their organizational design, and their interactions with the relevant ministries and politics. Taking these mergers as examples, issues of institutional culture (i.e. the internal perspective) and how they communicate with the outside world (i.e. the external perspective) will be linked to institutional design. Two other organizational issues will also be discussed and linked to the relevant LITER principles: firstly, the issue of how to combine the investigation and enforcement tasks of independent agencies, and secondly the issue of how to combine competition with regulatory tasks. In both cases authorities may opt for an integration or for a separation model. The separation model organizes the work within separate institutions, while the integration model bundles all activities within the same agency. These

draft downloadable from <http://www.oecd.org/gov/regulatory-policy/Governance%20of%20Regulators%20FN%202.docx> accessed 7 July 2014; CERRE, 'Independence, Accountability and Perceived Quality of Regulators' (2012) Brussels <http://www.cerre.eu/publications/independence-accountability-and-perceived-quality-regulators> accessed 7 July 2014.

[8] For a discussion of those aspects, see A T Ottow, 'Erosion or Innovation?: The Institutional Design of Competition Agencies—A Dutch Case Study' (n1).

institutional choices are highly relevant to the way market and competition authorities function and to how they organize their day-to-day work.

LITER Principles in the Context of Institutional Design

As shown in chapter 3, setting high ethical and professional standards should result in credibility, authority, and ultimately in legitimacy. These values are at the heart of the good agency principles. They provide the framework for the agency to perform its tasks and for stakeholders to assess the agency. How can agencies achieve these values from a design perspective?

In their research on agencies' institutional design Hanretty and Koop identified what they refer to as the 'model regulatory agency'.[9] They concluded from their research that a typical independent agency is managed by an agency head and has board members who serve for a fixed and renewable term of five years, who can be dismissed for reasons unrelated to their decisions, who cannot hold other offices in the public administration, and who need to be formally independent. The agency is typically obliged to submit an annual report to politicians, while politicians can issue policy instructions to the agency, launch an inquiry into the agency's operations, and control the budget. Lastly, the agency is formally independent, has exclusive competence, decides on its own internal organization and personnel policy, and makes policy decisions that cannot be reversed other than by a court. To achieve such a model independent agency, the legalization establishing the agency should—in the view of Hanretty and Koop—contain the following elements: (i) provisions for the executive board; (ii) provisions for board members; (iii) a relationship with political bodies; and (iv) decision-making, management, and finances.[10]

This chapter discusses the main elements of these four categories for the two case studies, also linking these to the LITER principles of legality, independence, transparency, effectiveness, and responsibility. Each LITER

[9] C Hanretty and C Koop, 'Comparing Regulatory Agencies: Report on the Results of a Worldwide Survey' (2009) European University Institute Working Paper RSCAS 2009/63 19. Their conclusions were based on the answers of 175 regulatory agencies from 88 countries. See also the book: M Fox and M Trebilcock, *The Design of Competition Law Institutions. Global Norms, Local Choices* (Oxford: Oxford University Press 2013), which provides a nice country overview with the different aspects of design.

[10] Compare C Hanretty et al, 'Independence, Accountability and Perceived Quality of Regulators, a CERRE Study' (2012) Brussels: Centre on Regulation in Europe. The CERRE report applies 13 criteria to test the core of legal independence. These 13 criteria essentially constitute a detailed fragmentation of all the elements related to independence. A regulator that meets all 13 criteria can be regarded as a 'model regulator'.

principle contains elements relevant to institutional design. Below, these elements are outlined first and elaborated upon subsequently, when discussing the various issues with regard to institutional design.

Legality

Although design is in principle an organizational matter, it must also fit the applicable legal framework. In view of the legality principle, institutional design has to follow some basic legal rules applicable to the decision-making process. These rules have consequences for the design, especially in the case of the fundamental rights as these set special rules for the imposition of sanctions. If an independent agency has the power to impose sanctions, it will have to comply with certain legal safeguards so as to ensure a fair process. This aspect, too, has certain design and organizational consequences. The various design options to be considered are discussed in depth in this chapter. There is a strong link between institutional design choices and the legality principle (in the form of the legal mandate of the agency) as without good design, the objectives of regulation will not be achieved, or at least not to the extent intended.

Independence

The principle of independence certainly forms the most important basis for the design of competition and market authorities. Agencies should be designed in such a way that they are able to take decisions objectively and without any undue influence. They should also have professional personnel, as well as adequate budgets and sufficient expertise to ensure high quality standards and integrity, both in their organization and in their decision-making. The way an agency's board is appointed can also strengthen its independence. Board members and heads of agencies should serve for a specified term, and reappointments and dismissals should be constrained. Furthermore, as discussed in chapter 3, agencies should explicitly operate independently of market players and political actors. It should be made clear, therefore, that holding positions in the corresponding regulated industries or political world is incompatible with board members' agency responsibilities, and institutional measures should be taken, wherever possible, to prevent such conflicts of interest arising. Agencies should also be clearly separated from their sponsoring ministry, both in terms of not receiving any ministerial instructions in individual cases and in not being able to be overruled by the minister.

When considering the requirements for independence, the difference between *de jure* and *de facto* independence has to be acknowledged: legal independence does not guarantee independence in day-to-day practice. At the same time, the legal and institutional measures constitute important ingredients and may strengthen, although not guarantee, factual independence.[11] Apart from the specific legal requirements, this chapter also therefore considers cultural and organizational aspects of the design.

Transparency

Requirements for independence represent one side of the coin; the other side is represented by requirements for accountability. Under the LITER principles' subvalues included in the transparency principle, accountability is an essential element in the design of any good agency. In institutional practice, accountability requirements translate into the provision of information in the form of the submission of annual plans and reports to political institutions and to the wider public, the scheduling of face-to-face meetings with relevant parliamentary committees and advisory bodies drawn from among the general public or relevant market players, and publication of reasons for and data underlying agencies' decisions.[12]

However, there should also be transparency in the processes revolving around the agency itself. Transparency is also needed in relation, for example, to the process for appointing board members, and in communications between the agency and its stakeholders. Transparency not only strengthens the independence—and, therefore, the legitimacy—of the agency, but also protects its integrity and creates trust in its decision-making. This is also confirmed in the CERRE study, which claims that 'What is more, independence and accountability are themselves positively related. This suggests that robust independence and accountability measures can effectively co-exist and contribute to better outcomes'.[13]

Effectiveness

Well-chosen governance structures will also increase organizational effectiveness and encourage competition and market authorities to improve the outcome of their work, within the limits of their legal framework and the

[11] There is criticism of a soley legal perspective on independence. Scholars from political sciences are sceptical whether legal provisions regarding independence translate into actual independence in the day-to-day work of these authorities. See for example: M Maggetti 'De Facto Independence after Delegation: A Fuzzy-Set Analysis' (2007) 1(4) Regulation & Governance 271; and K Yesilkagit and S Van Thiel 'Political Influence and Bureaucratic Autonomy' (2008) 8(2) Public Organization Review 137.

[12] These criteria are taken from the CERRE report (n7) 38.

[13] ibid 10.

objectives set by government.[14] If well chosen, these governance structures can be summarized as 'improving outcome through better governance'.[15] If the design of the organization leads to independence, this may also improve the organization's effectiveness and authority. Thus, the independence and effectiveness principles obviously correlate in institutional design: they reinforce each other, with a design respecting and strengthening independence forming an essential ingredient for the effective application of regulation and competition law. At the same time, a balance must be found between administrative efficiency and due process requirements.

Responsibility

The agencies themselves also have to set the right example and demonstrate good practice through their values, vision, and day-to-day work. They must not lose credibility by operating bad practices. Instead, they must seek to gain credibility, authority and, therefore, legitimacy by setting high ethical and professional standards. It is their own responsibility to earn independence and ensure that they perform their tasks according to a clear set of standards. By introducing clear internal compliance procedures, ethical codes, fair decision-making processes and providing external openness, they show authority and responsibility for their behaviour and actions. By communicating with their shareholders and taking firm but fair decisions, they can show the societal relevance and acceptance of their organization.

Introducing Two Cases of Institution Building

If we are to examine the issues vital to the design of independent agencies by taking two cases of agency mergers for which the existing structures have actually been rethought and redesigned, we have to start by describing their backgrounds. How were things structured before the agencies merged?

The first merger took place in the Netherlands. There, the Netherlands Competition Authority (NMa) merged with the Independent Post and Telecommunications Authority (OPTA) and the Consumer Authority (CA) into the new Authority for Consumers & Markets (ACM), which came into existence on 1 April 2013. The second merger was in the United Kingdom, where the Office of Fair Trading (OFT) and the Competition Commission (CC) merged to form the Competition & Markets Authority (CMA). The

[14] OECD report (n7) 19. [15] ibid 19.

CMA was launched in shadow form on 1 October 2013 and became fully operational on 1 April 2014, by which time the OFT and CC no longer existed.

The Netherlands: a brief agency background

The ACM is the result of the merger between the NMa, OPTA, and CA. These latter three agencies were relatively young organizations, with the oldest, OPTA, being established in 1997 as the new, independent regulator for the post and telecommunications sectors. Although its mandate, based on the Dutch Telecommunications Act 1997,[16] included both market regulation (aimed at achieving competitive markets) and consumer regulation (aimed at ensuring consumer protection), its main focus over the years was on achieving competition in the telecommunications markets. It was only in the last five years of its existence that it began to devote more and more attention to consumer issues, also in response to the introduction of additional regulations (such as those relating to telemarketing, spam, and internet security).

The NMa was originally created as an independent, single-purpose body under the Dutch Competition Act 1998. That same year, an independent energy agency, responsible for overseeing the gas and electricity markets, was also created, and this agency (the 'Office of Energy Regulation') was later transferred to the NMa. Although this chamber fell under the NMa board's responsibility, it acted relatively independently of the latter's general antitrust department. In 2004 the Transport Chamber, which was responsible for supervising the Dutch railway and public transport markets and Schiphol Airport, became part of the NMa.

The CA, which was established under the Dutch Consumer Protection (Enforcement) Act[17] in 2007 in response to EU legislation, was set up as a department of the Ministry of Economic Affairs and operated as such until merging with the other two agencies. Although its name suggests that it was responsible for overseeing the regulation of a broad spectrum of consumer interests, in reality it had a limited mandate and focused solely on unfair conditions in commercial trade that adversely affected the interests of multiple consumers.

[16] *Wet op de telecommunicatievoorzieningen* <http://wetten.overheid.nl/BWBR0028469/geldigheidsdatum_28-01-2011> accessed 15 September 2014.

[17] *Wet handhaving consumentenbescherming* <http://wetten.overheid.nl/BWBR0020586/geldigheidsdatum_16-09-2014> accessed 15 September 2014.

Under the legislation, the ACM will 'promote well-functioning markets, orderly and transparent market processes, and treat consumers with care'.[18] Improving quality was a priority, with the aim in combining these three organizations being to remove the overlap between their activities and to enable their knowledge to be used where it was most efficient.[19]

United Kingdom: another brief agency background

The Office of Fair Trading (OFT) was established by the Fair Trading Act 1973, which enforces both consumer protection and competition law. Its role was subsequently modified, and its powers changed, by the Enterprise Act 2002. Over time, the OFT's mission settled on making markets work well for consumers. The organization carried out market surveys (in what is referred to as phase 1 of the competition regime). If necessary, the OFT could launch consumer awareness campaigns and make recommendations to the UK government. These market surveys could lead to market investigations being referred to the Competition Commission (in phase 2 of the competition regime).[20]

The Competition Commission (CC) was created by the Competition Act 1998 and replaced the Monopolies and Mergers Commission on 1 April 1999. The majority of its powers were governed by the Enterprise Act 2002. Under this Act, the CC could conduct in-depth market investigations of or inquiries into mergers (in what is referred to as phase 2 of the competition regime). The CC was responsible for taking appropriate action and measures (known as remedies) following inquiries that identified competition problems and regulatory appeals. All CC inquiries were undertaken following reference by another agency, most often the OFT, or a sector regulator. After receiving a reference, the CC had to decide whether competition was indeed being prevented, restricted, or distorted and, if so, what action, if any, should be taken to remedy the adverse effect on competition or any resultant detrimental effect on customers (in the form of higher prices, lower quality, less choice of goods or services, or less innovation in relation to goods or services in any UK market).

The merger of the OFT and CC to create a single, new, competition authority (CMA) was at the heart of the competition regime reform as from

[18] Parliamentary Papers II 2012/13, Vol 33 622 No 2(2) under B, paragraph 5 <https://zoek.officielebekendmakingen.nl/dossier/33622/kst-33622-2?resultIndex=55&sorttype=1&sortorder=4> accessed 13 September 2014.

[19] Parliamentary Papers I 2012/13, No 17, 4

[20] Section 131 of the Enforcement Act 2002.

1 April 2014. The aims of this merger were clearly to eliminate inefficiency, duplication, and overlap in the markets and mergers regimes and to ensure a single agency with the right powers and flexibility to use the best processes in tackling competition problems. In addition, it sought to improve the allocation of resources and to establish a single, streamlined organization for enterprises to deal with.[21]

Governance Structure and Organizational Design

The boards of both the ACM and CMA had some freedom to choose the internal design they considered to be fit and appropriate, taking account of the legal framework applying and the tasks assigned to them. Although they are bound by the budgets that have been set, they can in principle decide for themselves how to allocate the resources within their organization.[22] This is an important ingredient for independence, given that the way in which resources are allocated can influence the choices made by an agency in terms of selection and prioritization. Prioritization in turn plays a major role in shaping the outcome of regulatory and competition policy, as discussed in chapter 5. Again, there is a direct link between the design and organization of the agency on the one hand and the outcomes and effectiveness of the agency on the other hand.

Legal entity of the agency

In general, having an adequate budget enables an agency to attract high-quality personnel and to deliver the required outcome. In the cases of the ACM and CMA, however, there are restrictions on budget and personnel which are directly related to the forms of the legal entities adopted by both agencies.

The ACM is an independent administrative body without legal personality. It operates under the Dutch Autonomous Administrative Authorities Framework Act.[23] The ACM's budget is part of the budget of the Ministry of

[21] Department for Business, Innovation & Skills, 'Competition and the Competition Regime; Government Response to Consultation' (2012) 4, 22 <https://www.gov.uk/government/uploads/system/uploads/attachment_data/file/31879/12-512-growth-and-competition-regime-government-response.pdf> accessed 21 August 2014.

[22] With the exception for energy and telecommunications, where contributions of the industry are collected specifically for those activities of ACM.

[23] According to Article 1 of the Dutch Autonomous Administrative Authorities Framework Act an autonomous administrative authority is a governing body with the task, adjudicated by law, of public government while not being hierarchically subjected to a Dutch minister.

Economic Affairs. Although the staff is under the authority of and accountable exclusively to the ACM and not to the responsible minister, they are civil servants and seconded from the Ministry of Economic Affairs.[24] Staff employed by the ACM receive instructions only from the agency's board. They are not allowed to seek instructions from the minister, and neither can the minister give instructions to ACM staff. This way, the crucial conditions for independent staff are enshrined in law. The ACM differs from the previous regulator, OPTA (one of the merged entities), as the latter was a completely independent, autonomous administrative authority with legal personality and its own budget and personnel. OPTA was funded by contributions from industry[25] and not restricted by any government policy on personnel, although it was also given instructions on cutting costs (as part of the government's general financial plan). Both the CA and the NMa, by contrast, were funded from the Dutch government's budget. The only exception was the energy division of the NMa, the Office of Energy Regulation, which, like OPTA, was funded by industry contributions. The Dutch parliament chose not to adopt the same legal structure for the ACM as such an entity would, in the parliament's view, be too large and too distant from government in terms of accountability. It is evident that the independence enjoyed by a completely independent, autonomous administrative authority (such as OPTA) is both *de jure* and *de facto* of a higher level than that enjoyed by an independent administrative body such as the ACM.

The CMA has been constituted as a Non-Ministerial Department (NMD). Being an NMD, the CMA is a government department albeit without being directly headed by its own minister, but instead usually headed by a statutory board. NMDs have their own budget (voted by parliament), their own annual report, and separate personnel. Although such departments have their own budget, they have to negotiate it with the responsible minister; in the case of the CMA, this is the Department for Business, Innovation & Skills (BIS).[26] This is necessary to ensure a minister can answer for the NMD's conduct in

[24] Article 5(1) *Instellingswet* <http://wetten.overheid.nl/BWBR0033043/geldigheidsdatum_23-08-2014#Hoofdstuk2_Artikel3> accessed 14 September 2014; Parliamentary Papers II 2011/12, Vol 33 186 No 3 (MvT) 11 <https://zoek.officielebekendmakingen.nl/kst-33186-3.html> accessed 13 September 2014.

[25] See for the influence on the independence of regulators with regard to the relationship with the regulated industry: K Johanssen, 'Regulatory Independence in Theory and Practice—a Survey of Independent Energy Regulators in Eight European Countries' (2003) AKF Forlaget <http://regulationbodyofknowledge.org/wp-content/uploads/2013/03/Johannsen_Regulatory_Independence_in.pdf> accessed 9 July 2014.

[26] The budget is set by the Treasury. As far as the budget goes, the initial budget awarded by the Treasury was a £51.2 million Resource Departmental Expenditure Limit (hereinafter: Resource DEL; of which £5.1 million was a ring-fenced budget) and a £1 million capital budget for the year

parliament and subsequently take action if necessary. NMDs are staffed by civil servants but are accountable to parliament through their sponsoring ministers.[27]

An adequate budget and highly qualified personnel form a buffer against undue influence and they are important ingredients of independence. By limiting an agency in its staffing or funding, the ministry can indirectly try to limit the agency's powers. Imposing a freeze on hirings, for example, can restrict an agency's power to enforce the law effectively, while depriving it of funds at the same time as increasing the regulatory requirements it has to fulfil can limit the resources available for spending on, for example, *ex officio* competition investigations. Funding models relying on compulsory contributions from industry are common in the regulatory area, where the need for an effective market can justify the need for regulation. Such funding models are less common, however, although not unheard of, in the area of competition.

Leadership structure: the board

The paper of the Organisation for Economic Co-operation and Development (OECD) on the principles for the governance of agencies states that independence in decision-making should also include 'explicit conditions and transparent processes for appointment and termination of appointments, including appeal procedures'.[28] Since an organization that lacks the right leadership or expertise will experience the adverse effects of this shortcoming on every level and in all its activities, appointing the right board members is one of the keys to organizational success.

An open and transparent appointment process is crucial.[29] The provisions governing the procedures for appointments in the Netherlands are laid down in the rules on the relationship between ACM and the responsible minister. The Dutch cabinet (in practice, the Minister of Economic Affairs) has to follow some general guidelines when appointing new

2014/2015, topped up by the BIS with £3 million. Later on, in the Autumn Statement 2013, the Chancellor of the Exchequer announced that the Resource DEL would be increased with another £12.6 million.

[27] J Ritter, *The Strange Case of Non-Ministerial Departments* (London: Institute for Government 2013).

[28] See OECD paper (n7) 36, where in paragraph 109 this statement was made.

[29] See also: European Commission, 'Ten Years of Antitrust Enforcement Under Regulation 1/2003: Achievements and Future Perspectives' (Communication) COM (2014) 453, 9 <http://ec.europa.eu/competition/antitrust/legislation/antitrust_enforcement_10_years_en.pdf> accessed 15 September 2014.

members of the ACM board, particularly with regard to the recruitment and selection of possible candidates.[30] The Dutch Minister of Economic Affairs appoints, suspends, and dismisses the members of the ACM board, which consists of three executive members.[31] Appointments reflect the expertise needed to carry out the ACM's tasks, as well as the societal knowledge and experience required.[32] The chair is appointed for a term of seven years, while other members are appointed for five years.[33] These periods have been chosen in implementation of EU obligations.[34] The UK appointment process is conducted in accordance with the Commissioner for Public Appointments' Code of Practice.[35] In the United Kingdom, the Secretary of State appoints the CMA board's 'chair'[36] for a maximum of five years.[37] Other than the chair, the CMA board consists of a chief executive, three executive directors, and seven non-executive directors. All CMA board members are appointed by the Secretary of State[38] in consultation with the chair.[39] Non-executive directors are appointed for up to five years, executives for three years.[40]

Apart from the rule that ACM board decisions are taken by plurality vote,[41] no further rules on the functioning of the ACM board have been set, and nor are the minutes of its meetings published externally. The rules in the case of the CMA are much more explicit: decisions by the CMA board are passed by ordinary resolution, with the chair or, in the absence of the chair, the person appointed to chair the specific meeting having a second or casting

[30] See the 'Relatiestatuut ACM en ministers 2013' (2013) Staatscourant nr. 9237 <https://zoek.officielebekendmakingen.nl/stcrt-2013-9237.html> accessed 21 August 2014.

[31] Article 3 *Instellingswet* (n24).

[32] ibid Article 3(2) *Instellingswet.*

[33] ibid Article 3(3) *Instellingswet.*

[34] Parliamentary Papers II Vol 33 186 No 8 (n24). The relevant European obligations are Article 35, fifth paragraph, of Directive 2009/72/EC of the European Parliament and of the Council of 13 July 2009 concerning common rules for the internal market in electricity and repealing Directive 2003/54/EC [2009] OJ L 211/52; and Article 39, paragraph 5 of Directive 2009/73/EC of the European Parliament and of the Council of the European Union of 13 July 2009 concerning common rules for the internal market in natural gas and repealing Directive 2003/54/EC [2009] OJ L 211/94.

[35] The Code of Practice for Ministerial Appointments to Public Bodies is available at <http://publicappointmentscommissioner.independent.gov.uk/wp-content/uploads/2012/02/New-Code-of-Practice-for-Ministerial-Appointments-to-Public-Bodies-August-2009.pdf> accessed 21 August 2014.

[36] According to section 1(1)(a) of the Enterprise and Regulatory Reform Act Schedule 4, part 1 (general), paragraph 1.

[37] Section 3(3) Enterprise and Regulatory Reform Act 2013.

[38] Section 1(1)(b) Enterprise and Regulatory Reform Act.

[39] Section 1(2) Enterprise and Regulatory Reform Act.

[40] Section 3(1) Enterprise and Regulatory Reform Act.

[41] The ACM board did not publish rules of procedure.

vote in the event of a tie.[42] The CMA board has collective responsibility for all decisions taken and will seek to achieve unanimity. Where members have concerns on a particular matter or proposed action that they are unable to resolve, these concerns should be recorded in the minutes of the meeting, which in the CMA's case are published externally.[43]

Although both the Dutch and UK legislation state the grounds for dismissal, these remain rather vague.[44] In the case of the ACM, suspension and dismissal are possible only in the event of unsuitability or incompetence for the position, or in the event of other serious reasons relating to the person concerned.[45] So clearly, the dismissal may not be related to a case or decision, but can only be done for reasons in relation to the person as such. An ACM board member can also be dismissed at his or her request.[46] In the UK, CMA board or panel members can resign at any time, providing they give appropriate written notice to the Secretary of State.[47] The latter may also remove a person from office at any time on the grounds of incapacity, misconduct, or failure to perform the allotted duties.[48] Dismissals of board members can be a delicate issue, especially if the political or governmental interests at stake are high. Board members should be protected against the threat of dismissal if they are to take objective and balanced decisions.

An important difference between the ACM and CMA is the fact that the latter has non-executive directors (NEDs) on its board (i.e. a one-tier board). The ACM has no supervisory board. While members of a supervisory board (i.e. a two-tier board) are responsible only for supervising the executive board, NEDs enjoy full board responsibility. The NEDs' role is to use their experience, qualifications, and skills to advise, guide, challenge, and support the executive team and other staff. Both NEDs and supervisory board members can obviously create added value by providing additional skills and expertise (from business, for example), as well as additional checks

[42] CMA 'Board Rules of Procedure' (2014) 18 <https://www.gov.uk/government/uploads/system/uploads/attachment_data/file/306124/CMA_Board_Rules_of_Procedure.pdf> accessed 21 August 2014.

[43] CMA Board Rules of Procedure (n42) 19.

[44] See OECD paper (n7) 39, where in paragraph 128 the grounds for dismissal are explicitly stated: bankruptcy, conviction of an indictable offence, misconduct, breach of the act he or she is responsible for enforcing, absence without leave, failure to disclose conflict of interest, engagement in paid employment outside the duties of his or her office without the minister's consent, physical or mental incapacity, refusing or neglecting to perform his or her functions or duties, or fitness to continue his or her duties.

[45] Article 3(6) *Instellingswet* (n24), see also Parliamentary Papers II Vol 33 186 No 3 (MvT) <https://www.eerstekamer.nl/behandeling/20120225/memorie_van_toelichting_2/document3/f=/vixdk501b9vj.pdf> accessed 21 August 2014

[46] ibid. 8.

[47] Article 6 *Instellingswet* (n24).

[48] ibid Article 7.

and balances, and by creating a buffer against agency bias. NED's however do not act as a supervisory board.

A question that can be raised from an accountability perspective is which system is preferable, and then whether a supervisory board should be installed alongside the agency's board. Both a supervisory board or a NED system can form an institutional element that not only strengthens the board's independence, but also ensures that the board is accountable to its stakeholders. These elements are currently missing in the case of the ACM, at least as far as the governance structure of its board is concerned. The ACM has only three full-time board members, all of whom are executives; it has neither non-executive board members nor a supervisory board. Although some independent administrative authorities in the Netherlands have a supervisory board, there are others that do not.[49] It would be advisable for the latter to install a supervisory board that has powers to appoint board members, to give certain strategic directions to the agency, and to control the quality of the organization (with regard, for example, to integrity procedures or financial issues). This supervisory board with controlling powers can serve as a buffer between the responsible minister, the cabinet, and the independent agency. This institutional framework will provide an appropriate balance between maintaining sufficient control over the agency on the one hand and the independence structure on the other hand. The members of the supervisory board should be appointed on the basis of their independence and expertise, with clear rules being set on appointments and on how to deal with conflicts of interest.

Both the CMA and the ACM have established policies on conflicts of interest and board members' integrity. In line with the CMA policy on handling such conflicts, it has also decided to maintain a register of board members' outside interests. As well as details of current employment (remunerated and otherwise), activities, and directorships, the register will also list details of relevant investments (including funds and investment trusts), membership of other organizations, past activities, and even positions held by family members.[50] The ACM has to comply with the integrity rules set by the Dutch

[49] Those with a supervisory board include the Dutch Healthcare Authority (NZa), the Netherlands Authority for the Financial Markets (AFM), and DNB, the Dutch central bank. The tasks and powers of these supervisory boards also differ, with most of them having solely an advisory function, and only a few have powers to appoint board members or give strategic advice.

[50] The CMA Register of Interests is <https://www.gov.uk/government/publications/cma-register-of-interests> accessed 8 July 2014. See also the CMA Board Rules of Procedure <https://www.gov.uk/government/uploads/system/uploads/attachment_data/file/306124/CMA_Board_Rules_of_Procedure.pdf> accessed 13 September 2014 and the Civil Service Management Code, which provides rules on conduct and discipline, downloadable at <http://resources.civilservice.gov.uk/wp-content/uploads/2011/09/civil-service-management-code-June2011_tcm6-3222.doc> accessed 24 September 2014.

Ministry of Economic Affairs[51] All employees must consequently give written notice of any current or future outside activity that may affect their role as an ACM employee. The secretary-general of the Ministry of Economic Affairs has also appointed a compliance officer within ACM; this officer has to give notice of and register any activities, especially those involving a financial conflict of interest, that may affect the ACM's work.

Organizational structure of ACM

It was decided that the ACM's organizational structure should reflect its mission and strategy. An essential aspect of this Dutch case is that although the new organization was built on the foundations of three existing organizations, they had a comprehensive mandate from the ministry to build the new organization in a way that maximized integration. The boards agreed to a fundamentally new approach to constructing the organization, one that combined the strengths of all three. An important condition for being more than just the sum of its constituent parts is having a comprehensive strategic vision of the new agency's core identity. This vision is meant to colour the regulatory philosophy, both internally and externally, and create opportunities for cross-sector synergies within ACM. Formulating this strategy has been a key element of the integration process and focus. The strategy was built around the legal mandate, which was reworded by the new board to read 'ACM creates opportunities and options for businesses and consumers'.

Regulatory and supervisory tasks have therefore been structured in a way designed to maximize synergy (see figure 3 in annex 4). This means housing all the NMa, OPTA, and CA consumer tasks within a single department: the Consumer Department. By transferring these powers to a single unit, the ACM can provide integrated and coherent consumer protection, thus enhancing the effectiveness of its enforcement. The Competition Department focuses on safeguarding and promoting competition, thereby providing companies with fair opportunities to do business and to innovate, the intended result being that consumers actually have something to choose from. This department aims to resolve the most important antitrust problems and so is responsible for handling all concentration and cartel investigation cases falling within the ACM's remit, as well as all cases involving abuse of dominance other than in the regulated industries.

The ACM's regulatory tasks have been concentrated in two departments. The first of these, the Energy Department, is responsible for regulating the energy

[51] The Regulation on Integrity of the Dutch Ministry of Economic Affairs is available at <http://wetten.overheid.nl/BWBR0032975/geldigheidsdatum_26-01-2014> accessed 22 August 2014.

and drinking water markets, while the second, the Telecoms, post, and transport department, is responsible for regulating the telecommunications, transport, and postal services markets. Competition in the latter department's markets is possible *between* or *on* networks. These two departments are also responsible for supervising potential abuses of dominant positions in these regulated industries. In this way the ACM is able to use its sector-specific knowledge as effectively as possible, and to tackle market failures in an integrated manner.

Horizontal teams have been created to handle many key issues, including prioritization policy, review teams, and cooperation on detection. A network of detection officers has been set up, for example, to collect and analyse tip-offs and indications and market information retrieved through various channels. All this information is used for ACM-wide prioritization of market and consumer problems. Such cross-departmental teams are formed wherever they are expected to result in an effective approach.

The Legal Department is responsible for punitive decisions (fines) and revision procedures and for all appeals. In addition it has advisory and coordination tasks, such as safeguarding the quality of the ACM's legal work and legislative affairs. The Corporate Affairs and Communication Department offers support to the board and is responsible for the communication of ACM. This department and the Office of the Chief Economist have ACM-wide tasks relating to strategy, national and international cooperation, communication and corporate affairs, and economic analyses and calculations. As such these departments, which are supporting both the departments and the board, form a vital link between the various divisions of the ACM, and their 600 employees.

Organizational structure of CMA

As figure 4 in annex 4 shows, the CMA has three directorates, each led by an Executive Director: Enforcement, Markets & Mergers, and Corporate Services.[52] These are supported by an Office of the General Counsel and an Office of the Chief Economic Adviser, which are both responsible for legal, economic, business, and financial analysis provided to the CMA board, case teams, and inquiry groups, and for appropriate and rigorous quality assurance. The Head of Professions (Legal, Economics and Delivery, as well as Business and Financial Analysts) also develops programmes to facilitate the continuing professional development of the staff, as well as

[52] See Competition & Markets Authority Annual Plan 2014/15 (2014) 19 <https://www.gov.uk/government/uploads/system/uploads/attachment_data/file/299785/CMA15.pdf> accessed 13 September 2013.

forming groups of professional expertise across the CMA. Detection intelligence is centralized throughout the organization. The CMA has over 500 employees.[53]

As in the case of the ACM, the way in which the CMA is organized also reflects its strategy. An important focus of the CMA's strategy is its ambition to deliver effective enforcement.[54] Establishing a separate enforcement directorate, where staff from different professional and organizational backgrounds are brought together in effective multidisciplinary teams, enables enforcement expertise to be bundled and exchanged between the different CMA tasks, as well as allowing all the competition and consumer measures at the agency's disposal to be combined. This also represents a response to the criticism that the outcome of cases handled by the previous organization, OFT, was disappointing and could be improved. By focusing on enforcement the CMA seeks to address emerging competition problems at an early stage and to increase the number and speed of cases handled.[55] The CMA intends to achieve its ambitions by delivering effective enforcement and developing integrated performance.[56]

Some independence issues raised by the ACM and CMA mergers

The CMA, as is also the case with the ACM, faces constraints on its personnel policy, and these restrict its ability to recruit expert staff. Government policy obliges both agencies to comply with strict rules on recruitment, thus limiting their freedom to target expertise and offer competitive salaries. Other regulatory authorities, especially in the United Kingdom, are offering higher salaries. They have this flexibility because they are funded by contributions from industry rather than being publicly funded. As the CMA cannot match these levels of remuneration, it has faced some difficulties when seeking to recruit personnel. This was one of the main reasons why the UK government sought to increase the CMA budget, even though it is still bound by

[53] See for instance: <https://www.gov.uk/government/organisations/competition-and-markets-authority/about> accessed 13 September 2014.

[54] Competition & Markets Authority, 'Vision, Values and Strategy for the CMA' (2014) 13. <https://www.gov.uk/government/uploads/system/uploads/attachment_data/file/274059/CMA13_Vision_and_Values_Strategy_document.pdf> accessed 15 September 2014.

[55] ibid 7.

[56] The other goals mentioned in the strategy document are: extend competition frontiers, refocus consumer protection, and achieve professional excellence. See for a critical analysis of the merger between OFT and CC: P Freeman, 'The Competition and Markets Authority: Can the Whole be Greater Than the Sum of its Parts?' (2013) 1(1) Journal of Antitrust Enforcement 4.

government rules on personnel policy.[57] By offering internal training programmes, both the ACM and CMA have been able, however, to invest in their staff and improve their professional standards.

Another independence aspect was raised during the establishment of the CMA. A unique characteristic of the UK competition system, and one reflected in the organization of the CMA, is the panel system. However, merging the OFT and the CC to create a single competition and markets authority would have ended the panel system. This was why it was decided that, despite the merger of these two agencies into the CMA, an internal separation should be maintained—in a two-phase system—between decision-making in merger investigations and market investigation studies. In the past, the OFT would determine in phase 1 whether or not there was a competition issue that needed to be addressed. If there was, it had to refer this to the CC, responsible for phase 2, who would conduct a more in-depth inquiry. Phase 1 decisions, regarding the initial assessment, are now taken by the CMA board, while phase 2 decisions, the in-depth inquiry, are in the hands of a panel of independent experts.

Concerns were expressed during the consultation round on the formation of the CMA that the removal of the two agency system would increase the risk of 'confirmation bias' in phase 1, and phase 2 reviews would henceforth be conducted by the same agency and no longer by a separate agency such as the CC. The CMA has recognized this issue, but firmly believes that the concerns have been fully addressed,[58] now that the UK government has sought to resolve these concerns through the composition and structure of the CMA, and specifically by including the continued use of panels of experts in phase 2 investigations.[59] Decisions on markets and mergers in phase 2 work are consequently still taken by independent groups of panel members. Each panel group has a chair and at least three members. Panel

[57] See for the budget of both the Office of Fair Trading and Competition Committee the 2013-2014 Annual Report and Accounts. Available at <https://www.gov.uk/government/uploads/system/uploads/attachment_data/file/322820/9988-2901757-TSO-OfT_Annual_Report_Web_ACCESSIBLE.pdf> and <https://www.gov.uk/government/uploads/system/uploads/attachment_data/file/322811/40626_2902424_Web_Accessible_v1.1.pdf> respectively, accessed 22 August 2014.

[58] D Currie, 'The New CMA: How Will it Promote Competition?' (2013) Beesley lecture 7 November 2013 2, 12 <https://www.gov.uk/government/speeches/the-new-competition-and-markets-authority-how-will-it-promote-competition> accessed 15 September 2014.

[59] J Aitken and T Lamb, 'What the New Competition and Markets Authority Means for the UK Market' [2012] International Financial Law Review <http://www.iflr.com/Article/3094618/What-the-new-Competition-and-Markets-Authority-means-for-the-UK-market.html> accessed 22 August 2014.

members are appointed by the Secretary of State,[60] after consultation with the chair,[61] for a maximum of eight years.[62] They are appointed—in open competition—for their experience, ability, and diversity of skills in competition economics, law, finance, and business.[63] The board's oversight role does not extend to the substance of decisions by groups on phase 2 work. The groups make their decisions independently of the board. The board is kept informed about resourcing, efficiency, application of CMA policy, and the staff processes supporting the panel's work.[64]

Interference with Ministers and Politics

From a legal perspective, the most common instruments for intervening in an agency's activities are general instructions (or general guidelines), a right of approval, and a veto right granted to the minister for certain types of agency decisions. The situations for the ACM in the Netherlands and the CMA in the United Kingdom are described in the following two sections.

In the Netherlands

To ensure that the ACM is independent, the Act establishing the ACM[65] stipulates firstly that the minister may not give instructions in individual cases, and secondly that ACM board members and staff must not seek or accept instructions from the minister.[66] The legislation refers, however, to three situations in which the minister may intervene.

The first situation is the right of the minister to overturn a negative merger decision by the ACM in a particular merger case.[67] If the latter refuses to license implementation of a concentration, the addressee of the decision can request the minister to grant the licence. The licence may then be granted if the minister believes that the ACM's decision should be overturned because important reasons in the public interest outweigh the restriction of competition that will result from the merger. This ministerial power, however, has never been used. If it were, the decision would have to be issued transparently; moreover,

[60] Section 1(1)(b) Enterprise and Regulatory Reform Act 2013.

[61] Section 1(2) Enterprise and Regulatory Reform Act 2013.

[62] Section 3(2) Enterprise and Regulatory Reform Act 2013.

[63] See: <https://www.gov.uk/government/organisations/competition-and-markets-authority/about/our-governance#cma-panel> accessed 13 September 2014.

[64] ibid. [65] *Instellingswet* (n24). [66] ibid Article 9 *Instellingswet.*

[67] Article 47 of the Dutch Competition Act <http://wetten.overheid.nl/BWBR0008691/geldigheidsdatum_14-09-2014>accessed 14 September 2014.

the minister cannot act alone, and the decision has to be taken by the cabinet (the executive body of Dutch government comprising the ministers and their state secretaries). Without such a pressure valve, parliament could arguably, in times of financial crisis and as has happened in other EU member states, adopt legislation that allows decision-making on politically sensitive mergers to by-pass the competition authority entirely.

The second situation is the right granted to the Minister of Economic Affairs to approve general policy rules of ACM on, for example, the application of competition law in relation to sustainability issues.[68] Under the Dutch Competition Act, a decision to adopt such general policy rules has to be presented to the ministry for approval prior to publication (i.e. an *ex ante* approval right) as such decisions involve issues of policy. This right also extends to general policy rules concerning consumer issues. Areas covered by sector-specific regulation are exempt from this obligation. The minister needs to refrain from giving instructions in individual cases.[69] If the ACM adopts general policy decisions beyond its powers (*ultra vires*), the minister has the right to object against the adaptation of such policy guidelines. Under the Act streamlining the ACM,[70] however, the power to annul ACM policy decisions cannot be used in respect of sector-specific regulation in the energy, postal, telecommunications, or transport sectors.[71]

The third situation is the minister's right to issue general policy guidelines.[72] In the past, the relationship between the Minister of Economic Affairs and the NMa came under pressure after the minister issued the NMa with general guidelines for calculating gas companies' transport tariffs.[73] Under the Dutch Competition Act, the minister could not give instructions in individual cases. In this case, however, the state believed there to be no question of an individual policy rule and the instructions to be of a purely general nature. The Dutch

[68] See the draft position paper on Policy Rule on Competition and Sustainable Development: 'The Assessment of Anticompetitive Practices as a Result of Sustainability Initiatives in Practice' (2013) <https://www.acm.nl/en/publications/publication/11733/Opportunities-for-collaborations-with-regard-to-sustainable-development/> accessed 29 September 2014.

[69] Article 23a *Wet Onafhankelijke Post- en Telecommunicatieautoriteit* (n16).

[70] Article 10(3) *Instellingswet* (n24). See under F: <https://www.eerstekamer.nl/behandeling/20140703/publicatie_wet/document3/f=/vjl4b3is9wzg.pdf> accessed 13 September 2014.

[71] Parliamentary Papers II 2013/14 Vol 33 622 No C (MvA) <https://zoek.officielebekendmakingen.nl/dossier/33622/kst-33622-C?resultIndex=12&sorttype=1&sortorder=4> accessed 15 September 2014. To this end, the proposal to the *Stroomlijningswet* adds a third paragraph to Article 10 of the *Instellingswet ACM*. 'Wet van 25 juni 2014 tot wijziging van de Instellingswet Autoriteit Consument en Markt en enige andere wetten in verband met de stroomlijning van het door de Autoriteit Consument en Markt te houden markttoezicht' (Act streamlining the ACM). The Act was published 3 July 2014. <https://www.eerstekamer.nl/behandeling/20140703/publicatie_wet/document3/f=/vjl4b3is9wzg.pdf> accessed 9 July 2014.

[72] Article 5a Competition Act and Article 10 *Instellingswet* ACM.

[73] The Office of Energy Regulation (DTe), which changed its name to Energy Chamber later on, was part of the Netherlands Competition Authority.

Trade and Industry Appeals Tribunal (CBb) disagreed with this view and ruled the board's decision on this 'general' policy rule to be invalid.[74] The Trade and Industry Appeals Tribunal believed that the instructions constituted individual instructions regarding the rates charged by the state-owned company GTS, and that these were incompatible with the (old) Dutch Competition Act.[75] The legislator had deemed it important for there to be no scope for political interference in individual decisions taken by the competition authority's board. In this case the state had a clear interest in charging high transport tariffs as this had a substantial influence on its revenues. The transport tariffs set in the competition authority's new decision (taken after the CBb's ruling) were substantially lower.

In 2012 an incident occurred in which fines imposed by ACM became an issue in the Dutch political world. Fines imposed by the competition authority as a result of enforcement decisions may be treated by the government as a source of funding. In his budget forecasts at the end of 2012, the Minister of Economic Affairs forecast that fines collected by the ACM in 2017 could amount to 125 million euros; this was four times higher than previously estimated. The ACM operates independently in taking decisions and imposing fines. Although the minister is obviously free to forecast amounts expected to be raised from fines, even the minister made it clear, when questioned by the legislature,[76] that such forecasts do not affect the ACM budget. The ACM is completely independent in deciding whether to impose fines and in determining the level of any fine in an individual case, but does not in any event receive the income generated by its fines. The minister subsequently commissioned a report, in August 2013, to look into the forecasts and informed parliament in writing that the amounts originally stated were unlikely ever to be attained.[77] This incident nevertheless indicates that government suggestions

[74] College van Beroep voor het bedrijfsleven, *EnergieNed en VEMW v NMa en Gas Transport Services B.V.*, LJN: BM9470, NJB 2010 1499.

[75] This case is discussed in: A T Ottow, 'The Different Levels of Protection of National Supervisors' Independence in the European Landscape' in S Comtois and K de Graaf (eds), *On Judicial and Quasi-Judicial Independence* (Netherlands Institute for Law and Governance Series 7 Den Haag: Boom Juridische Uitgevers 2013) 139.

[76] See for the 125 million euros in fines budget forecast and the independence of the ACM: B Baarsma, 'Ontwikkelingen in het mededingingstoezicht. Essay in het kader van het WRR-project Toekomst van toezicht' (2012) SEO Economisch Onderzoek, commissioned by the de Wetenschappelijke Raad voor het Regeringsbeleid <http://www.seo.nl/uploads/media/2012-94_Ontwikkelingen_in_het_mededingingstoezicht.pdf> accessed 9 July 2014.

[77] The letter from the Minister of Economic Affairs is available at <http://www.rijksoverheid.nl/documenten-en-publicaties/kamerstukken/2014/02/11/brief-aan-de-tweede-kamer-boetebeleid-autoriteit-consument-en-markt.html> accessed 9 July 2014. The report issued by the minister and executed by Strategies in Regulated Markets (SRM) is available at <http://www.rijksoverheid.nl/documenten-en-publicaties/rapporten/2014/02/11/afschrikwekkende-werking-van-boetes-van-de-autoriteit-consument-en-markt.html> accessed 9 July 2014.

of targets for fines may also be seen by the media and the general public as an attempt by the government to influence the agency's behaviour.

These examples show how delicate the relationship between the independent agency and the minister can be. There is a thin line between general policy guidelines and interference in individual cases, with the latter clearly conflicting with the principle of independence. Individual or (subtle) organizational interventions can be used as a possible way to influence an agency's behaviour and, as a result, to interfere in the outcome of cases. In view of the importance of the independence principle, this relationship has to be analysed with care.

In the United Kingdom

The relationship between the CMA and the UK Department for Business, Innovation & Skills (BIS) is governed quite differently. In its response to consultation, the UK government explicitly stated that the CMA is and must be seen to be independent. It therefore decided to constitute the CMA as a Non-Ministerial Department (NMD):

> This status will ensure that the CMA is free from influence from Ministers, whilst also ensuring transparency of decision making and sound accountability. Its budget will be set by HMT [Her Majesty's Treasury, the UK's economic and finance department] and will be protected for the Spending Review period, so that its decisions on cases will not be influenced by their possible impact on future budgets. This will ensure that there is no appearance of Governmental interference in the CMA's decisions on cases.[78] [...] As an NMD, the CMA will be free to prioritise its own resources and annual plans of activity.[79]

In order, however, to increase transparency in the way in which BIS engages with the CMA and to give the CMA some general directions, the minister issued a strategic steer following consultation.[80] This steer outlines the government's long-term goals for competition and growth and provides an open and transparent statement upon which the CMA can reflect. In my view, the steer is to be welcomed from the perspective of the transparency principle. Some concerns may be raised, however, from the perspective of the independence principle. The CMA will have to take note of this high-level strategic steer and follow the general directions it gives in practice. In response,

[78] Government Response to Consultation (n21) 92. [79] ibid 14.

[80] Department for Business, Innovation & Skills, 'Competition Regime, Response to Consultation on Statement of Strategic Priorities for the CMA' (2013) <https://www.gov.uk/government/uploads/system/uploads/attachment_data/file/245607/bis-13-1210-competition-regime-response-to-consultation-on-statement-of-strategic-priorities-for-the-cma.pdf> accessed 9 July 2014.

however, to concerns raised during the consultation process, the government stressed that the steer would in no way seek to reduce the CMA's independence, or to dictate its day-to-day work.[81] According to the government, the strategic steer is of a 'have regard' nature and does not seek to constrain unduly the CMA's ability to prioritize its activities or to develop improved processes, and should also not be seen as biasing CMA decisions. David Currie, the CMA chair, stated the following in respect of the strategic steer:

> Some have pointed to the strategic steer that Government has given us as a weakening of that independence. I could not disagree more strongly. It is important that any regulator, including the competition authority, is sensitive to both political currents and political realities. And it is important that there is a continued dialogue between the regulator and Government (as well as other stakeholders) on a 'no surprises, no veto' basis. The strategic steer makes that high-level communication, which might otherwise be covert, open and transparent.[82]

Indeed, the steer provides transparency in the relationship between the minister and the agency. It also, however, contains some important guiding principles on the CMA's work. According to the steer, the CMA's central task is to ensure that the forces of competition are fully harnessed to support a return to strong and sustained growth. The CMA should consequently seek to identify markets where competition is not working well and, in doing so, take account of consumer behaviour. The government considers consumer behaviour issues to be central to the CMA's analysis of whether markets are working well and, where relevant, that these issues should inform the remedies put in place.[83] The steer also contains provisions on the enforcement level. It clearly indicates that the CMA should be a strong defender of fair competition and enforce breaches of antitrust rules robustly and fairly, thus sending the message that the UK will not allow infringements against competition law that harm consumers.

Comparing this strategic steer with the strategy documents of the CMA and ACM, it can be observed that elements of the BIS steer can be found in the ACM's strategic document. These include taking account of consumer behaviour and longer-term dynamic competition, and the key advocacy role that the competition authority has to play in challenging government if the latter creates barriers to competition. This suggests that the ACM has set

[81] Government Response to Consultation (n21) 92 and the Department for Business, Innovation & Skills, 'Competition regime' (n80) 5, paragraph 8.

[82] D Currie, 'The Case for the British Model of Independent Regulation 30 years on' (2014) The Currie Lecture, Cass Business School, London 11.

[83] Response to Consultation on Statement of Strategic Priorities for the CMA (n80) 10, paragraph 6.

these elements independently, while the CMA is more influenced by a policy guideline from government. At the same time the steer provides solid support from the government for a strong competition policy and enforcement strategy. Hyman and Kovacic regard political support as the most important factor in the success of an agency's design.[84] According to them, a new agency is doomed if it lacks a supportive constituency or generates political opposition, whereas a positive political context will give a substantial impulse to the new organization and help it achieve its goals. The strategic steer can be seen as a vehicle for ensuring continued political support. As long as it does not contain or lead to individual interventions in CMA decisions (which it would not seem to), such a steer remains clearly within the institutional boundaries of the principle of independence.

The UK Secretary of State also has a legal right to intervene in the CMA's decision-making in merger cases if the 'public interest' is at stake. This is taken to include issues of national security, media quality, plurality and standards, and financial stability.[85]

Institutional Culture and Legitimacy

As explained in chapter 3, good governance will enable market and competition authorities to gain acceptance and legitimacy for their work. But their governance structure alone is not, as such, sufficient. Agencies themselves also have to set the right example by setting high ethical and professional standards and demonstrating good practices in their day-to-day work. They must seek to gain credibility, authority and, therefore, legitimacy by applying the values that form the basis for the good agency or LITER principles and that also provide the framework for the agency's performance and for stakeholders' assessment of this.

Leadership of the organization is, in my opinion, a crucial ingredient of institutional culture and essential for the independence, integrity and, therefore, legitimacy of the organization:

> Independence is fragile—in the Netherlands, too. Much influence can be exercised by appointing people—and by implementing budgetary measures as well. However,

[84] W Kovacic and D Hyman 'Competition Agencies with Complex Policy Portfolios' (n4).

[85] As laid down in section 58 of the Enterprise Act 2002; Competition & Markets Authority, 'Guidance on the CMA's Jurisdiction and Procedure' (2014) <https://www.gov.uk/government/uploads/system/uploads/attachment_data/file/270256/CMA2_Mergers_Guidance.pdf> accessed 15 September 2014; and Public Bill Committee 'Enterprise & Regulatory Reform Bill' (2010) 12th sitting cc512-24 <http://www.publications.parliament.uk/pa/cm201213/cmpublic/enterprise/120710/am/120710s01.htm> accessed 23 August 2014.

the most important factor for fostering respect for independence lies with the board of the regulator itself, hence the subtitle of my statement: 'noblesse oblige.' Regulators should keep up their independence themselves, and more or less earn it—not from an ivory tower or by acting like a child throwing tantrums when criticized or pressured, but as a self-confident, professional organization that listens and knows there is not just one truth, and who can be trusted by all parties.[86]

Leadership of the board of an agency, be it a new or an existing agency, is key to ensuring that the agency achieves its intended results. Setting a clear mission and priorities, built around a transparent strategy, will create credibility, both within and outside the agency, and give the organization a strong drive to succeed. The agency's success depends on people's willingness to make it succeed, to achieve improvements, and to be receptive to innovation. An important element should be a focus on identifying a common culture, based on key values and a core vision. This requires continual investment in conveying the agency's message and ensuring that the tone at the top is embedded in the culture. In case of an institutional change, it must be recognized that this change contains 'the risk of disruption of the regulatory ecosystem'.[87] Within established organizations a fundamental strategic review may, however, need a disruptive change in order to ensure the possibility of innovation and new initiatives. This change will trigger a cultural change within the organization, thus resulting in a new strategic approach, as has been the case with the ACM and CMA. At the same time, it is the responsibility of the agency's board to ensure cohesion within the new entity in order to avoid conflicts and destructive effects.[88] How agencies can build and achieve the right institutional culture is examined in the following section from both an internal and an external perspective.

Internal agency perspective

Independence constitutes an important element for achieving the right culture in the light of the LITER principles of good agency behaviour, and various organizational measures can be taken to protect agencies' independence. Capture can be avoided by agencies' institutional design: sophisticated design mechanisms should be considered as a way to minimize capture.[89]

[86] Translation of: C A Fonteijn, 'De toezichthouder is onafhankelijk, maar "noblesse oblige"' (2011) 2(3) Tijdschrift voor Toezicht 64.

[87] Hyman and Kovacic, 'Competition Agencies with Complex Policy Portfolios' (n4) 33–34.

[88] A T Ottow 'Erosion or Innovation?: The Institutional Design of Competition Agencies—A Dutch Case Study' (n1).

[89] R Barkow, 'Insulating Agencies: Avoid Capture Through Institutional Design' (2010) 89 Texas Law Review 15, 37, 39.

Staff rotation, for example, can be an important remedy against capture[90] and tunnel vision, while participation in interdisciplinary, problem-oriented teams and flexible deployment of staff are ways of ensuring access to broader-ranging expertise, providing they are accompanied by careful cross-training. There will always be a need to rotate certain staff in order to prevent the creation of new silos. The risk of this must be regularly monitored and scrutinized. An important feature of the mergers in both the Netherlands and the United Kingdom was the major reshuffling of personnel. No staff members were given assurance prior to the actual merger that they would keep their jobs. Everybody had to apply for a new job, which was a very complicated, demanding and, for the individuals concerned, stressful process. However, this measure helped improve integration and created new teams throughout the organization.

Extra safeguards against bias should also be built in at the level of internal procedures. The CMA decided, for example, to take advantage of the fact that the panel system is now under the same roof by also seeking recourse to the panel members' expertise on case decision groups (CDGs) on investigations under the Competition Act after a provisional decision or a statement of objections has been adopted. These panel members can provide a fresh assessment of the merits of Competition Act cases, while the extra safeguard ensures greater efficiency throughout the decision-making process. By robustly scrutinizing Competition Act cases, the panel members enhance the capability and credibility of the CMA's decision-making process in such investigations. This is an important benefit resulting from the merger of the two competition agencies.

Another organizational means to create the right culture within the organization is by establishing an academy. The ACM and CMA academies have been set up to provide professional training for staff at all levels. The academy has an important role to play in implementing the organization's strategy through training and education, and through ensuring a common style of enforcement and cooperation between departments. The academies of both these agencies are responsible for in-house training of staff and for building relationships with fellow agencies and the academic world. Professional courses at all levels of experience have been set up to provide education and training in skills and expertise. These programmes will deliver higher standards of professionalism and improve the outcome of the agencies' work. Chisholm[91] also stresses the need for professional capacities, with professionalism of the

[90] Barkow (n89) 30–34.

[91] Chisholm, 'Problem-Solving and Institutional Design' (n4) 464.

organization and its personnel (in the form of education and training) resulting in better performance and increased independence.

External agency perspective

Externally, too, the independent agency must show that it adheres to the LITER principles. This requires it to demonstrate a sufficient degree of openness and transparency. Openness is one of the core values of both the ACM and CMA. This value forms the basis for the transparency principle, which in addition contains the subvalues of accountability, and participation of and communication with stakeholders. On the accountability level, both agencies are legally obliged to provide information to the public. The CMA is accountable to parliament, and is required to set out and publicly consult on its annual plan for the following year. At the end of the year it also has to report on how it has performed. The ACM is obliged to publish an annual plan and to send its annual report to parliament.[92] Both agencies have to show that they have delivered according to set outcome criteria.[93] In the CMA strategic steer the minister points out that robust and swifter enforcement should not, however, be at the expense of making correct decisions and fairness. Once again, a balance must be struck between the instrumental and safeguard dimensions of the LITER principles. According to the legislation that created the CMA, procedures and decision-making should become more efficient in order to improve the outcome of the competition (and consumer protection) regime. At the same time the decision-making process also needs procedural fairness that takes account of the interests of all parties concerned (including the regulatory burdens for business).

Both agencies organize consultations on various issues and host roundtable meetings to enable discussions with industry, fellow agencies, and other possible stakeholders. In addition to the 'hard' organizational structure, a number of other important measures have been taken to encourage everyone at the agency to cooperate with external stakeholders, to promote the philosophy of 'looking inwards from the outside',[94] and to support an integrated approach to dealing with market and consumer problems.

[92] Article 6 *Instellingswet* (n24).

[93] For the CMA these criteria can be found in the 'Performance Management Framework' <https://www.gov.uk/government/uploads/system/uploads/attachment_data/file/274146/bis-14-559-competition-and-markets-authority-performance-management-framework.pdf> accessed 9 July 2014. For the ACM the assessment criteria are still under construction.

[94] See 'ACM Strategy Document' available at <https://www.acm.nl/nl/publicaties/publicatie/11991/Strategie-Autoriteit-Consument-en-Markt/> accessed 22 August 2014.

An example of these measures includes the consultations that the ACM initiated on discussion of its agenda, both on social media and on its website, in order to reach a broader audience than just the 'usual suspects'. The *Consuwijzer*, the ACM consumer information desk offering consumers practical tips and advice on their rights, also plays a critical role in all the ACM's spheres of activity, and lessons can be learned from the experience gained in this respect. The corresponding *Consuwijzer* website provides consumer support in the form of checklists, specimen letters, success stories, and information on other consumers' experiences. The ACM has also set up an business information desk to offer enterprises a 'one-stop shop' covering the entire spectrum of the agency's activities, while stakeholders will also be regularly involved in round-table discussions, workshops, and consultations.

The ACM and CMA also plan to use their networks at a European level (the European Competition Network, the Body of European Regulators for Electronic Communications, and the Agency for the Cooperation of Energy Regulators) and international level (the Organisation for Economic Co-operation and Development and the International Competition Network) so as to develop and obtain active feedback on best practices and to learn from others' experience.[95]

Investigation and Enforcement: Separation or Integration?

A special design issue within market and competition authorities involved in enforcement and sanctioning is the question of how to combine the tasks of investigation, prosecution, and sanctioning. Many agencies around the world combine these functions within the same institution. In those cases, however, there may be a lack of checks and balances in the decision-making process.[96] There may also be a 'prosecutorial bias'; in other words, the team handling the case may have a natural tendency to look at the facts in a way that favours the finding of an infringement. This type of bias can be particularly prevalent among staff at an agency that has powers of both investigation

[95] C Sabel and J Zeitlin, 'Learning From Difference: The New Architecture of Experimentalist Governance in the EU' in C Sabel and J Zeitlin, *Experimentalist Governance in the European Union: Towards a New Architecture* (Oxford: Oxford University Press 2010).

[96] OECD 'Country Studies, European Commission—Peer Review of Competition Law and Policy' (2005) <http://www.oecd.org/daf/competition/prosecutionandlawenforcement/35908641.pdf> accessed 18 July 2014.

and adjudication.[97] The question is what we can do from a design perspective to prevent this bias. This section analyses the various design options in the light of the LITER principles of legality, independency, transparency, and effectiveness as the relevant principles in this context, while other enforcement aspects are dealt with in chapter 5.

Two models: bifurcated model and single-tier model

Looking at the institutional design of market and competition authorities shows there to be two possible models.[98] The first of these is the separation model, also called the bifurcated or two-tier model, while the second is the integrated, or single-tier, model.

The separation model divides the tasks of investigation and decision-making (adjudication) between two different institutions, with two possible ways of structuring the separation. In the first of these (the 'bifurcated judicial model'), the competition authority goes to court for enforcement following an alleged infringement. A good example of this is the United States of America, where an investigation may be followed by a decision by the Department of Justice's Antitrust Division to file a suit to prove its case in a federal court.[99] In this bifurcated judicial model, private parties usually have their own right, parallel to that of the competition authority, to conduct their own investigation and to bring a case to court. In the second variant of the separation model (the 'bifurcated agency (or tribunal) model'), the competition authority goes to a specialized agency, rather than to a court, for enforcement.[100] This latter variant is designed to counter the concern that a court dealing with both criminal and civil matters will not have sufficient knowledge of the highly specialized cases brought to court by a competition authority or, if possible, a private party. Which of these two bifurcated models is chosen for the design of national competition authorities will

[97] D Slater, S Thomas, and D Waelbroeck, 'Competition Law Proceedings Before the European Commission and the Right to a Fair Trial: No Need for Reform?' The Global Competition Law Centre Working Papers Series GCLC Working Paper 04/08.

[98] See the ICN Advocacy Working Group report 'Advocacy and Competition Policy' (2002) ICN's Conference Naples, Italy <http://www.internationalcompetitionnetwork.org/uploads/library/doc358.pdf> accessed 12 July 2014.

[99] For more on this subject, see: H First, E M Fox, and D Hemli, 'Procedural and Institutional Norms in Antitrust Enforcement: The U.S. System' (2012) New York University Law and Economics Working Papers paper 303 <http://lsr.nellco.org/cgi/viewcontent.cgi?article=1307&context=nyu_lewp> accessed 19 July 2014.

[100] E Fox and M Trebilcock, *The Design of Competition Law Institutions. Global Norms, Local Choices* (Law and Global Governance Series, Oxford University Press 2013).

depend on multiple factors, including but not limited to the strength of the institutions, the regulatory and competition culture, and the strength of the national courts. The bifurcated agency model has its advantages, particularly in developing countries, where courts can be weak. In countries with strong and independent courts, however, the bifurcated judicial model is usually the preferred option.

The opposite of the separation model is the integrated model, where the tasks of investigation, prosecution, and decision-making are in the hands of a single institution. Market and competition authorities operating an integrated model also have two options when it comes to their internal design.[101] The first of these is a functional separation, whereby even though one institution is responsible both for investigating a case and for making a decision on it, different and separate groups or directorates within that institution have the task of investigating the case or of making the final decision. This ensures that the different tasks are handled by different people within the institution and as independently as possible. An example of this can be seen in France, where the country's competition authority is structured on an integrated basis, but with a functional separation.[102] The competition authority's Investigation Services are responsible for initiating cases and starting an investigation, led by the General Rapporteur. The College, which is the body responsible for adjudicating the case, has no involvement or say in the proceedings of the investigation. After the investigation has been concluded, the General Rapporteur sends the case to the parties concerned and to the College. The latter then decides whether the referred practices fall under the scope of the French Commercial Code or whether the referral is inadmissible. If the referral is admissible, all the parties will be fully heard in the proceedings before the College.[103] It is then the College that decides on the case and on whether to impose sanctions.

The second option is that of a fully integrated agency, with no formal separation into different entities for the tasks of investigation, prosecution, and decision-making, as in the case of the ACM in the Netherlands. Different

[101] See the European Commission Staff Working Document 'Enhancing Competition Enforcement by the Member States' Competition Authorities: Institutional and Procedural Issues' <http://ec.europa.eu/competition/antitrust/legislation/swd_2014_231_en.pdf> accessed 23 July 2014.

[102] For the design of the French Competition Authority and a brief overview of the investigation and adjudication process see: B Lassèrre, 'The New French Competition Authority: Mission, Priorities and Strategies for the Coming Five Years' (2009) <http://www.autoritedelaconcurrence.fr/doc/intervention_bl_autorite_trustubusters_09.pdf> accessed 23 July 2014.

[103] For the full procedure and powers of the College see Articles L462-1 to L462-9 and Articles L463-1 to L463-8 of the French Commercial Code.

departments within the agency—such as the legal department alongside the relevant expert department—may, however, be involved in handling a case. The problem of the lack of separation of powers is addressed in the legislation that obliges the ACM to install an effective 'Chinese wall' at an employee level. This is designed to ensure that the people involved in investigating and assessing the report are not involved in the decision-making or in the actual imposition of any fine,[104] and also that those taking decisions on the alleged infringement and the possible sanctions look at the matter with a fresh pair of eyes and without an enforcement bias.[105]

The system used by the ACM is similar to that followed within the CMA.[106] When the CMA opens a formal investigation, the case is allocated to a team leader, a project director, and a senior responsible officer, who together form the investigation team. Regular review and scrutiny are a key part of the investigation process, and this function can be performed by senior officials and advisers, both internal and external.[107] A case decision group is appointed once a statement of objections has been issued.[108] To provide for a fresh perspective and an independent assessment, there is a clear disctinction between the two teams so that the final decision is taken by officials who were not involved in the decision to issue the statement of objections.

These two examples of the Netherlands and the United Kingdom need to be distinguished from the situation applying within the European Commission, where the team responsible for investigating possible infringements of Articles 101 and 102 of the Treaty on the Functioning of the European Union (TFEU) is the same as the team responsible for subsequently imposing any sanctions required as a remedy. Within the European Commission, the task of investigating the case and the process of decision-making is consequently in the hands of the same team.[109] There are several weaknesses in such a system. The first is the fact that decisions are made by an expanding group of political

[104] Article 12q *Instellingswet* (n24).

[105] The functional separation through the Legal department of the NMa was accepted by the CBb: College van Beroep voor het bedrijfsleven, 30-08-2011, AWB 09/824 <http://uitspraken.rechtspraak.nl/inziendocument?id=ECLI:NL:CBB:2011:BR6737> accessed 23 August 2014.

[106] Explained in: CMA, 'Competition Act 1998: Guidance on the CMA's Investigation Procedures in Competition Act 1998 Cases' (2014) <https://www.gov.uk/government/uploads/system/uploads/attachment_data/file/243700/1-guidance-on-cma-investigation-procedures-in-ca98-cases-consultation.pdf> accessed 24 September 2014.

[107] CMA, 'Administrative Penalties: Statement of Policy on the CMA's Approach' (2013) Consultation document, 47 <https://www.gov.uk/government/uploads/system/uploads/attachment_data/file/212288/CMA4con_-_Administrative_penalties.pdf> accessed 29 September 2014.

[108] ibid 64.

[109] I Forrester, 'Due Process in EC Competition Cases: a Distinguished Institution with Flawed Procedures' (2009) 34(6) European Law Review 817.

appointees (i.e. one commissioner for each member state) instead of by an independent agency. These political appointees may be influenced by political considerations, especially during the decision-making process. The team involved in investigating the case is also responsible for proposing a decision and for deciding whether to impose a penalty or other remedy. Finally, although the party concerned can state its case and opinion to the case team, there is no opportunity for a fair and public hearing of the case before the institution making the final decision. Some internal checks are, however, available within the integrated design of the European Commission, including the fact that the case team's investigation is subject to peer review so as to provide a 'fresh pair of eyes'.[110] Other forms of internal checks include the review by the chief economist and the existence of the hearing officer,[111] while there are also two final internal checks in the form of the opinions issued by the Advisory Committee and the Legal Service. The Advisory Committee, consisting of member state representatives, delivers a written opinion on preliminary draft decisions by the European Commission.[112] Although the Commission is not bound by this written opinion, it will take it into account and inform the board of how it has done so.[113] However, although these internal checks must be welcomed and form additional safeguards, they do not provide a functional separation within the European Commission.

Separation or integration in the light of LITER: fair trial as a central theme

The following section discusses various aspects of the good agency or LITER principles in relation to the choice for the separation or the integration model. The principles of relevance here—legality, independence, transparency, and effectiveness—have a common theme running through them: the right to a fair trial.

[110] See for this, and more, internal checks within the EU framework: P Marsden, 'Checks and Balances: European Competition Law and the Rule of Law' (2009) 22(1) The Antitrust Marathon: Antitrust and the Rule of Law 51; and European Commission Competition, 'Proceedings for the Application of Articles 101 and 102 TFEU: Key Actors and Checks and Balances' <http://ec.europa.eu/competition/antitrust/key_actors_en.pdf> accessed 19 July 2014.

[111] P Marsden (n110).

[112] This procedure is followed for the following type of decisions: a prohibition decision, an interim measure, a commitment decision, finding inapplicability, and the imposition of a fine or a periodic penalty payment.

[113] See D Geradin, A Layne-Farrar, and N Petit, *EU Competition Law and Economics* (Oxford: Oxford University Press 2012) and 'Proceedings for the Application of Articles 101 and 102 TFEU' (n110).

Legality principle: fundamental rights

The legality aspects of the choice of separation or integration of the investigation and enforcement tasks revolve around Article 6 of the European Convention on Human Rights (ECHR). This article concerns the right to a fair trial and states that a person may invoke the rights laid down in it as soon as a criminal charge is brought against him. The charge does not have to be considered criminal under national law; it is sufficient, therefore, to establish that the charge falls within the sphere of criminal law and is meant to be both deterrent and punitive.[114]

One of the most important rights laid down in this article is the right of access to a 'fair and public hearing by an independent and impartial tribunal'; in other words, judgement should be issued by an independent and impartial tribunal fulfilling all the conditions of Article 6 ECHR. The European Court of Human Rights (ECtHR) ruled in the *Menarini* case[115] that even though the agency concerned operated an integrated model and therefore combined the investigative and adjudicative functions (and so could not be qualified as an independent or impartial tribunal), such a system may nevertheless be compatible with Article 6 ECHR. Since that judgement, it has been possible for a single 'administrative authority' to combine prosecution with the subsequent finding of an infringement and, if applicable, the imposition of sanctions, providing the party concerned is able to challenge that decision before an institution that meets all the criteria following from Article 6 ECHR (i.e. an independent court or tribunal).[116]

The *Menarini* judgement shows that the integrated model may accord with the law, as long as there is the opportunity of appeal before a tribunal meeting the criteria of Article 6 ECHR. However, the judgement in that case does not explicitly state what is meant by 'full judicial review' and which criteria need to be fulfilled. Full judicial review means that the impartial tribunal has powers not only to review the decision (i.e. the amount of the fine and so on), but also to review the factual evidence of the case.[117] In other words, it

[114] See for this European case law: *Öztürk v Germany* (1984) 6 EHRR 409, A/123; *Bendenoun v France* (1994) 18 EHRR 54, A/284.

[115] ECHR *Menarini Diagnostics S.R.L. v Italy* (2011) 43509/08.

[116] W Wils, 'The Combination of the Investigative and Prosecutorial Function and the Adjudicative Function in EC Antitrust Enforcement: A Legal and Economic Analysis' (2004) 27(2) World Competition 201.

[117] M Botta and A Svetlicinii, 'The Right of Fair Trial in Competition Law Proceedings: Quo Vadis the Courts of the New EU Member States?' (2014) Centre for Antitrust and Regulatory Studies, University of Warsaw 9th ASCOLA Conference on Procedural Fairness in Competition Proceedings.

can review the investigative task of the agency, as well as the decision-making process and the decision itself. In conclusion, it is important for a decision made by an independent agency with an integrated design to be subject to review by a court having 'full jurisdiction' to examine the legitimacy of that decision and the factual evidence. This aspect is dealt with in more detail in chapter 6 on review by the courts.

Independence, transparency, and effectiveness

These legal aspects are closely related to the independence principle as the right to a fair trial is linked to an impartial and independent judgement of the case. As the focus of Article 6 ECHR is on the court or tribunal, independent agencies can take some measures internally to ensure an independent decision-making process in enforcement cases. Independence, as discussed in chapter 3, is also related to the impartiality of the agency itself.

Bias must also be prevented. Within enforcement teams there is 'perhaps a natural, psychological inclination for an official entrusted with investigative duties to search for and give greater weight to evidence that support his belief that an infringement has occurred'.[118] This bias is referred to as prosecutorial or confirmation bias and can cause a narrow focus on evidence presented to establish an infringement, while contra-arguments or contra-evidence may be ignored or considered less important. Procedures or design solutions can be established in order to prevent such risks from arising.

Another important element is the transparency of the decision-making process, given that ensuring a fair process means it has to be made clear who is deciding what, and how the parties involved can participate in the process and get access to the data room and evidence.

However, there can also be an overkill of procedures and protection of rights, and this can frustrate the agency's enforcement activities. Here, too, therefore, a fine balance has to be found between the safeguard and instrumental dimensions of the LITER principles. From an institutional perspective, maintaining a strict division between prosecution and sanctioning may lead to extra costs, lengthy procedures, and ineffective enforcement. These elements also, therefore, need to be taken into consideration when selecting the institutional design model for enforcement and the internal procedures to be followed.

[118] D Geradin and N Petit, 'Judicial Review in European Competition Law' in M Merola and J Derenne (eds), *The Role of the Court of Justice of the European Union in Competition Law Cases* (Bruges: College of Europe, Global Competition Law Centre 2012) 21.

Conclusion

In my view the separation model is not the preferred option. Such a strict separation of tasks results in substantial extra costs and duplication of work,[119] whereas solutions can also be found within a single, integrated organization. It is crucial for the first-instance decision-making process to comply with the principles of legality, independence, and transparency. Improving the quality of the decision will achieve better case outcomes. These improved outcomes will in turn give the agency as a whole more authority. Within the integrated model, the French example provides the best guarantees against bias, with legal safeguards and a clear distinction being made between the two phases. However, I also consider the models of the Netherlands and the United Kingdom to be sufficient, although they provide only minimal guarantees and safeguards. These agencies consequently have to ensure they provide sufficient transparency in order to show that there is no interference between the two teams and that the decision-making process follows a clear set of rules.

Coordination Between or Integration of Agencies?

Looking at the design options of single or multiple agencies, as set out in chapter 2, the key question is which model can be regarded as the optimal institutional design from the perspective of the LITER principles. In this section the focus is on the different combinations of functions in relation to competition and regulatory work. Should this be done by separate agencies or should combinations be made?

Two questions should be asked in relation to market and competition authorities. The first is a general question of relevance to all single or multiple agencies: does coordination of activities within the same entity produce better results than coordination between separate entities? This is a more general question concerning situations in which a single institution is to be created in order to facilitate coordination. The second question builds on the first question and relates more specifically to market and competition agencies: should an *ex post* competition law agency be combined with an *ex ante* market authority? Is the combination of the two types of activities ideal? These questions are complex as there are pros and cons in both models, and

[119] Compare R Nazzini, 'Administrative Enforcement, Judicial Review and Fundamental Rights in EU Competition Law: a Comparative Contextual-Functionalistic Perspective' (2012) 49 Common Market Law Review 971, 1002. Here he states 'a full second-tier review would be wasteful, as long as there is confidence in the quality of the first instance decision-making'.

there is no 'black and white' answer. In other words, there is no single, overriding model, and different countries around the world have made different choices for their institutions.

This section discusses various aspects of these questions and illustrates the various scenarios and the differences, based on the ACM and CMA, without seeking to suggest that one system will automatically work better than another. In the case of both these agencies, competition tasks are concentrated under a single roof and combined with consumer protection functions. The essential difference between the two agencies is in their relationship with regulatory authorities. The CMA does not have a regulatory function, but operates in an environment which is based on considerable coordination tools and working relationships with the sectoral regulators in the United Kingdom. The ACM, meanwhile, integrates these functions under the same roof and is also the exclusive market authority for the energy, telecommunications, postal services, transport, and water sectors, which means it combines *ex ante* and *ex post* oversight activities.

Integration versus coordination models

The first question to be answered when seeking to establish the optimal institutional design for a competition or market agency, is whether a single-function agency that coordinates its actions with other agencies performs better or more effectively (coordination model) than an integrated agency, where functions are combined under a single roof (integration model). Scholars disagree on whether rivalry and competition between agencies is good or bad. They also differ in their views on the advantages and disadvantages of jurisdictional overlap and the process of coordination. Pierson points out that the dynamics of agency design mean that actions by agencies have many unintended consequences and that, as a result, any rational-instrumental approach towards institutional design has its limits.[120] Design choices are 'partially but intrinsically subjective'.[121] This makes it difficult to identify the rationale behind every design and to come up with the optimal result.

Many different institutions have been created from organizations of the past and put together from differing bits and pieces.[122] Bringing separate institutions under one roof does not in itself create integration and innovation. There is

[120] P Pierson, 'The Limits of Design: Explaining Institutional Origins and Change' (2000) 13(4) Governance 475, 494.

[121] Chisholm, 'Problem-Solving and Institutional Design' (n4) 467.

[122] D Carpenter, 'The Evolution of National Bureaucracy in the United States' in J D Aberbach and M Peterson (eds), *Institutions of American Democracy: The Executive Branch* (Oxford: Oxford University Press 2005) 43.

always a risk that cohesion will fail to be achieved and that the new design will create separate operating units for each function within the single organization. These units will then, once again, become rivals and fight for larger proportions of the portfolio, headcount, and budgetary resources.[123] A combination clearly has more potential for synergy and efficiency if it brings together complementary tasks.[124] This should also ensure fewer internal disagreements. In short, having a single, combined agency produces cost savings and avoids agency rivalry. Since issues such as cost and available capacity may cause concerns, these circumstances may result in a decision to have a single, combined agency.

A separation of powers allows enterprises the possibility to go 'forum shopping' and to choose the most favourable agency for their purposes. If separated agencies are to be prevented from being played off against each other, their actions will need to be coordinated intensively. While rivalry between agencies, as may occur in a coordination model, may give rise to different or even conflicting views and cause more conflicts, it could also simultaneously give rise to greater transparency as both agencies will have to provide good reasons for their views and decisions, thus demonstrating their expertise in the matter and justifying their approaches and interventions. However, conflicting outcomes attributable to conflicting decisions can be detrimental for the markets and parties concerned and lead to costly litigation (for agencies and enterprises alike). The transaction costs of a coordination model are also higher. However, good and constructive cooperation (if properly managed) can result in improved quality and also in additional quality checks.

Regulatory competition scholars argue, however, that regulatory outcomes improve in the event of overlapping powers and rivalry between institutions. These institutions will, they claim, have an incentive to perform better as they will have to compete with the other agencies for power and reputation.[125] Others argue that separate agencies, with shared jurisdiction, have to coordinate their actions, and that this can result in conflicting assessments and profound disagreements on the optimal solution.[126] Jurisdictional overlap can lead, in their view, to jurisdictional chaos and border disputes, and even to 'territorial disputes' between agencies,[127] as well as to forum shopping by complainants and extra transaction costs (through the duplication of teams and coordination costs). They point out moreover

[123] Hyman and Kovacic, 'Competition Agencies with Complex Policy Portfolios' (n4) 25.

[124] ibid 38.

[125] A O'Connell, 'The Architecture of Smart Intelligence: Structuring and Overseeing Agencies in the Post-9/11 World' (2006) 94 California Law Review 1655; J Gersen, 'Overlapping and Underlapping Jurisdiction in Administrative Law' (2007) Public Law & Legal Theory Working Papers No. 161.

[126] Hyman and Kovacic, 'Competition Agencies with Complex Policy Portfolios' (n4) 29.

[127] ibid 24–25.

that the fact that a single-function agency has to coordinate means it will be exposed to a greater risk of capture and political influence.

Combination of competition and regulatory tasks

The second institutional question is whether *ex post* competition and *ex ante* regulatory tasks should be combined into a single organization. The answer to this question 'depends on the balance of output-related effects and input costs'.[128] There are many pros and cons in each of the two models.

Although a market regulator, with specific sector knowledge, is better suited to applying regulations and competition law to a sector, it may lack expertise in competition. Building this expertise will involve substantial investments in people and knowledge. A single, combined agency may therefore create a bias in favour of *ex ante* regulatory remedies ('sectoral activity will overwhelm competition law').[129] Given the *ex ante* approach of regulation, this may also lead to underperformance of competition law. Whether this is a good or bad thing also depends on how market interventions are regarded from an economic perspective. These differing views account for many of the differences in perspective between competition and market authorities, with these differences resulting in different approaches and in potential conflicts between the two types of agencies. Although it may seem easier to resolve potential conflicts in situations involving one board, under one roof, problems in such situations may also be brushed under the carpet and so not come out into the open.

At the same time, if powers are separated, the competition authority can act as a regulatory appeals body for regulatory agencies (as in the United Kingdom)[130] or provide competition advice to the regulatory agency. This may also prevent the greater risk of regulatory capture, which exists when the personnel of a single-sector market regulator have intense contacts with a single industry in their day-to-day practice.

Some scholars have concerns that a multifunctional agency may result in a lack of focused enforcement. Antitrust lawyers fear that consolidating the

[128] M Cave and J Stern, *Competition and Regulatory Policy and Institutional Design for Scotland* (2013) The David Hume Institute, Research Paper No. 11/2013, 8.

[129] ibid 9.

[130] ibid 9. Cave and Stern conclude by stating that 'Our preference is for separation between competition and regulatory agencies, based largely on concern about regulatory opportunism and about the resulting suppression of multiple viewpoints'. For other authors in favour of separation: F Trillas, 'The Institutional Architecture of Regulation and Competition: Spain's 2012 Reform' (2013) IESE Business School Working Paper No. WP-1067-E; J Laffont and D Martimort, 'Separation of Regulators Against Collusive Behaviour' (1999) 30(2) RAND Journal of Economics 232.

different regulatory areas may dilute traditional antitrust law, while regulatory experts are afraid that all priorities and resources will be directed towards antitrust enforcement. Consumer lobbyists meanwhile are concerned that the agency will not be sufficiently focused on consumer interests. In other words, all camps fear the erosion of substantive law (whether competition law or sector-specific regulation) as a result of institutional choices. As they see it, prioritizing actions in a multifunctional agency will lead to the erosion of goals and tasks. Biber argues that such an agency will have so many things to do that ultimately it will do nothing.[131] On the other hand, multifunctional agencies can also combine expertise and integrate policies in order to improve the agency's effectiveness in dealing with complex regulatory issues.[132]

Coordination or integration in the light of the LITER principles

Translating these arguments into the good agency or LITER principles, the question of coordination or integration relates mainly to the principles of legality, independence, transparency, and effectiveness. Does regulatory competition between agencies lead to better results because of their having to 'fight' for their authority or even their existence?

The legal mandate of the agencies concerned, irrespective of whether they are a single or multifunctional agency, is crucial. Decision outcomes depend not only on the organizations' structure, but also on their mandate. Creating two separate agencies with overlapping powers or even conflicting goals creates a risk of rivalry and conflicting decisions. While coordination is key in such a scenario, it will also be a complicating factor and slow down the decision-making process. This in turn may lead to a loss of competition in dynamic markets. Legislators need to consider these aspects when formulating agencies' mandates. In the event of combined powers, on the other hand, consideration must be given to whether these powers create an agency that is too powerful, and whether the countervailing powers are sufficient.

From the independence perspective, it can be argued that highly specialized agencies run a higher risk of being captured. Capture or bias may be prevented by the fact that, in a coordination model, other independent agencies, or other specializations within the same agency, will also examine matters.

[131] E Biber, 'Too Many Things to Do: How to Deal With the Dysfunctions of Multiple-Goal Agencies' (2009) 33(1) Harvard Environmental Law Review 62; P Freeman, 'The Competition and Markets Authority: Can the Whole be Greater Than the Sum of its Parts?' (2012) 1 Journal of Antitrust Enforcement 1.

[132] Cseres, 'Integrate or Separate' (n4) 33–36.

A multifunctional agency may be less sensitive to capture as it will have to deal with many different parties and interests.

Competition and coordination between agencies may lead to greater transparency if the coordination procedures are clearly set and all agencies provide openness on discussions taking place between them. This is not always, however, the case in practice, and that may lead to differing decisions. While these decisions may give insight into different views, they may also lead to conflicting results, which may be detrimental to the markets and parties involved.

From a transaction cost perspective (cf. effectiveness principle), the arguments are clearly in favour of the integration of agencies as this can produce substantial cost savings. Expertise can also be shared and combined, which can result in a more effective enforcement practice of the agency. From an effectiveness perspective, therefore, integration may be the optimal model. However, greater efficiency does not automatically mean greater effectiveness: a multifunctional agency may become too big to handle or result in choices that undermine other tasks of the agency. A focus will therefore have to be found within the agency through a clear strategy that combines the various tasks for which the agency is responsible.

The Netherlands: integrating competition and regulation tasks in an integrated agency

From a political perspective, the primary rationale behind the merger of the NMa, OPTA, and CA in the Netherlands was financial. The Dutch Minister of the Interior and Kingdom Relations submitted the central government's budget-cutting programme to parliament in February 2011. This included a proposal to combine various regulatory agencies responsible for non-financial sectors. Following that proposal, the Dutch Minister of Economic Affairs informed parliament in March 2011 of the plans to consolidate the NMa, OPTA, and CA. Another reason for this merger was the belief that consolidation would increase the efficiency and effectiveness of competition oversight and market regulation in that a consolidated agency would be able to anticipate developments in a flexible and integrated manner, and make better use of its consolidated knowledge and expertise.[133] Under the legislation, the ACM will 'promote well-functioning markets, orderly and transparent market processes, and treat consumers with care'.[134]

[133] Parliamentary Papers II 2011/12 Vol 33 186 No 6, 17–18 <https://zoek.officielebekendmakingen.nl/dossier/33186/kst-33186-6?resultIndex=44&sorttype=1&sortorder=4> accessed 15 September 2014.

[134] Parliamentary Papers II 2012/13 Vol 33 622 No 2 (n18).

It was only later, during the parliamentary discussions, that these arguments were elaborated upon and substantiated.[135] The view was taken that increasing choice and transparency for consumers would result in a better balance between price and quality, and also in more innovation, insofar as these three organizations were responsible for those tasks.[136] Improving quality was a priority, with the aim in combining these three organizations being to remove the overlap between their activities and to enable their knowledge to be used where it was most efficient.[137] As the legislator argued, the ACM can approach cases from an integrated perspective and adopt a balanced, integrated approach, instead of being restricted by the limited scope of the three individual agencies. According to the legislator, this merger is intended to strengthen sector-specific regulation by making it easier to use the other agencies' knowledge. The previous division of powers between the three institutions was seen as being inconsistent and unclear, and this apparently created confusion for consumers and enterprises alike,[138] resulting in a fragmented approach to resolving problems.[139]

It should be noted, however, that the three organizations already had close working relationships with each other and, most importantly, had already agreed before the merger to establish the consumer information helpdesk *Consuwijzer*. In addition, energy regulation was already part of the NMa's remit, with general competition law on the abuse of dominant positions and energy regulation being combined and coordinated. This was possible because of these tasks also being the responsibility of the NMa board (including the Energy Chamber). Although the organizations had previously agreed cooperation protocols for setting informal rules on cooperation and allocating cases in order to prevent forum shopping, some regulatory competition continued to exist in practice between the organizations, mainly between the NMa and OPTA, and mostly in cases where the legal boundaries were less clear and views on the need for market interventions varied.[140] One famous case in which the organizations successfully cooperated was the *Reggefiber* case.[141] In this case, the companies KPN Telecom and Reggefiber notified a

[135] Parliamentary Papers I 2012/13, No 17, 4.

[136] Parliamentary Papers II 2011/12 Vol 33 186 No 6, 11 <https://zoek.officielebekendmakingen.nl/dossier/33186/kst-33186-6?resultIndex=44&sorttype=1&sortorder=4> accessed 15 September 2014.

[137] Parliamentary Papers I 2012/13, No 17, 4.

[138] Parliamentary Papers I 2012/13, No 17, 5

[139] Parliamentary Papers I 2012/13, No 17, 8

[140] A T Ottow, *Telecommunicatietoezicht. De invloed van het Europese en Nederlandse bestuurs(proces)recht* (The Hague: Sdu Uitgevers 2006).

[141] NMa decision of 19 December 2008 in case 6397/*KPN-Reggefiber*, downloadable in Dutch from <https://www.acm.nl/nl/download/bijlage/?id=2840> accessed 27 September 2013.

joint venture to the NMa under the merger regulation, whereas at the same time OPTA had to investigate whether KPN Telecom could be regarded as having a significant market power. The different regimes applying meant that the two cases could have had different outcomes. In the end, however, the two independent agencies coordinated their decisions and the remedies imposed were fully synchronized. This success, however, was mainly due to the NMa and OPTA chairs' personal commitment to ensuring the agencies worked closely together on this occasion and ultimately took fully coordinated and interlinked decisions.[142]

The merger that created the ACM must be seen against the background of societal change in the Netherlands, where market competition is now being looked at more critically and attention has been redirected towards issues of public interest. Introducing competition as such is no longer accepted as the sole remedy for market failures; instead, additional remedies are seen as being required in order to ensure societal needs are protected.[143] This view also puts pressure on competition and market authorities to take these concerns into account when considering market interventions and formulating remedies.[144]

Consumers, therefore, have a central position in the ACM strategy.[145] Indeed they can be regarded as the cement of the new building: this principle applies to all ACM activities, ranging from the execution of specific consumer protection tasks to the application of industry-specific regulation and competition rules. The various types of legislation enforced by the ACM affect consumers in different ways. The competition, regulation, and consumer protection legislation enforced tends to focus on seeking to further the interests, either directly or indirectly, of consumers and consumer welfare. The ACM can combine these approaches, and thus improve the market for consumers, by ensuring that consumer protection is geared towards protecting more vulnerable consumers and consumers in regulated or other markets where products and services are dangerous or complicated or viewed as basic necessities. Consumers will be empowered through the provision of choice and information, as well as by an increased awareness of their rights and the means of redress available to them.[146] This strategy will ensure further

[142] P Kalbfleish, 'The Assessment of Interest in Competition Law: A Balancing Act' in M Monti et al (eds), *Economic Law and Justice in Times of Globalization—Festschrift for Carl Baudenbacher* (Baden-Baden: Nomos Verlagsgesellschaft, 2007) 455.

[143] K Cseres, 'The Controversies of the Consumer Welfare Standard' (2007) 3(2) Competition Law Review 133.

[144] T Prosser, *The Regulatory Enterprise—Government, Regulation and Legitimacy* (Oxford: Oxford University Press 2010).

[145] ACM Strategy Document (n94) 4.

[146] ACM Strategy Document (n94) 4–6.

integration of the organization and can lead to more effective enforcement, as illustrated in chapter 5 on enforcement.

However, there are concerns that a multifunctional agency may result in a lack of focused enforcement. In the case of the ACM in particular, some lawyers fear that such consolidation could result in antitrust law being diluted. Alternatively, too much weight, and therefore too many resources, could be diverted away from regulatory work and assigned to enforcing antitrust provisions, while concerns have also been expressed about the possibility of a declining focus on consumer interests. While these concerns have to be taken seriously, the ACM believes that it will actually be in a better position to carry out its duties. Combining regulation, competition, and consumer protection in an integrated manner will enable better solutions to be devised: the agency will be able to choose from a wider range of instruments in its toolkit. In the ACM's view the three areas of the law—antitrust, regulatory, and consumer protection law—will not be eroded by bringing them under a single roof. On the contrary, the new organization has triggered a process of cross-fertilization and a better combination of tools and instruments for resolving problems in the various areas. Given the scarcity of resources, priorities will obviously need to be set, but a balanced portfolio should ensure enforcement in all three areas.

Merging the *ex ante* teams with the abuse of dominant position teams within the sector directorates—as is now the case within ACM—will allow regulation and competition law, for example, to be integrated, while also allowing the development of a multifunctional approach to cases within a single team. For merger cases, new integrated teams combining competition law expertise and sector knowledge are formed in the event of sector mergers, as in the *Reggefiber II* case,[147] where a single, integrated team prepared the decision. This contrasted with the *Reggefiber I* case,[148] which was dealt with by two separate teams (OPTA and NMa), thus creating the need for coordination mechanisms and for two boards to agree on the process and outcome, resulting in additional transaction costs and less efficiency.

A key question when building the organization was to decide whether to have all functions (such as legal units and detection teams) in all departments, or to centralize certain activities in a separate department. Rather than complete centralization around specific tasks, it was decided to apply a mix of choices, both for historical reasons and due to the availability of

[147] On 6 May 2014, the ACM decided that for the proposed merger, KPN needed to apply for a permit for the proposed concentration. When that application would have been received, further investigation would be needed with regard to the case.

[148] NMa decision *KPN-Reggefiber I* (n141).

expertise. It was decided to concentrate all work relating to regulated sectors (including cases relating to the abuse of dominant positions) in the sectoral departments and to give each department its own detection team, while concentrating all consumer-related work in the Consumer Department, and to introduce horizontal coordination procedures and incentives to encourage cooperation between the departments. A network of detection officers has, for example, been created to collect and analyse indications and market information retrieved through various channels. All this information is being used for an ACM-wide prioritization of market and consumer problems. Such cross-departmental teams will be formed wherever they are expected to result in an effective approach.

It could be claimed that having integrated teams within the same organization will lead to bias and a resultant suppression of multiple viewpoints, as Cave and Stern argue. This possible risk has been identified within the ACM and resolved by assigning the legal counsel and chief economist the task of acting as independent reviewers. These views must be presented to the board and form part of the decision-making process. This procedure should strengthen the impartial and independent position of ACM. At the same time, this requires continuous attention of the board and management.

Another important observation should, however, be made from the perspective of the legality and independence principles. The formation of a multifunctional agency has clearly attracted criticism, with claims that combining all these functions into a single agency will result in the ACM becoming too big and too powerful.[149] A lack of countervailing powers will create a risk of abuse of powers and regulatory failure. This situation requires that a sufficient control is exercised by the appeal bodies that are responsible for adjudicating on ACM decisions. In the case of just a marginal review of decisions, this could result in a lack of democratic control. Therefore, there is a clear link between the institutional design of the agency and the required intensity of the review by the courts. This element is discussed in more detail in chapter 6, which examines the process of judicial review.

United Kingdom: integrated competition agencies in a coordination model

The situation in the United Kingdom is different. There, a different institutional approach has been chosen for dealing with the problem of how to achieve an

[149] R Ebbers, 'Nieuwe Big Brother' (2012) VNO NCW Forum <http://www.vno-ncw.nl/SiteCollectionDocuments/Forumartikelen/Forum_1912_ACM_17651.pdf> accessed 29 September 2014.

effective alignment of regulation and competition law. The merger of the CC and OFT to form the CMA is an example of how two competition agencies can be integrated into a single competition agency.[150]

Before the merger, the competition agency model in the UK was based on coordination between the OFT and CC. This contrasted with the single competition model existing in the Netherlands. The OFT and CC worked together on reviews of merger, market inquiries, and remedial orders. In February 2009, the two agencies agreed a Memorandum of Understanding (MoU), in recognition of their interlinked, albeit distinct, statutory roles in relation to the variation and termination of companies and orders. This MoU explained how the OFT and CC would work together to deliver these responsibilities. An updated version of the MoU was published in March 2011. The fact that the OFT and CC published this MoU jointly indicates their close working relationship, as also underlined by the following statement on the final page of the MoU:

> In addition to the discussions between the OFT and the CC in relation to specific individual reviews, CC and OFT staff primarily responsible for merger, monopoly and market remedies will meet on a regular basis to discuss issues relating to remedies generally. To the extent that policy issues arise in relation to variation and termination of orders and undertakings they may be discussed in such forums.[151]

In 2011, the UK government decided to review the UK competition regime and, in March that year, announced a consultation.[152] Its response to the consultation was published a year later.[153] The government emphasized that although the country's competition regime was already world class, the government nevertheless had some specific concerns about key elements of the regime, including its efficiency and the regulatory burdens of the dual body relationship between market studies (phase 1) and market investigations (phase 2), difficulties in successfully prosecuting antitrust cases at reasonable cost and in reasonable time, and the scope for delivering more streamlined and consistent decision-making processes.[154] In addition, the government stated that it is

[150] In this section the specific consumer tasks and the change of the consumer protection regime will not be discussed.

[151] See 'Memorandum of Understanding between the OFT and Competition Commission on the Variation and Termination of Merger, Monopoly and Market Undertakings and Orders Under the Fair Trading Act 1973 and Enterprise Act 2002' (2009). This MoU was later revised: 'Revised Memorandum of Understanding Between OFT and Competition Commission on the Variation and Termination of Undertakings' (2011).

[152] 'A Competition Regime for Growth: A Consultation on Options for Reform' (March 2011) <https://www.gov.uk/government/uploads/system/uploads/attachment_data/file/31411/11-657-competition-regime-for-growth-consultation.pdf> accessed 22 August 2014.

[153] Government Response to Consultation (n21).

[154] ibid 22.

committed to reducing the number and cost of public bodies, and to reduce the burden that such bodies impose on the businesses with which they deal. Having two wholly separate competition bodies imposes some additional costs, and more importantly for the economy, prevents more flexible allocation of resources across the competition regime. It is right that the Government considers whether the institutions can be rationalized to the benefit of the regime and to reduce the cost to the taxpayer.[155]

The UK government stressed four benefits of creating the CMA. Establishing the CMA would, firstly, create a scope for long-term cost savings, and, secondly, a single advocate able to speak powerfully for competition across the economy, whether British, European, or global. Furthermore, creating the CMA would improve coherence in the competition practice and streamline the approach in decision-making through strong supervision of the end-to-end case management process. Lastly, as a fourth benefit, resources would be utilized more flexibly to address the most important competition problems of the day, while the incentives to use antitrust and market tools to deal with competition problems would be enhanced. Taken together, these four benefits are considered

favourable to consumers and [will] lead to long run improvements to UK productivity and growth. The risks associated with the creation of the CMA will be mitigated, in part through the retention of a two phase process for mergers and markets and independent panels for phase 2 and through careful transition planning. [...] The creation of the CMA is not expected to result in savings over and above those which need to be achieved as a result of the Spending Review, but will facilitate these.[156]

The OFT and CC expressed during the consultation their support for the merger and for creation of the CMA.[157]

Alongside its newly created single competition agency, the UK also has regulatory agencies that not only have *ex ante* regulatory powers, but also—in most cases—concurrent powers. Examples of these agencies include Ofwat (for water and sewerage), Ofcom (for communications and broadcasting), and the CAA (for aviation). These agencies can consequently seek recourse to the specific *ex ante* remedies based on the sector regulation *and* to those available in competition law to resolve competition issues in the relevant market. The concurrency system is a specific characteristic of the UK competition system.

It was suggested during this period of external review that the sectoral regulators in the UK previously focused too much on *ex ante* regulatory approaches and remedies relative to the *ex post* competition policy approach.[158]

[155] ibid 22–23. [156] ibid 26. [157] ibid 24.

[158] M Cave and J Stern, 'Competition and Regulatory Policy and Institutional Design for Scotland' (2013) Research Paper No. 11/2013, The David Hume Institute 2.

The 2014 reform of the competition regime resulted in an enhanced regime being introduced. The CMA was given a new remit to work with sectoral regulators so as to ensure fuller use of competition law and policy in sectoral markets.[159] The agency now has a greater role to play in ensuring that competition in regulated sectors is addressed because the new competition regime has reinforced cooperation and information sharing between the CMA and sectoral regulators.

These new instruments include the provision whereby, before using their direct regulatory powers of enforcing licensing conditions, sectoral regulators first have to consider whether it is more appropriate to apply competition law. The CMA is now also empowered to decide which body (the sectoral regulator or the CMA itself) should lead a case. If it is satisfied that this will benefit consumers by encouraging greater competition, the CMA has the power to take a case over from a sectoral regulator.[160] This new approach reflects the increasing role that the legislator has chosen for competition law in the regulated sectors. A partnership approach with the sectoral regulators has been chosen for the CMA in order to achieve this primacy of competition law. As cooperation is an important principle in the enhanced concurrency arrangements, the CMA and sectoral regulators have agreed to establish the UK Competition Network as the basis for further cooperation.[161]

The UK model is obviously, therefore, a coordination model, where the competition authority and market agencies remain separate organizations, but work closely together. At the same time, the CMA clearly has to act as the leading competition authority, while enjoying the support of the sectoral regulators. In addition to the legal measures, the UK market and competition authorities have agreed to establish practical forms of cooperation, including the collecting and sharing of information (both on cases and more generally), staff secondments, general pooling of resources, and the provision of advice and training,[162] all with the aim of enabling fuller use of competition law in the regulated sectors.

[159] Speech by A Chisholm, 'CMA Mission and Strategy' (2013). See for the application of competition law to regulated markets: CMA, 'Regulated Industries: Guidance on Concurrent Application of Competition Law to Regulated Industries' CMA 10, 2014.

[160] See for a detailed description of this new regime: CMA, ''Baseline' annual report on concurrency—2014' (2014) 5–6.

[161] The UK Competition Network brings together the CMA, CAA, FCA, Ofcom, Ofgem, Ofwat, the ORR, and the Utility Regulator of Northern Ireland. The UKCN was mentioned in the 'UKCN Statement of Intent' published on 2 December 2013, available at <https://www.gov.uk/government/uploads/system/uploads/attachment_data/file/262996/UKCN_Statement_of_Intent_FINAL.pdf> accessed 8 July 2014.

[162] CMA Baseline report (n161) p 56.

In practice, the CMA and its fellow sectoral regulators have signed memoranda of understanding, laying down the principles on which their cooperation will be based. The CMA has made considerable efforts to establish relationships with these other agencies in order to improve the application of competition law. An example of this is the provision for market investigation referrals, a specific power that allows the CMA to look into competition issues in selected markets.[163] Sectoral regulators can request the CMA to perform such investigations, which can ultimately lead to remedies being imposed by the CMA (i.e. by its panel members). When preparing a possible reference, the sectoral regulator and CMA also work closely together to identify possible competition problems that may occur.[164]

In the United Kingdom, the panel system also operates as an appeal body for certain regulatory decisions.[165] The separation of institutions allows this, whereas other countries, such as the Netherlands, have structured their review procedures within the agency, while still allowing the possibility of an appeal to specialized courts.

Conclusion

Two questions have been analysed in this section. Firstly, the question of whether a coordination model of separate agencies with overlapping tasks is preferable, or whether an integrated model involving agencies being brought into a single organization is the preferred option. Concentrating competition under a single roof, as in the case of the CMA, not only creates more efficiency, but also greater effectiveness. Expertise can be combined and procedures can be streamlined, while at the same time also respecting the panel system for phase 2 decisions in merger cases and market investigations. Integrated agencies clearly have certain pros and cons. This model

[163] On market investigation references, see for example: D Chetty, Y Njisane, M Mbikiwa, and C Martin, '"Knowledge is power". The Role of Market Inquiries in Assessing the State of Competition and Facilitating Ex Ante Regulation of Markets' (2014) Eighth Annual Competition Law, Economics and Policy Conference; R Whish and D Bailey, *Competition Law* (Oxford: Oxford University Press 2012) 467; Competition Commission 'Guidelines for Market Investigations: Their Role, Procedures, Assessment and Remedies' (2013) <https://www.gov.uk/government/uploads/system/uploads/attachment_data/file/284390/cc3_revised.pdf> accessed 24 September 2014.

[164] See, for example: Ofgem, Consultation on a proposal to make a market investigation reference in respect of the supply and acquisition of energy in Great Britain, London, 27 March 2014. Available at <https://www.ofgem.gov.uk/ofgem-publications/86807/cmamarketreference09072014.pdf> accessed 8 July 2014.

[165] See for an overview of the appeals system in the United Kingdom: HM Government, 'Streamlining Regulatory and Competition Appeals' (2013) Consultation on Options for Reform.

allows expertise and integrated policies and instruments to be combined, thus improving the effectiveness of how the different issues at stake are dealt with. However, potential synergy must then be present. If there is no overlap or common interest, the merger bringing the agencies together will not provide many benefits. The argument for separation can be found in the phenomenon of regular competition: competing agencies keep each other sharp. However, the separation model gives rise to additional transaction costs and may also create more uncertainty, with different agencies possibly delivering different outcomes, thus putting considerable regulatory burdens on the parties.

The second part of this section analysed whether the bringing together of competition tasks and regulatory tasks is a good idea. An example of this can be seen in the Netherlands, in the case of the ACM. Having integrated teams within the same organization can lead to bias, and multiple viewpoints may be suppressed. The ACM has resolved this issue by assigning the task of acting as independent reviewers to its legal counsel and chief economist. The UK regime must obviously be considered against the background of the concurrency system, which clearly has various pros and cons and is non-existent in most other countries. Important aspects when answering this second question are whether a multifunctional agency will result in a lack of sufficiently prioritized high-impact enforcement (i.e. doing lots of different things and, therefore, nothing in any depth), and whether multifunctionality may lead to underperformance of competition law because of the agency preferring to take on cases involving *ex ante* regulatory remedies. These are realistic risks that must be taken into account and that demand special attention from the agency's board.

Conclusion

From an institutional perspective, the LITER principles of independence, transparency, and effectiveness play a key role in the choices made when designing an agency and in its relations with its stakeholders. These principles form the basis for the legality of an agency and have a direct and intrinsic influence on the responsibility demonstrated by the agency, its board, and its staff. In my view, independence should be seen as a leading principle in this respect. The relationships between the independent agency and the responsible minister and ministry are something of a delicate issue. Agency independence requires the minister to remain at a distance and to refrain from involvement with individual cases, while drawing on the expertise of the independent agency can also improve the substantive quality of the rules and result in a better understanding of each other's position. However, *de jure* independence is not enough. Independence must also be earned by the agencies themselves, through good practices and through the high quality of their decisions. Leadership and institutional culture are crucial to ensure the quality of the organization itself, its practices, and its results. The ambitions for the right agency's culture must be led from the top of the agency's leadership so as to ensure integrity and impartiality. The quality of the organization and its personnel requires a continual investment in infrastructure and education.

Having a clear strategy will give the agency a clear direction, thus making focus and priorities possible and providing cohesion between the organization and the desired agency branding. Stakeholders' involvement in defining the strategy will improve the independent agency's openness and transparency, which are important elements of the good agency or LITER principles. Building relationships with stakeholders, fellow agencies, and the academic world meanwhile will add quality to the organization and create critical followers. These institutions' input is important in delivering better results and in preventing the agency from developing tunnel vision.

5
Enforcement

Introduction

Enforcement is the key activity of market and competition authorities. The agencies' enforcement task—in other words, their oversight of companies—is seen as their very *raison d'être*. General principles for enforcement should accordingly be developed for that purpose. This chapter maps out these enforcement principles on the basis of the LITER principles of legality, independence, transparency, effectiveness, and responsibility.

In the good agency model, enforcement is an important but often missing link, or at least an aspect that should receive more explicit attention. Although the legal literature and case law on competition and regulatory enforcement focus mainly on sanctions, formal sanctions are just one aspect of enforcement practice. Agencies must master the art of choosing the right enforcement style, rather than simply opting for vertical instruments of oversight (i.e. sanctions). Greater differentiation of the enforcement toolkit will improve not only the extent to which substantive rules are accepted, but also the impact of the oversight performed by the agencies. Proper enforcement is a question of creating the right mix of instruments; a process that depends on such things as the rules to be enforced, the nature of the supervised enterprise, and the phase of the market's development. Or, in other words, a process that depends on the specific circumstances of the case. A major mistake that agencies make in practice is to opt for one specific style of enforcement as a general strategy, sometimes driven by an ideological preference for a certain style, and sometimes for cultural, historical, or legal reasons. In order to ensure compliance, it is in any event essential to understand which tool is most effective in each specific case.

This chapter takes the general LITER or good agency principles as the basis for further elaborating on the enforcement activities, and specifically those elements of enforcement that are relevant for market and competition authorities. The word 'enforcement' is used in the broad sense in this chapter: meaning not just formal actions (i.e. decisions) by the agencies, but informal actions as well, whereby the agency intervenes by other means, such as advocacy or informal meetings. As in the case of other issues, a code of good practice is needed for enforcement principles too, given that a specific characteristic of enforcement activities is that they can have serious implications and create burdens for the enterprises involved. This consequently needs to be taken into account when designing procedures and remedies. Procedural fairness and the proportionality of the measures are important elements when seeking to ensure that cases lead to fair outcomes. Here, the guardian dimension of the LITER principles comes into play. Whereas market and competition authorities focus mainly on effective outcomes from an enforcement perspective (cf. the effectiveness principle), supervised companies are keen to have fewer burdens and to ensure fair procedures (cf. the legality principle). This chapter translates the LITER principles into principles of enforcement in order to show the various options for selecting enforcement styles. Lastly, examples from the Netherlands and the United Kingdom are used to illustrate these options. Rather than advocating a specific style of enforcement, this book aims to provide insight into the pros and cons of the various options against the background of the good agency or LITER principles, and to give market and competition authorities a framework for resolving their enforcement dilemmas. These enforcement principles provide insight into the factors to be weighed against each other and into the trade-offs that can be made. Clearly, 'developing principles to guide enforcement conduct is a start, but it is only that'.[1] Translating these general principles into day-to-day practice requires expertise, skills, and an adequate institutional infrastructure. Inevitably, the principles will sometimes conflict and a balance will have to be struck. A degree of flexibility is also required in order to adapt the principles to the circumstances of the case or to the problem to be resolved. In other words, enforcement demands craftsmanship rather than a standard approach.

Principles of Enforcement

In order to establish principles of enforcement, firstly we have a look at some important sources that can be used to identify the principles of enforcement.[2]

[1] J Black, 'Managing Discretion' (2001) ARLC Conference Papers, Penalties: Policy, Principles and Practice in Government Regulation, 26–29.

[2] Parts of this section are taken from: A T Ottow, 'Developing a Common Framework for Good Performances by Agencies' in P Lugard, *The International Competition Network at Ten* (Antwerpen: Intersentia 2011) 251–66.

After discussing the enforcement principles put forward by these sources, I arrive at the LITER principles where I discuss the five umbrella concepts that together compose these good agency principles.

Hampton Report and Regulators' Compliance Code

In seeking to establish the enforcement principles, reference can be made to practice in the United Kingdom where, following the Hampton Report,[3] new enforcement principles, including a more risk-based approach, were introduced.[4] This report recommended that problems should be approached on the basis of the principle of risk assessment so that 'the burden of enforcement falls most on high-risk business, and least on those with the best records of compliance'.[5] This report was followed in 2007 by a Regulators' Compliance Code,[6] which introduced enforcement rules stating that comprehensive risk assessments should be used in order to allocate resources to the areas that need them most, agencies should give authoritative and accessible advice in an easy and cheap way, enterprises should not have to provide unnecessary information, no inspections should take place without a reason, and independent agencies should be accountable for the efficiency and effectiveness of their activities while remaining independent in the decisions they take. An amended version of the Regulators' Compliance Code,[7] which was published in April 2014, clarified certain pre-existing provisions so that independent agencies, and those they supervise, would have a clear understanding of what was expected of them. The new provisions included a requirement for agencies to perform their activities in such way (while giving advice and providing guidance) that it helps the regulated businesses and bodies not only to comply with the law but also to facilitate compliance

[3] P Hampton, *Reducing Administrative Burdens: Effective Inspection and Enforcement* (HM Treasury, London 2005) (here referred to as the 'Hampton Report').

[4] Discussed in T Prosser, *The Regulatory Enterprise. Government, Regulation and Legitimacy* (Oxford: Oxford University Press 2010) 206–07, 211–14.

[5] Hampton Report (n3) 24.

[6] Department for Business, Enterprise and Regulatory Reform, 'Regulators' Compliance Code: Statutory Code of Practice for Regulators' (2007). This was supplemented in 2008 by the Code of Practice on Guidance in Regulation and the Macrory Review of regulatory penalties (R Macrory, 'Regulatory Justice: Making Sanctions Effective—Final Report' (2006) Cabinet Office), followed by the Regulatory Enforcement and Sanctions Act 2008.

[7] The UK government promised in its 2012 Autumn Statement to review and refresh the Regulators' Compliance Code, see: Chancellor of the Exchequer by Command of Her Majesty, 'Autumn Statement 2012' CM (2012) 8480, 76 and 79. Subsequently, the Department for Business, Innovation & Skills published a Consultation Paper on revising the code, see: Department for Business, Innovation & Skills, 'Consultation Paper Amending the Regulators' Compliance Code' (2013).

in the future. The focus of the Regulators' Compliance Code and the new legislative provisions is clearly on lessening the burdens for business and on working as efficiently as possible. The code also devotes attention to the agencies' advisory and advocacy roles. Although the code is not applicable to market regulators, it can clearly be used by market and competition authorities as a general framework.

Principles for Economic Regulation

The *Principles for Economic Regulation* report focuses specifically on market regulators, but does not contain any very specific elements with regard to enforcement. Of particular relevance is the previously identified principle of focus, where it is stated that:

i) The role of economic regulators should be concentrated on protecting the interests of end users of infrastructure services by ensuring the operation of well-functioning and contestable markets where appropriate or by designing a system of incentives and penalties that replicate as far as possible the outcomes of competitive markets.
ii) Economic regulators should have clearly defined, articulated, and prioritised statutory responsibilities focused on outcomes rather than specified inputs or tools.
iii) Economic regulators should have adequate discretion to choose the tools that best achieve these outcomes.[8]

The important aspects here are the focus on outcome (and not the tools) and the discretion that the independent agency should have to choose the tools (best suited to achieving these outcomes). In practice, it is often the output—such as the number of decisions or the total amount of penalties—that is taken into account as it is obviously easier to develop performance indicators based on concrete numbers (i.e. output) than indicators based on outcome. Although the outcome and effects on industry and consumer welfare are more difficult to measure, they say more about the real effects of the oversight and enforcement than the total number of decisions or interventions. Proving the effectiveness of enforcement is a hurdle that market and competition authorities have to overcome.

[8] Department for Business, Innovation & Skills, 'Principles for Economic Regulation' (2011) <https://www.gov.uk/government/uploads/system/uploads/attachment_data/file/31623/11-795-principles-for-economic-regulation.pdf> accessed 25 July 2014.

OECD reports on enforcement and inspections

Another important document is the report on enforcement published by the Organisation for Economic Co-operation and Development (OECD). Based on two expert papers,[9] an extensive review of practices in OECD and non-OECD countries, and on research conducted on this topic from the 1980s to around 2010, the OECD has devised 11 principles on enforcement:

1. Evidence-based enforcement. Regulatory enforcement and inspections should be evidence-based and measurement-based: deciding what to inspect and how should be grounded on data and evidence, and results should be evaluated regularly.
2. Selectivity. Promoting compliance and enforcing rules should be left to market forces, private sector, and civil society actions wherever possible: inspections and enforcement cannot be everywhere and address everything, and there are many other ways to achieve regulatory objectives.
3. Risk focus and proportionality. Enforcement needs to be risk-based and proportionate: the frequency of inspections and the resources employed should be proportional to the level of risk and enforcement actions should be aiming at reducing the actual risk posed by infractions.
4. Responsive regulation. Enforcement should be based on 'responsive regulation' principles: inspection enforcement actions should be modulated depending on the profile and behaviour of specific businesses.
5. Long term vision. Governments should adopt policies and institutional mechanisms on regulatory enforcement and inspections with clear objectives and a long-term road-map.
6. Co-ordination and consolidation. Inspection functions should be co-ordinated and, where needed, consolidated: less duplication and overlaps will ensure better use of public resources, minimise burden on regulated subjects, and maximise effectiveness.
7. Transport governance. Governance structures and human resources policies for regulatory enforcement should support transparency, professionalism, and results-oriented management. Execution of regulatory enforcement should be independent from political influence, and compliance promotion efforts should be rewarded.

[9] OECD, 'Reform of Regulatory Enforcement and Inspections in OECD Countries' <http://www.oecd.org/fr/reformereg/34976533.pdf> accessed 8 September 2014; and OECD, 'Inspections Reforms: Why, How and With What Results' <http://www.oecd.org/gov/regulatory-policy/Inspection%20reforms%20-%20web%20-F.%20Blanc.pdf> accessed 8 September 2014; both presented to the OECD Regulatory Policy Principles at its 7th meeting in November 2012.

8. Information integration. Information and communication technologies should be used to maximise risk-focus, co-ordination, and information-sharing—as well as optimal use of resources.
9. Clear and fair process. Governments should ensure clarity of rules and process for enforcement and inspections: coherent legislation to organise inspections and enforcement needs to be adopted and published, and clearly articulate rights and obligations of officials and of businesses.
10. Compliance promotion. Transparency and compliance should be promoted through the use of appropriate instruments such as guidance, toolkits, and checklists.
11. Professionalism. Inspectors should be trained and managed to ensure professionalism, integrity, consistency, and transparency: this requires substantial training focusing not only on technical but also on generic inspection skills, and official guidelines for inspectors to help ensure consistency and fairness.[10]

Here, too, focus and outcome are important ingredients. However, the report also mentions transparency, compliance strategies, and a risk-based approach (as in the Hampton Report). The OECD principles point to evidence-based oversight, which has clearly received more attention in the years since 2005. Data and evidence play a prominent role in enforcement practice, leading not only to high standards of proof for market and competition authorities (cf. the transparency principle), but also to burdens on business through the requirement for them to provide information. In an extreme case, the evidence-based approach can form an obstacle to effective enforcement if the burden of proof is not proportionate to the goals of the regulation. Economic evidence (and review by the courts) is dealt with in chapter 6.

Legal approach

A more legal approach to enforcement is followed by Black, who identifies the following enforcement principles: legality, consistency, proportionality, non-discrimination, due process, transparency and accessibility, efficiency, and expertise.[11] Basically these are the standard administrative law requirements referred to in chapter 3. These requirements can be divided into three categories: (i) scope of the remedy (legality, consistency, proportionality, and

[10] OECD, 'Regulatory Enforcement and Inspections' (2014) <http://www.keepeek.com/Digital-Asset-Management/oecd/governance/regulatory-enforcement-and-inspections_9789264208117-en#page1> accessed 25 July 2014.

[11] J Black (n1) 26–29.

non-discrimination); (ii) procedural fairness (due process, and transparency and accessibility); and (iii) effectiveness (efficiency and expertise). The first two categories refer to the guardian dimension of the law, while the final category relates directly to the effectiveness principle, which has been identified as one of the LITER or good agency principles.

Closely related to these legal requirements are the fundamental rights aspects of enforcement by independent agencies. As stated in chapters 3 and 4, the law on fundamental rights forms an integral part of supervisory law and principles. Article 6 of the European Convention on Human Rights (ECHR) is of particular importance in this respect. This provision includes several requirements that, when taken together, ensure a fair trial. The rights arising from this Article 6 accrue to anyone charged with a criminal offence. Although the imposition of an administrative fine is strictly speaking an administrative act, it is classified in the ECHR as a criminal charge due to the nature and severity of the penalties.[12] Under the ECHR, the agency must inter alia respect various rights: firstly, the presumption of innocence, which means that the accused (enterprise) is considered innocent until proven guilty; secondly, the enterprise's right to remain silent and its privilege against self-incrimination;[13] and lastly the fact that any trial has to be held within a reasonable but adequate period of time. Apart from procedural aspects, fundamental rights can also influence the design of the remedies and the intensity of a court's review of enforcement decisions.

The influence of the European Union is also relevant in the enforcement context. In principle, member states are free to determine how EU law is enforced in their national courts. The European Court of Justice (ECJ) has, however, imposed limits on national procedural autonomy. *Greek Maize* is undoubtedly the leading case on the requirements of EU law with regard to national enforcement.[14] In this case the Greek state failed to fulfil its obligation to initiate all the criminal and disciplinary proceedings provided for in national law against the perpetrators of fraud. The ECJ ruled that Article 4(3) of the Treaty on European Union (TEU) requires member states to take all measures necessary to guarantee the application and effectiveness of EU law: 'For that purpose, whilst the choice of penalties remain within their discretion, they must ensure in particular that infringements of EU law are penalized under conditions, both procedural and substantive, which

[12] *Öztürk v Germany* (1984) 6 EHRR 409.

[13] The practice of this principle is complicated, especially since there may be some sort of obligation to cooperate in the field of economic supervision; see, for example, *Saunders v UK* ECHR 1996 43/1994/490/672 and *Funke v France* ECHR case A/256-A.

[14] Case C-68/88 *Commission v Greece (Greek Maize)* [1989] ECR 2965.

are analogous to those applicable to infringements in national law of a similar nature and importance and in which in any event, make the penalty effective, proportionate and dissuasive'.[15] The essential criteria for enforcement measures are that they have to be effective, proportionate, and dissuasive. These criteria are based on the European principle of effectiveness, but have so far remained rather vague. It can be argued on the basis of case law, however, that the ECJ has taken a rather punitive approach. It is also clear that member states, including independent agencies, have to take action and have an enforcement obligation (an in-principle obligation) in the event of infringements of EU law.[16]

LITER principles in the context of enforcement

Based on the good agency or LITER principles of legality, independence, transparency, effectviveness, and responbility, the following important elements can be identified with regard to enforcement.

Legality

The *lex certa* principle, i.e. the principle of legal certainty, should be mentioned in this context as enforcement cannot be based on vague legal or other norms or concepts, or even principles. The legal norm infringed should be sufficiently concise, clear, and transparent. Supervised enterprises must be able to know which rules they have to comply with. Otherwise, the lack of legal certainty implies that enforcement is impossible. Rights and obligations must be explicitly stated. This clearly forms an important element of the legality principle's safeguard dimension. By translating general legal norms into guidelines, independent agencies provide not only legal certainty, but also greater (*ex ante*) transparency.

In addition, enforcement should be proportionate. The principle of proportionality, mostly in relation to the selection and formulation of remedies, is an important element of enforcement. Actions, interventions, and remedies must be tailored around problems and the specific circumstances of the case. Minor infringements require minor sanctions, although recidivism may result in more severe sanctions. Proportionality also means that the only

[15] *Commission v Greece (Greek Maize)* (n14) paragraph 24. See, for example, K de Weers and A T Ottow, 'Towards a European Enforcement Toolkit' (dissertation, Europa Institute, Utrecht University) 4 <http://www.uu.nl/SiteCollectionDocuments/REBO/REBO_RGL/REBO_RGL_EUROPA/ThesisKoendeWeersFINALVERSION[2].pdf> accessed 1 July 2014.

[16] A T Ottow, *Telecommunicatietoezicht: De invloed van het Europese en Nederlandse bestuurs(proces)recht* (dissertation, University of Amsterdam, SDU Uitgevers, Den Haag 2006).

burdens to be imposed on the enterprises concerned should be those that are strictly necessary for the purpose.

Procedural fairness, including the principle to hear both sides, forms an important element in enforcement procedures. There must be clarity on the rules and processes to be followed during an enforcement case so as to ensure procedural fairness. The parties involved will then be able to deliver the evidence needed to substantiate their case and to defend their rights in an infringement procedure within a reasonable period of time. An agency that does not comply with the procedural rules will be considered unfair and will lose its credibility. The outcome of the case can also be challenged in court as not being in compliance with administrative rules on procedural fairness. Agencies must be alert to the need to take these formalities into account.

As discussed in chapter 4, the separation of the fact-finding stage from the sanctioning stage of the procedure is a delicate issue in procedures involving administrative sanctions, such as penalties. The protection of fundamental rights plays an important role in that respect, not only for the institutional design of the decision-making process, but also in the consequences it has for how independent courts have to review sanctioning decisions.[17]

Independence

The OECD report also clearly highlights another aspect of enforcement: the important link between the institutional environment of the independent agency and its enforcement practice. Agencies must be able to set their own enforcement priorities. Political influence on the enforcement choices an agency makes can represent a significant impediment to effective enforcement. This can also result in unequal treatment of market parties and in potential risks for business and consumers, thus infringing the non-discrimination principle. This is especially true if the state is involved as a market player and distorts competition. In such circumstances, the independent agency must be able to initiate investigations against the enterprise, without any pressure from the government or politicians to prevent it from doing so. The agency must be able to take its own decisions, based on the circumstances of the case and on objective considerations. This is also true with regard to the kind of enforcement measure to be taken. If a penalty is considered appropriate, the way the penalty is calculated must be based on objective and non-discriminatory guidelines. In some cases it may be the legislator or responsible minister who prescribes the general framework for

[17] See for more: A Scordamaglia-Tousis, *EU Cartel Enforcement. Reconciling Effective Public Enforcement with Fundamental Rights* (International Competition Law Series, volume 54, The Hague: Wolters Kluwer Law & Business 2013).

calculating the fines, but it is up to the market or competition authority to apply those guidelines to the individual case, as discussed in chapter 3.[18]

In relation to enforcement, bias is of special importance. The rotation of personnel and organizing a fresh pair of eyes can improve the impartiality and prevent the development of tunnel visions. Independent agencies can be easily blamed for pro-enforcement bias, being too much results-oriented. The collection of sufficient evidence and the evaluation of the available evidence must be done in a cautious and careful way. There is always the risk of confirmation bias, where evidence which does not confirm the theory of harm is consciously or unconsciously ignored or interpreted in a pro-enforcement way.

Transparency

The decisions must be based on data and evidence, while the agency must also be able to publish its enforcement decisions. By publishing its decisions, the agency can provide evidence of its interventions and effectiveness. Publication is an important tool in accountability. Communications, too, can be an enforcement tool as publication of data, decisions, or infringements can have both a preventive and a deterrent effect. Publication will also result in equal treatment (cf. the non-discrimination principle) and prevent deals being reached 'behind closed doors'. Well-reasoned and published decisions serve the interests of transparency, accountability, and predictability.

Clear communication on the agency's agenda of priorities, identifying the specific areas of attention, should also be expected. The same applies to the publication of prioritization principles or penalty guidelines, which give guidance to stakeholders, as well as to the need for the agency to have a clear framework to refer to in its decisions. However, tailor-made solutions can come at the expense of less predictability and less legal certainty, while enforcement actions must sometimes be taken unexpectedly (for example, dawn raids). Enforcement may entail an element of unpredictability if it is to be effective. This tension between transparency and effectiveness must be recognized, and the two principles will not always be compatible.

Effectiveness

Enforcement is directly related to effectiveness: the outcome of enforcement must be effective if it is to attain the goals of the applicable regulation. Which tools and instruments should be chosen to optimize the result of compliances

[18] See the general guidelines of the Dutch Minister of Economic Affairs, 'Beleidsregels van de Minister van Economische Zaken voor het opleggen van bestuurlijke boetes door de ACM' available at <http://wetten.overheid.nl/BWBR0033327/geldigheidsdatum_02-08-2014> accesssed 25 July 2014.

or to reduce risks? This is the key question, but there is no standard answer. In the years since 2005, independent agencies have invested considerable time and energy in developing more sophisticated strategies and tools, and in seeking to identify more hybrid and flexible approaches to enforcement. As well as applying the classical sanctioning approach, they have also tried to find solutions for specific problems. However, identifying these solutions remains the biggest challenge facing these agencies.

A complicating factor is the impact assessment of the choices made. Stakeholders are demanding more and more 'hard' results and still focusing too much on output rather than outcome. The measurement of impact in competition law and regulation is still underdeveloped, while demonstrating the effectiveness of enforcement action, and more generally the interventions of the independent agency, also remains a weak spot in the oversight system. How, for example, should an agency prove that the mere existence of the regime has prevented damage from occurring (i.e. anticipation effects)? Informal interventions can also be very effective, but how can these be shown and proven?[19]

Effectiveness is also influenced by the extent and nature of coordination with other agencies. Cooperation with fellow independent agencies can produce better results and reduce burdens and the extent of overlap. Adopting a partnership approach can allow sharing of expertise and skills, and resolution of any problems, in a coordinated way.

With regard to enforcement, a delicate balance has to be found between *effective* enforcement and *careful* enforcement. While effective enforcement focuses on getting quick results through efficient procedures and problem-solving solutions, careful enforcement takes account of procedural fairness and proportionality, and may consequently result in longer procedures and a more formal approach towards remedies. This creates a tension, which is discussed throughout this chapter.

Responsibility

Agencies have to take responsibility for enforcement in the light and context of their roles and tasks. The way the agency sees its roles and tasks has a major influence on the choices it makes on the enforcement side. Is it very proactive, or does it choose to adopt a more reactive role? If it considers consumer protection to be an important task, it will tend to be more interventionist, while others may see this as paternalistic. Their responsibility relates not only

[19] See for the benefits and use of the informal intervention: ACM, 'Annual Report 2013' 118 <http://jaarverslag.acm.nl/downloads/JaarverslagACM2013.pdf> accessed 25 July 2014.

to their repressive tasks, but also to their advisory, advocacy, and reflective roles, as discussed in chapter 2. As the reports on enforcement discussed earlier in this chapter clearly state, advocacy is seen as a core element of independent agencies' tasks, including providing sufficient guidance in the form of toolkits, checklists, and guidelines.

As discussed in chapter 3, the attitude towards responsibility also influences the enforcement strategy an agency selects. If it assigns more responsibility to the enterprises themselves, it will follow more of a compliance approach than if there is less confidence that self-regulation or compliance by the industry will work. Agencies' views on society and the role of the state will also influence their enforcement style and the enforcement choices they make. Do they, for example, see it as their responsibility to protect only vulnerable consumers, or to take preventive measures benefiting all consumers? The design of their enforcement tools will reflect these choices and they will take responsibility in linc with these various options. The responsibility principle obliges independent agencies in any event to accept a degree of responsibility that accords with the goals of the applicable regulations and the tasks entrusted to them.

Responsibility is also related to responsiveness. Enforcement literature refers to this as 'responsive regulation':[20] in other words, the agency must be responsive to and design its enforcement around the specific circumstances of the case.

Conclusion

From an enforcement perspective the LITER or good agency principles reflect the continuous movement of the enforcement pendulum, swinging from calls for more and stricter interventions (cf. effectiveness principle) to demands for fewer burdens and lower costs for the industry (cf. legality principle). Although independent agencies are being assigned increasing numbers of tasks, there is also a clear desire to restrict their powers, while at the same time calls regularly go out for more, and for more stringent, oversight. These calls and trends have repercussions for how independent agencies perform their enforcement tasks. A greater focus on reducing the burdens for industry and on working more efficiently will force agencies to make other choices and will put them under more pressure to demonstrate effective outcomes.

[20] For example an 'enforcement pyramid', a range of enforcement sanctions extending from persuasion through warning and civil penalties up to criminal penalties, licence suspensions, and license revocations. See R Baldwin and J Black, 'Really Responsive Regulation' (2005) LSE Law, Society and Economy Working Papers.

While this tension is felt by the agencies in their day-to-day work, they may bring the other LITER principles of independence, transparency, and responsibility into play to come to balanced decisions on strategy and enforcement in the longer run. The weight that both the agencies and society confer to each of these principles influences the choices made and the reasoning behind these enforcement choices.

Prioritization

An important issue in enforcement is the problem of prioritization. Limited capacity and budgets force independent agencies to set priorities. Although in some countries the agencies have a general obligation to enforce and follow up complaints,[21] it is also recognized that they cannot pursue all cases, given their capacity and budget constraints. Which criteria can and should agencies use when selecting their enforcement priorities?

Discretion in setting the enforcement agenda

It is not always clear how market and competition authorities set their priorities. Sometimes they have a statutory duty to perform certain tasks (for example, the requirement for market assessments in the telecommunications sector). In practice, however, agencies largely have a considerable margin of discretion in setting their enforcement agendas. It should, however, be mentioned that the enforcement tasks of market and competition authorities are not done by individual inspectors, but instead based mainly on written evidence assessed by multidisciplinary teams (lawyers, economists, political scientists, and so on) working together on a case; in other words, enforcement work is team-based.

Supervised enterprises usually visit the relevant agency to present their case. On-site inspections are made only in exceptional circumstances. This makes enforcement work less 'visible', more abstract, and bureaucratic. Individual case officers consequently have less discretion and autonomy to make choices, with the risk of less flexibility to adapt to the circumstances of the case. At the same time, working in teams can provide a mechanism for

[21] In the Netherlands, for example, case law is available on the discretionary powers of the competition agency and other regulators on the right to and limits of prioritization, for example judgement of the Trade and Industry Appeals Tribunal (CBb) of 20 August 2010, *LJN* BN4700. From this case law it follows that the independent agencies may set priorities and refuse to take on a case, but they need to reason this sufficiently and argue why further investigation is not required.

preventing tunnel vision and capture. External or unpredicted events may trigger activities or force agencies to initiate procedures, while in other cases action may be taken in response to complaints or at the agency's initiative.

From the perspective of the legality and transparency principles, it will be preferable to publish prioritization guidelines, containing objective and general criteria for independent agencies to use as the basis for selecting their enforcement cases. The UK Competition & Markets Authority (CMA), for example, has published its prioritization principles.[22] Social media can be used to consult markets and consumers (and their associations) to set the prioritization agenda.

In view of the independence principle it should in any event be clear that the agency itself must set its own priorities and select the cases it considers appropriate in the light of its overall strategy. Budgets for litigation must also be separated from the agency's normal budgets. If the responsible ministry does not compensate the agency for the costs of litigation or if severe limits are imposed on litigation costs, this could influence the cases that the agency will choose to take on. This could ultimately lead to an enforcement portfolio containing only certain types of cases (probably easy cases, where the litigation risks are low). In addition, the minister may use budgets as a way of influencing the type of cases selected by the agency, and this would conflict with the principle of independence. The agency must, therefore, have full discretion to build its portfolio of cases.

Balanced enforcement portfolio

It is important for market and competition authorities to have a balanced portfolio of cases. Their portfolio-building must take several aspects relating to the goals of the regulation and the agency's tasks into account. These include the kind of harm involved and the extent to which consumers are at risk, as well as the need to ensure a balance between small and larger cases, easy and difficult cases, cases that can set precedents or where the deterrent effects are significant, cases involving different levels of risk appetite, and cases with short-term effects and those with longer-term implications. Ultimately, strategic enforcement choices and, therefore, the selection of cases should be driven by the agency's overall strategy. This requires flexible budgets, a project-based approach, and dynamic allocation of resources. Opting solely for smaller, easier cases will not demonstrate great overall effectiveness

[22] Competition & Markets Authority, 'Prioritisation Principles for the CMA' (2014) CMA16 <https://www.gov.uk/government/publications/cma-prioritisation-principles> accessed 25 June 2014.

on the part of the agency. It will therefore have to take account of the various tasks assigned to it and allocate its capacity and budget accordingly. If, for example, the energy sector is seen as an important industry facing competitive concerns, cases in this area will be searched for, while infringements involving considerable detrimental effects on consumers should be included in the portfolio if vulnerable consumers are an important focus in the strategy. Multifunctional agencies in particular run the risk of choosing cases that will have the greatest political impact (consumer cases, for example) or the highest branding effects for the agency.

As an example of how to balance the portfolio, the CMA Prioritisation Principles[23] specify a list of factors that the UK competition authority will consider when deciding whether to take on a case. The strategy set by the agency is essential for determining which problems to select for further investigation. The CMA focuses its efforts and resources on deterring and influencing the behaviour that poses the greatest threat to consumer welfare. In seeking to target both its resources and enforcement strategy, the CMA considers various factors, including the direct and indirect impact on consumers, strategic significance, risks, resources, and the effects on efficiency and productivity, as well as the capacity and interests of its fellow independent agencies. Strategic planning is an import aspect of the prioritization process. By considering how to assess the progress achieved in meeting strategic objectives, the CMA can select the cases most closely targeting these objectives and ensure that these cases adhere to these goals. By setting an example in certain areas it may also have a preventive and deterrent effect in others, thus creating clear spill-over benefits. Its planning should also include decisions to terminate investigations and not to continue them without good reason as case teams may otherwise find it difficult to stop investigations and may tend to postpone 'no-go' decisions (i.e. a 'stranded cost' bias). Regular reviews of these processes are necessary in order to avoid allocating capacity to weak cases that cannot meet the standards of proof. The longer a case continues, the more difficult it will be to decide that there is insufficient evidence to establish an infringement. Agencies must realize this and build in safeguards.

Prioritization is a delicate exercise as the independent agency may be blamed (and sometimes even held liable) for selecting the wrong cases and, therefore, taking no action in other cases. Most cases relating to negligence

[23] Competition & Markets Authority (n21). See also: International Competition Network, 'Agency Effectiveness. Competition Agency Practice Manual. Chapter 1L Strategic Planning and Prioritisation' (2010) 29–45 <http://www.internationalcompetitionnetwork.org/uploads/library/doc744.pdf> accessed 6 September 2014, which also provides interesting case studies on prioritization.

are about *not* taking action or *not* having seen the problem, or having seen it too late. Can an agency be held liable for such negligence? This question is dealt with in detail in chapter 6. Put briefly, however, and as explained in the following two sections on styles, and tools and instruments of enforcement, the answer depends on the view taken on enforcement: in other words, on how active the agency should be, and on what is seen as the optimal enforcement style or tool.

Styles of Enforcement

Translating the enforcement principles into appropriate methods of enforcement is one of the most difficult tasks facing market and competition authorities and is a struggle on a daily basis. Conflicting goals in the underlying regulations may also form an impediment to making the right enforcement choices. Various tools and instruments are available, and it is not always certain how effective they are. Although enforcement trends can be identified, these change over time, and the choices made are greatly influenced by views on society and on the different roles that agencies, enterprises, and consumers should play in achieving compliance and reducing risks. Is it seen as the responsibility of governments and authorities to protect public interests, or does society demand that enterprises and consumers should take responsibility and organize self-regulatory oversight for themselves? This relates to the LITER principle of responsibility: in other words, who is taking regulatory responsibility? Can stakeholders trust the industry to comply with the rules and avoid risks, based on self-interest and social responsibility, or is the agency responsible for arranging the capacity required to take on oversight?

We can see a difference in views and attitudes before and after the financial crisis of the years 2007 to 2014. Before the financial crisis, closer cooperation between market and competition authorities and supervised enterprises was clearly seen as an important option. This horizontalization (referred to by Andenas and H-Y Chiu as 'self-regulatory governance')[24] is a response to an increasingly complex society, in which it is virtually impossible to continue adhering to top-down steering and in which agencies are being charged with an increasing number of tasks. Cooperation between social stakeholders is necessary—in that view—in order to achieve the objectives, while also

[24] M Andenas and I H-Y Chiu, *The Foundations and Future of Financial Regulation: Governance for Responsibility* (Routledge 2013) 85.

leaving scope to respond effectively to new developments. In its report on the future of the rule of law, the Dutch Scientific Council for Government Policy[25] stated, for example, that the classic pattern of vertical state steering had passed its prime and was in need of modernization. This view was based on the belief that there should be more horizontal steering, based on target requirements, with enterprises having a certain leeway in deciding for themselves how to achieve the desired results, and the Scientific Council advised placing more emphasis on enterprises' own responsibility. Such a system creates greater flexibility and allows a more alert response to changes in the social and technical environment. This more 'market-based governance' is based on the 'perception by industry participants that self-regulatory standards will stave off more costly regulatory intervention'.[26]

However, more has been expected from the market and competition authorities after the financial crisis. Since there is greater distrust in market players' self-cleansing abilities, there have been calls for more stringent oversight. At the same time, agencies are being 'lumbered' with more and more tasks, and higher expectations, and these are forcing them to look for better and more efficient ways of enforcement. Owing to historical, legal, and cultural differences, many national differences obviously still exist.[27] These vary from sector to sector, although certain trends and choices can be said to have been copied by agencies in many sectors and countries.

Rather than listing all the different options, this chapter analyses a few of the most important ones.[28] Enforcement styles that have had an important influence on many agencies' work are analysed against the LITER principles. In all the cases examined the independent agency is looking for the optimal approach in terms of effectiveness. The latter is the overriding principle in the context of enforcement, sometimes at the cost of the transparency or legality principles. Agencies' choices are very much driven by how they divide the responsibilities between the agency and the enterprises it oversees, and thus allocate resources and costs.

[25] *Wetenschappelijke Raad voor het Regeringsbeleid* (WRR)

[26] Andenas and H-Y Chiu (n24) 91.

[27] This conclusion is based on the research done by Yane Svetiev and myself on the enforcement practices of financial market authorities in the EU. During the research we found that different approaches exist across the EU and its member states, leading to different enforcement styles in the field of financial regulation. These preliminary conclusions have been presented in a draft paper: A T Ottow and Y Svetiev, 'Institutional Innovation in Financial Supervision in the Interstices between Public and Private Law' (2014) European Regulatory Private Law and Financial Services Third Annual Workshop, European University Institute, Florence.

[28] See for an extensive overview: R Baldwin, M Cave and M Lodge, *Understanding Regulation: Theory, Strategy and Practice* (Oxford: Oxford University Press 1999) chapter 11.

Vertical style of supervision

Theory broadly distinguishes two styles of oversight: vertical and horizontal. Vertical supervision, resulting in vertical enforcement, employs conventional instruments for oversight (such as cease-and-desist orders, administrative fines, and punitive sanctions) to uphold the law and is a classic command-and-control model.[29] Steering is vertical because conduct is dictated top-down. The force of law is used to prohibit certain types of conduct, to demand positive action, or to lay down conditions for access to a certain industry. The infringement of the law is seen as the starting point for intervention. This contrasts with horizontal supervision, where the focus is on collaborating with the supervisee. There are other terms for distinguishing between these two practices: informal versus legalistic or formal supervision or oversight, and cooperative versus adversarial supervision or oversight, while De Bruijn et al. distinguish between the sanction style and the accommodative style.[30]

An example of the vertical approach is the way in which the European Commission responded to the financial crisis in October 2008, when it instructed Jacques de Larosière to propose recommendations for strengthening the European financial supervisory system. The financial crisis had exposed serious gaps in cooperation, coordination, consistency, and trust between national regulatory authorities, and the Commission wanted to take steps to reform financial oversight at a European level.[31] De Larosière concluded that effective, convergent sanctioning regimes were of paramount importance for a new supervisory system:

> Supervision cannot be effective with weak, highly variant sanctioning regimes. It is essential that within the EU and elsewhere, all supervisors are able to deploy sanctioning regimes that are sufficiently convergent, strict, resulting in deterrence.[32]

The European Commission's 2010 Communication on reinforcing sanctioning regimes in the financial services sector[33] shows the Commission's concerns about traditional methods of financial regulation. The Commission

[29] R Baldwin, M Cave, and M Lodge (n28).

[30] H de Bruijn, E ten Heuvelhof, and M Koopmans, *Law Enforcement. The Game Between Inspectors and Inspectees* (Boca Raton, Florida: Universal Publishers 2007).

[31] European Commission, 'European Financial Supervision' (Communication) COM (2009) 252.

[32] The de Larosière Group, 'High-level Group on Financial Supervision in the EU chaired by J de Larosière' (2009) 50 <http://ec.europa.eu/internal_market/finances/docs/de_larosiere_report_en.pdf> accessed 24 September 2014.

[33] See Commission, 'Communication on Reinforcing Sanctioning Regimes in the Financial Services Sector' COM (2010) 716.

specifically draws attention to existing differences between member states' financial regulators with regard to sanctioning tools and stresses that the effectiveness of such tools should be guaranteed throughout the member states.[34] The Commission also addresses the importance of severe sanctions for specific infringements by referring to tools in criminal law and to high levels of fines.

The issue of fines, as a single strategy, can become rather formalistic and legalistic. The deterrent effect of sanctions must be considered in each case separately and must not create an automatic approach to infringements. Sanctions are an *ex post* approach, where the damage has already occurred. This sanctioning approach does not focus on preventing damage in the future, although the sanctioning of infringements may have some deterrent effect. The underlying problems also need to be analysed, and the independent agency must consider possible alternatives to sanctions (see the discussion of responsive regulation and problem-solving approaches elsewhere in this chapter).

Horizontal style of supervision

The vertical enforcement style contrasts with a horizontal approach, where the focus is on collaborating with the supervisee. This alternative is based on trust, and this trust is the point of departure in the relationship between the agency and the supervisee. The relationship here is more cooperative than in the case of vertical supervision. The agency forms 'regulatory partnerships with the regulated and other market participants'.[35] Examples of horizontal supervision include self-regulation, co-regulation, covenants, and voluntary compliance programmes.

Back in the 1990s, a host of social sciences publications pleaded for a less vertically-oriented approach to monitoring enterprises' compliance with the rules and highlighted the benefits of a different approach to enforcement in terms, for example, of public administration, organizational studies, and business ethics. The social scientists arguing in favour of such an approach demanded attention for horizontal instruments for complying with the rules, on the basis that they believed it would be more effective to give enterprises more responsibility for complying with and enforcing certain rules. These non-legal disciplines also highlighted the drawbacks of a one-sided, vertical

[34] Conclusion drawn from the research done by Y Svetiev and myself for the European University Institute, of which the preliminary conclusions have been presented in a draft paper (n27).

[35] Andenas and H-Y Chiu (n24) 78–83.

approach and advocated a more integrated approach combining the two (vertical and horizontal) styles of oversight.[36]

As the horizontal alternative is based on trust between the agency and the supervisee, this enforcement style demands a different tack, not only in enforcement practice, but also in enforcement law. Its practice is designed to give supervisees more responsibility and uses instruments such as covenants and compliance agreements, while the agency maintains a greater distance. The search for new forms of horizontal supervision is creating tensions between law and practice as these new forms of enforcement are not easy to accommodate within the administrative law system. This is because the conventional administrative law instruments are more vertical and repressive. Here, the principle of legality comes into play. In most cases, there is no legislation specifically granting the agency explicit powers to establish covenants or compliance agreements, and such initiatives are usually undertaken by the supervisee and the agency on a voluntary basis. In the dynamic environment that characterizes many markets, the principle of legality should be seen in a proper perspective and should not stand in the way of a more horizontal approach to oversight. It would be preferable, however, for the legislature to lay down these powers in special rules. This has evident advantages: not only does it prevent disputes on the powers of these agencies, but it also offers a foothold for embedding this form of supervision in administrative law and then linking it to procedural safeguards (such as a requirement for transparency), which are currently lacking in many cases.

If seen from the perspective of the agency's tasks, the transfer of responsibility to the enterprises it supervises gives rise to another form of tension. Does this transfer mean that the agency will still perform the tasks entrusted to it? Or will it in fact undermine the agency's very *raison d'être*, i.e. its supervising of enterprises? Independent agencies must keep a constant finger on the pulse and ensure proper compliance with competition and regulatory rules. Horizontal supervision, after all, is *not* a question of turning a blind eye to infringements; rather it is designed to ensure that there are no infringements of the law. Opting for non-public-law or for less conventional instruments does not mean non-compliance; compliance with the rules is the point

[36] For an example of a more integrated approach of enforcement, see the responsive regulation model, which uses an enforcement pyramid, in I Ayres and J Braithwaite, *Responsive Regulation: Transcending the Deregulation Debate* (New York: Oxford University Press 1992). The enforcement pyramid is discussed on pages 38–39. For a critical perception about the effectiveness of this pyramid model: see R Baldwin and J Black (n20); N Gunningham and P Grabosky, *Smart Regulation* (Oxford: Clarendon Press 1998); J Mendeloff, 'Overcoming Barriers to Better Regulation' (1993) 18 Law and Social Inquiry 711; and R Johnstone, 'Putting the Regulated Back into Regulation' (1999) 26 Journal of Law and Society 378.

of departure as the enterprise involved must abide by the law. Horizontal supervision also requires the agency to actively monitor compliance, but does so by encouraging enterprises to comply of their own accord. The agency should see prevention of breaches as an important part of its task. There are few administrative law instruments for such preventive oversight, however, and the agency will therefore have to come up with appropriate but creative solutions, which are not always available in the traditional administrative law channels.

This approach clearly also entails risks for the independent agency. The agency's informal or cooperative involvement with the industry may lead to capture and, therefore, conflict with the principle of independence. Another difficult aspect of self-regulatory enforcement regimes can be the enforceability of the arrangements. This places the agency in a dilemma: on the one hand it uses horizontal arrangements in order to give enterprises more responsibility and to allow them to organize their own enforcement mechanisms, while on the other hand it needs instruments to check whether these arrangements are being complied with and to ensure they remain adequate. The self-regulation process will lose much of its speed and flexibility if the arrangements are formally incorporated into a regulatory decision. The agency also has to monitor whether voluntary implementation is simply 'window dressing' and whether it creates a false sense of security. The arrangements may also be less transparent than otherwise, and the lack of transparency may allow the process to be surrendered. Lastly, all market parties must be involved in ensuring that the legal principle of non-discrimination is respected.

Risk-based approach

The risk-based approach was pushed in the United Kingdom in the Hampton Report and has since remained popular, especially in the financial sector.[37] The essence of risk-based enforcement is the prioritization of enforcement interventions in accordance with an assessment of the risks identified in the areas falling within the agency's regulatory scope.[38] In this approach, risks have to be identified, assessed, and assigned a risk profile ranging from high to low. Resources are then allocated accordingly, on the basis of risk calculation, and efficiency and cost-benefit analyses. 'The influence of the risk-based approach lies in the purported cost-effectiveness, proportionality and

[37] Andenas and H-Y Chiu (n24) 78–83.

[38] R Baldwin, M Cave, and M Lodge (n28) chapter 13; and J Black, 'The Emergence of Risk-based Regulation: Choices, Practices and Lessons Being Learnt' in OECD, *Risk and Regulatory Policy: Improving the Governance of Risk* (2010).

flexibility in assessing risk and determining appropriate regulatory action, reflecting the limitations of regulatory resources in the decentred regulatory space'.[39] In the case of the lower categories of risk, the agency trusts that internal compliance or control mechanisms will ensure compliance.[40]

The biggest risk facing the independent agency in this approach is the risk of wrongly categorizing enterprises and, therefore, of allocating insufficient resources to certain businesses. The factors used to weigh risk must be carefully selected, while risk-profiling can also be labour-intensive. Another question that needs to be resolved concerns what kinds of controls or tools to apply to what kinds of risks. Risks may also change, and enterprises' categorization into certain risk profiles may no longer be up-to-date. Another regulatory risk is the risk that enterprises that do not attract the agency's attention will remain 'under the radar' and become 'forgotten regulatees'[41] as they no longer have any incentive to comply with the rules. Consequently, certain enterprises may not be supervised adequately, thus resulting in higher risks. Andenas and H-Y Chiu point out that the financial crisis that hit some UK banks could have been caused by such misperceptions of banks' financial health.[42]

As Black pointed out, this risk-based approach could result in greater transparency and accountability. Her argument is that this approach allows the agency to provide clarity on the risks/enterprises that it will not supervise and, therefore, to create more acceptance among politicians and the wider public that independent agencies 'cannot ensure that each and every one of its objectives will always be met'.[43] This in turn legitimizes the existence of several different levels of intensity of oversight, correlating with the different risk profiles. The financial crisis showed, however, that the market authorities always get blamed ('Where was the regulator?') and that the risk-based approach did not give them sufficient protection. The financial market authorities were blamed for not having performed their supervisory job properly. Explaining priorities and the selection of cases will remain difficult whenever something goes wrong that the independent agency did not see, or where it miscalculated the risks.

Independent agencies adopting a risk-based approach, in my view, regularly have to re-evaluate whether their categorization of risks and their risk assessment factors are still up-to-date. They also need to continue investing

[39] Andenas and H-Y Chiu (n24) 82.

[40] Labelled by Andenas and H-Y Chiu as a 'form of self-certifying discipline' (n24) 80.

[41] R Baldwin, M Cave, and M Lodge (n28) 285.

[42] Andenas and H-Y Chiu (n24) 79.

[43] J Black, 'The Emergence of the Risk-Based Regulation and the New Public Risk Management in the United Kingdom', (2005) 3 Public Law 19.

resources in supervised enterprises with lower risks so as to ensure that their compliance systems are still in place and not just a tool for 'window dressing'.

Responsive regulation

The best-known work on responsive regulation is that of Ayres and Braithwaite.[44] These authors developed the responsive regulation model, which uses an enforcement pyramid to examine which enforcement instruments to deploy, based on a hierarchy of sanctions graded from light to heavy, and from horizontal to vertical. The base of the pyramid comprises the most cooperative instruments for ensuring compliance, while the heaviest or most severe instruments, such as fines and the withdrawal of permits or licences, are located at the top. The message in the model is clear: an independent agency must first establish whether cooperation and consultation is possible, and should opt for heavier sanctions only as a last resort (i.e. a bottom-up approach). At the same time, the model acknowledges that there should be scope for imposing heavier sanctions as a means of pressuring supervisees into ensuring better voluntary compliance. The instrument the agency selects should depend not only on the characteristics of the enterprises concerned and the nature of the standards to be complied with, but also—for market and competition authorities—on the specific circumstances of the relevant markets and the interest (public or otherwise) to be protected. In this approach, knowing the supervised enterprises also enables independent agencies to choose the right form of intervention. Responsive regulation assumes that agencies are able to identify which response is most suited to the behaviour of the supervised enterprise. Ayres and Braithwaite recognize that their model focuses specifically on situations where agencies and the supervised enterprises repeatedly interact with one another, and thus have many opportunities to influence each other.[45]

This model has attracted criticism from a legal perspective, specifically with regard to the non-discrimination principle. Flexibility is one of the characteristics of the pyramid approach: the ability to climb up and down the pyramid to ensure effective and efficient outcomes facilitates a swift change in strategies, but may also lead to less predictability and greater uncertainty, and ultimately also to tension with the principle of non-discrimination.[46] This

[44] I Ayres and J Braithwaite, *Responsive Regulation: Transcending the Deregulation Debate* (n36). For a series of articles on responsive regulation, see the special issue of Regulation & Governance (2013) 7.

[45] J Etienne, 'Ambiguity and Relational Signals in Regulator-Regulatee Relationships' (2013) 7 Regulation & Governance 33.

[46] P Westerman, 'Pyramids and the Value of Generality' (2013) 7 Regulation & Governance 89.

approach also requires considerable discretionary powers as the independent agency has to decide which instrument or approach is best in the given circumstances. The responsive regulation approach clearly holds a tension between the effectiveness principle on the one hand and the legality principle on the other hand. The agency needs to be aware of this tension and not only to focus on the specific case at hand, but also to take account of similar cases and the choices made there.

Problem-solving

Other leading research, by Sparrow,[47] argues that although the pyramid provides a useful way of deciding which sanction is appropriate for which form of non-compliance, there are also situations in which risk is not correlated with lawbreaking, but that are nonetheless of concern to independent agencies. Sparrow suggests that the focus should be on the problems that occur or could occur (i.e. a problem-oriented approach) and that the agency should choose those tools from its toolkit that it believes may adequately resolve the problem or cushion its effects. Sparrow views problem-solving from a different angle and focuses on identifying the relevant problems and developing effective solutions ('Find a problem and fix it!'),[48] recognizing that different problems require different solutions.

This approach can be illustrated by financial regulation. The focus in current EU financial regulation is on disclosure and transparency in order to protect the investor/customer against specific risks. It is understood that risk disclosure and the provision of sufficient information enable investors to make informed decisions. This approach is followed in countries such as Germany and France, where the independent agency checks whether the necessary information has been provided and then leaves it up to the professional investor to decide whether to accept the product and the specified risk. This rather formal, legalistic approach, where the independent agency does not look at the actual risks of the financial product, but merely at how the information on the product has been delivered, contrasts with the approach in countries such as the Netherlands and the United Kingdom, where the financial market authorities are involved at the development stage of the product. If they consider a product to be detrimental to customers, they will advise the financial institution to withdraw it or to redesign it in an

[47] M K Sparrow, *The Regulatory Craft* (Washington DC: Brookings Institution Press 2000); and M K Sparrow, *The Character of Harms. Operational Challenges in Control* (Cambridge: Cambridge University Press 2008).

[48] Sparrow, *The Regulatory Craft* (n47).

acceptable way. This is a much more preventive approach to problem-solving and results in a more interventionist agency, which is also involved in the supervised enterprises' product development.

The problem and its solution are the central focal point in the problem-solving approach, and any possible legal impediments are disregarded. Sparrow has clearly shown that problems identified may not necessarily correspond with infringements of the law. As he points out, 'There are [...] situations in which risk is not correlated so closely with lawbreaking'.[49] In cases where there is no specific legal basis for resolving the problem identified, the independent agency may come into conflict with the legality principle. In any event, reconciliation with legal requirements may prove to be difficult. Sparrow pleads for sufficient discretion for independent agencies in order to allow them to exercise their professional judgement in choosing the right solutions.[50] He also points out that responsiveness to problems may conflict with the values of equity and consistency,[51] thus recognizing that reconciling or balancing these different values can be a challenging exercise. Agencies need to be aware of this and to seek to deal with problems consistently. What is important is that agencies realize that by focusing only on infringements of the law, they may miss other important problems and risks in the outside world. Identifying these risks may enable them to find ways to alert the stakeholders involved and to take steps within the boundaries available to them in law.

Behavioural economics

Behavioural economics is increasingly being used as a method for identifying consumer or business biases that may cause competition problems. This behavioural knowledge is subsequently used to design better and more effective solutions and to draft more appropriate remedies.[52] Behavioural economics is not, therefore, an enforcement strategy in itself, but is used as a tool within an enforcement strategy and, as such, can be considered a style of enforcement.

[49] ibid 41.

[50] ibid 246. See also A T Ottow, *Telecommunicatietoezicht* (n16) where I also plead for wide discretionary powers so as to enable authorities to take new situations into account (dynamic approach).

[51] Sparrow, *The Regulatory Craft* (n47) 251.

[52] The best known work is that of R H Thaler and C R Sunstein, *Nudge. Improving Decisions about Health, Wealth and Happiness* (New York: Penguin Books 2008). See also Bennett et al, 'What Does Behavioural Economics Mean for Competition Policy' (2010) 6 Competition Policy International Journal.

In its Strategy Document the Dutch Authority for Consumers & Markets (ACM) states that consumer empowerment will form an important part of its work, while competition law will be used to give consumers greater choice and lower prices.[53] A well-functioning market provides the best guarantee that consumers' interests will be properly served. Influences from behavioural economics[54] and consumer choice in antitrust theory will be used to ensure that the choice provided is actually of use to consumers, or at least that consumers understand how they should apply this choice.[55] This involves devoting more attention to resolving consumer problems *ex ante*, and placing more emphasis on empirical evidence.[56] The focus is on long-term resolution of problems, if necessary involving private enforcement of competition law, mediation roles, and alternative dispute resolution, rather than on short-term ad hoc intervention. The ACM can also explore the use of behavioural economics by emphasizing the importance of the demand side in making markets work efficiently.[57] Behavioural biases highlight important synergies between consumers and competition policy, and may also have implications for anticompetitive behaviour. Behavioural economics can be used in various ways to help understand consumers' problems and to improve the application of both competition law and consumer protection law.[58]

Already before it merged with the CMA, the UK Office of Fair Trading (OFT)[59] was innovative in its approach to behavioural economics. The OFT's stance towards the theoretical exploration of new uses for behavioural economics reflected a desire to shape the incorporation of the new theory into general practice. This said, even the OFT's leading behavioural researchers understood that this approach represented only an 'incremental advance' on

[53] The following sentences are taken from A T Ottow, 'Erosion or Innovation? The Institutional Design of Competition Agencies—A Dutch Case Study' (2014) 2(1) Journal of Antitrust Enforcement 25.

[54] OECD Global Forum on Competition, 'The Interface between Competition and Consumer Policies, Background Note' (2008) 4 DAF/COMP/GF 7–12.

[55] K J Cseres, 'The Controversies of the Consumer Welfare Standard' (2007) 3(2) Competition Law Review 121.

[56] W E Kovacic, 'Competition Policy, Consumer Protection and Economic Disadvantage' (2008) 25 Washington University Journal of Law and Policy 101.

[57] ACM, 'Behavioural Economics and Competition Policy' (2013). See also, for example, the Financial Conduct Authority, 'Applying Behavioural Economics at the Financial Conduct Authority' (2013) Occasional Paper No. 1, London.

[58] M. Bennett et al, 'What Does Behavioural Economics Mean for Competition Policy?' (2010) 6 Competition Policy International 1, 4,7.

[59] The following text on the OFT cases on behavioural economics is (with permission) taken from and prepared by B Nunez, master student of Law and Economics at Utrecht University, for his master thesis: 'The Application of Behavioural Economics by Regulators in the UK: A Theoretical and Practical Analysis' (2014).

previous policy and that it should not occasion the replacement of traditional practices. The evaluation of the OFT's study into online games, which is discussed as an example of enforced self-regulation at the end of this chapter, reveals how additional behavioural insights can be used to improve an agency's understanding of the indicators of consumer harm and to devise solutions to problems.

Conclusion

This chapter presents enforcement choices and styles as different classifications. However, situations are never 'black and white'; instead, different combinations and choices have to be made in different circumstances. The distinctions and labelling used here are made for the sake of clarification and analysis. Supervisory approaches and instruments are in most cases complementary and need not be seen as mutually exclusive. This is also referred to as 'ambidexterity',[60] or the 'carrot and the stick', with soft and hard approaches both being present and able to be used simultaneously. In practice, these models are combined when independent agencies attempt to find the right mix of instruments[61] or, as I put it, perform customized enforcement.[62] It could be said that 'a good supervisor has no enforcement strategy'.[63] In my opinion, it is important for an independent agency to take on an active role and to look for innovative, effective solutions to ensure compliance with the law and to achieve the goals of the legislation. In that search it has to respect the legal boundaries of its powers, and set fair and transparent procedures. At the same time the legislator has a responsibility to provide the expert agency with the flexible powers it needs to ensure it can adapt its enforcement approach to the circumstances of the case, and if new or unexpected problems arise. Nowadays, agencies perform their duties in a constantly changing, highly dynamic environment, with many new technological and other developments. Whatever approach they take, they must be careful not to get 'locked-in'[64] to a certain choice for a certain enforcement approach. Problems and risks change over time. Flexibility is therefore needed on the part of

[60] This terminology is used by C A Fonteijn, chair of the Netherlands Authority for Consumers & Markets (ACM) in his speeches.

[61] See A T Ottow, *Mastering the Market? Exploring New Forms of Market Supervision* (inaugural lecture 18 September 2008, University of Utrecht, The Hague: Boom Juridische Uitgevers 2009).

[62] Introduced in A T Ottow's inaugural lecture '*Mastering the Market?*' (n61) 12.

[63] Interview with M Dankers, AFM, on 19 February 2014 for the research on the enforcement practices of national regulatory authorities for the European University Institute by Y Svetiev and A T Ottow.

[64] R Baldwin, M Cave, and M Lodge (n28) 288.

agencies, legislators, and policymakers. This requires independent agencies to remain alert at all times and to look critically at any choices made.

Tools and Instruments

This section analyses a selection of systems, tools, and instruments, ranging from a more vertical to a more horizontal approach, in the context of the enforcement principles.

Sanctions

The imposing of sanctions represents a traditional approach to enforcement in the field of regulation and competition law. A regime focusing on sanctions ('command and control' enforcement style), which is by definition oriented *ex post*, leads to a more formalistic, legal style of enforcement, as in the case of the financial sector in Germany, where sanctions are imposed on financial institutions that fail to obey the rules. This contrasts with countries such as the Netherlands and the United Kingdom, where independent agencies are more *ex ante* oriented and apply a risk-based, interventionist approach.

A distinction has to be made between administrative and criminal sanctions. Although both are regarded as punitive sanctions and thus fall within the meaning of a criminal charge following from Article 6 of the European Convention on Human Rights (ECHR), these two types of sanctions have distinct characteristics, with administrative sanctions generally being seen as less severe than criminal sanctions. In some countries individuals, too, can be subject to administrative fines.

Criminal sanctions

Criminal law is completely vertical and repressive. In other words, this instrument is at the top of the enforcement pyramid. Whether criminal law sanctions need to be introduced in addition to or instead of administrative law sanctions so as to improve the enforcement of competition law or regulation is an issue subject to continual debate. Sanctions clearly need to be in place and must be applied to ensure that there is sufficient pressure on enterprises to opt for voluntary compliance. This raises the question of which sanctions are necessary. In general, most countries currently operate market oversight through administrative sanctions, while a dual system of administrative law and criminal law sanctions is used only in niche areas such as financial supervision.[65] The debate on the criminalization of competition law is still high on many countries' agendas and is being given consideration in more and more countries around the world.[66]

How should a dual—administrative and criminal—system be viewed? There are sound arguments both for and against such a system, and this makes it difficult to reach clear conclusions. Advocates of such as system attach great importance to the deterrent effect of criminal law sanctions such as prison sentences. As they see it, the regulating effect of these sanctions could prevent cartel breaches.[67] Those in favour of this deterrent effect refer to criminal law enforcement in the United States of America and argue that this prevents many breaches.[68] Criminal sanctions, such as imprisonment, are deemed necessary, given that the profits that can be made from cartel agreements exceed the administrative fines many times over.[69] Administrative sanctions cannot therefore—in this view—prevent such behaviour.[70] This line of reasoning consequently argues for criminalization,[71] although some claim that it may be fairer and more effective to penalize the individuals directly responsible rather than the enterprise as a whole and that the decision-makers in the enterprise should be held accountable. Opponents, on the other hand, believe

[65] The question arises in what way the European legislator can oblige the member states to establish sanctions of criminal law. On the criminalization of EU Competition Law on EU level and, possibly, the level of member states, see: G Hukopian, 'Criminalisation of EU Competition Law Enforcement—A possibility after Lisbon?' (2010) 7(1) The Competition Law Review 157. See also: ECJ 13 September 2005, case C-176/03, *Commission of the European Communities, supported by: European Parliament v Council of the European Union*, paragraphs 38–51 <http://curia.europa.eu/jcms/upload/docs/application/pdf/2009-02/cp050075en.pdf> accessed 25 July 2014. From the judgement in *Commission v Council* follows that, in this case, there was no legal basis to issue a sanction.

[66] Countries criminalizing cartel conduct include, among others, Australia, Canada, Germany, Mexico, Russia, and the United States of America; see J Clarke, 'The Increasing Criminalization of Economic Law: a Competition Law Perspective' (2012) 19(1) Journal of Financial Crime 76.

[67] For five reasons in favour of the imprisonment of individuals, see: W P J Wils, 'Is Criminalization of EU Competition Law the Answer?' (2005) 28(2) World Competition 117.

[68] See, for example, W P J Wils (n67) 117, 159.

[69] This is mentioned by, among others, A P Reindl, 'How Strong is the Case for Criminal Sanctions in Cartel Cases?' in K.J. Cseres et al, *Criminalization of Competition Law Enforcement, Economic and Legal Implications for the EU Member States* (Cheltenham: Edward Elgar Publishing Limited 2006) 116.

[70] See J M Connor, *Price-Fixing Overcharges: Legal and Economic Evidence* (2005) Staff Paper No. 04-17, Purdue University; P Whelan, 'A Principled Argument for Personal Criminal Sanctions as Punishment Under EC Cartel Law' (2007) 4(1) The Competition Law Review 7; OECD, 'Report on the Nature and Impact of Hard Core Cartels and Sanctions Against Cartels Under National Competition Laws' (2002) DAFFE/COMP; and OECD, 'Report Cartels: Sanctions Against Individuals' (2005) DAF/COMP.

[71] See W P J Wils (n67).

that criminal law sanctions have no more than a minimal impact on preventing breaches and that enterprises are likely to take much greater account of the potential damage to their reputation that a breach could cause.[72]

There are also economic reasons for focusing on the deterrent and preventive effects of criminal sanctions,[73] although economists point out that it also has to be established whether the costs of criminal law enforcement exceed the benefits of reducing the number of breaches. This is because criminalizing competition law demands investments in the public prosecution apparatus, both in terms of staffing and expertise. Practice in the United Kingdom has shown that this aspect of capacity and expertise is indeed often underestimated. Criminalization in the United Kingdom has not yet produced the anticipated results, which was mainly due to a lack of expertise and capacity on the part of the OFT. The CMA may strike quite a different note in this regard. Building the specific criminal expertise, and experience of procedures and evidence, in this field of law and preparing cases takes time and requires skilled people, who are not always available within a competition agency, and, even if time and people are available, can be at the expense of other enforcement activities.

Administrative sanctions

In most cases, independent agencies have the power to issue administrative sanctions. The focus of these sanctions, which have been competition authorities' most important enforcement tool over the years, has been on improving the procedure and on introducing leniency programmes to improve the detection of cartels.[74] Many competition authorities have published penalty guidelines that lay down criteria for calculating fines. These guidelines provide clarity and greater legal certainty for the imposition of fines. Examples of them include the *Administrative penalties: statement of policy on the CMA's*

[72] See, for example, J M Karpoff and J R Lott, 'The Reputational Penalty Firms Bear From Committing Criminal Fraud' (1993) 36 Journal of Law and Economics 757; and J M Karpoff et al, *The Cost to Firms of Cooking the Books* (University of Washington 2006).

[73] B C J van Veldhoven and P W van Wijck, *Recht en efficiëntie. Een inleiding in de economische analyse van het recht* (Deventer: Kluwer 2007) chapter 10; and P Buccirossi et al, 'Deterrence in Competition Law' (2009) Discussion Paper no. 285, Governance and the Efficiency of Economic Systems.

[74] For more on the topic of leniency programs, see: M Motta and M Polo, 'Leniency Programs and Cartel Prosecution' (2003) 21 International Journal of Industrial Organization 347; C Aubert, P Rey, and W E Kovavic, 'The Impact of Leniency and Whistle-Blowing Programs on Cartels' (2006) 24 International Journal of Industrial Organization 1241; and K Bisset and L Thomas, 'Lenciency Program: A New Tool in Competition Policy to Deter Cartel Activity in Procurement Auctions' (2004) 17 European Journal of Law and Economics 5.

approach[75] and the European Commission's *Guidelines on the method of setting fines imposed pursuant to Article 23(2)(a) of Regulation No 1/2003.*[76] In addition to the calculation bases and the categories of infringements (ranging from light to heavy), the aggravating and mitigating circumstances are important elements. If, for example, an enterprise provides full cooperation, this may be taken into account as a mitigating factor. Another mitigating factor could be the existence of a compliance programme. Whether the existence of compliance programmes can provide immunity from or reduce any fines imposed is an issue for discussion. According to Wils, this should not be the case as it would be unfair and would undermine important incentives created by the competition authorities' leniency programmes.[77] This view is contested by Geradin, who claims that compliance programmes should be taken into account.[78] The existence of an adequately functioning compliance programme (which the enterprise concerned can demonstrate) can in many countries clearly constitute mitigating circumstances, providing this programme is not merely 'window dressing'.[79] In my opinion, this can certainly lead to better and more preventive results, as long as the programme is properly constructed and implemented. As I see it, competition authorities also have a responsibility to take preventive measures and stimulate compliance. Appropriate programmes should consequently be actively encouraged and also taken into account when an infringement occurs.

The independence principle can also come into play in the context of a sanctioning regime. Fines imposed by independent agencies in market or competition enforcement may be treated as a source of funding by governments, and may even influence the agency's budget. The government may therefore have a financial interest in interfering with the fines imposed by an independent agency. This issue has been extensively debated with regard to the ACM in the Netherlands. In his budget forecasts at the end of 2012, the Dutch Minister of Economic Affairs estimated that fines collected by the ACM could amount to around 125 million euros in 2017,

[75] Competition & Markets Authority, 'Administrative Penalties: Statement of Policy on the CMA's Approach' (2013) <https://www.gov.uk/government/publications/administrative-penalties-statement-of-policy-on-the-cmas-approach> accessed 27 June 2014.

[76] Guidelines on the method of setting fines imposed pursuant to Article 23(2)(a) of Regulation No 1/2003 [2006] OJ C 210/02.

[77] W Wils, 'Antitrust Compliance Programmes and Optimal Antitrust Enforcement' (2013) 1(1) Journal of Antitrust Enforcement 52.

[78] D Geradin, 'Antitrust Compliance Programmes and Optimal Antitrust Enforcement: A Reply to Wouter Wils' (2013) 1(1) Journal of Antitrust Enforcement 325.

[79] See, for example, the speech of the ACM chair, C A Fonteijn, before the ICC in The Hague where he clearly makes this point: Speech 24 January 2014 for seminar Compliance, organized by the ICC in The Hague, <www.ACM.nl> accessed 23 September 2014.

which was four times higher than previous estimates.[80] In principle, the ACM is independent in deciding whether to fine and on the level of fine to impose, but is bound by the framework for calculating fines laid down in the General Guidelines of the Minister of Economic Affairs on imposing administrative fines by the ACM.[81] Although the minister, too, is free to forecast the revenues expected to be generated from fines in the future, his decision to give a forecast implied that the ACM should raise the level of its fines. When questioned by the legislature, however, the minister made it clear that such estimates did not affect the ACM's budget. Subsequently, in August 2013, the minister commissioned a report to look into the forecasts and wrote to parliament to acknowledge that it was unlikely that the amounts originally stated would ever be achieved.[82] This incident nevertheless indicates that any suggestion by the government that fining targets may be set may also be seen by the media and the general public as a means of influencing the agency's behaviour.

Naming and shaming

Another way of sanctioning is the 'naming and shaming' of enterprises. Publication of decisions establishing an infringement, as well as identifying the enterprises concerned, may have a deterrent effect.[83] This is standard practice in many countries, while in other countries, including the Netherlands, the publication of agency decisions on the agency's website

[80] This statement was published in the Coalition Agreement 'Bruggen slaan' on 29 October 2012, available at <http://www.rijksoverheid.nl/documenten-en-publicaties/rapporten/2012/10/29/regeerakkoord.html> accessed 28 July 2014.

[81] See the General Guidelines of the Dutch Minister of Economic Affairs: 'Beleidsregels van de Minister van Economische Zaken voor het opleggen van bestuurlijke boetes door de ACM' available at <http://wetten.overheid.nl/BWBR0033327/geldigheidsdatum_02-08-2014> accesssed 25 July 2014.

[82] The official report of July 2013 showed the forecast of the target could not be reached: 'Boete inkomsten ACM', 3 July 2013 <http://www.rijksoverheid.nl/documenten-en-publicaties/rapporten/2013/07/03/boete-inkomsten-acm.html> accessed 26 July 2014. This report was followed by an official letter from the Minister of Economic Affairs stating the findings of the report: 'Kamerbrief over boetebeleid Autoriteit Consument en Markt', published 27 August 2013 <http://www.rijksoverheid.nl/documenten-en-publicaties/kamerstukken/2013/08/27/kamerbrief-over-boetebeleid-autoriteit-consument-en-markt.html> accessed 26 July 2014. Currently there is an online consultation on a proposed new law concerning the possible increasing of the fining maximums currently set for the ACM. See <http://www.internetconsultatie.nl/wetsvoorstelverhoging boetemaximaacm> accessed 24 September 2014.

[83] For more on the topic of naming and shaming, see: J van Erp, 'Reputational Sanctions in Private and Public Regulation' (2008) 1(5) Erasmus Law Review 145; K Yeung, 'Government by Publicity Management: Sunlight or Spin' (2005) 1 Public Law 360; J B Owens, 'Have We No Shame?: Thoughts on Shaming 'White Collar' Criminals, and the Federal Sentencing Guidelines' (2000) 49(5) American University Law Review 1047.

has raised concerns about the legal protection of supervisees. The argument against publication is that it cannot take place while the decision is still under appeal and the highest court has not issued a final judgement. Until then, publication could cause irreversible reputational and other damage to the enterprise concerned. Applying the LITER principles to this issue shows a clear clash between the principle of legality on the one hand and the principles of transparency, effectiveness, and responsibility on the other. From a legal perspective, the enterprise's position must be safeguarded and protected against interventions that have not yet been tested and that have irreversible consequences. An appeal court must have verified the decision before details of the infringement are published and the enterprise identified. From the agency's perspective, non-publication of a decision prevents the agency from giving a full account of its activities, and from allowing consumers or competitors to become aware of the infringement. This in turn may cause additional damage or risks, and prevent claims for damages being issued. Moreover, no deterrent effect can take place if the enforcement decision is not published. The highest administrative court in the Netherlands has decided that the independent agency (in this case the former Dutch post and telecommunications regulator OPTA) must be able in principle to publish the sanctioning decision, given:

> [T]hat it is appropriate in view of OPTA's supervisory task that decisions to impose sanctions are made public, so that the task of supervising compliance with regulations and the related power to act against infringements of these regulations can be enforced.[84]

However, the enterprise concerned must be given the opportunity—before publication of the agency's decision—to ask an interim court to rule on whether publication of the infringement decision is lawful. This solution combines the safeguard dimension of the LITER principles with the instrumental dimension: effectiveness is safeguarded by a quick test by the court, with the starting point being that publication is necessary. At the same time, the rights of the enterprise concerned are respected by giving it an opportunity to bring the publication decision before a court. However, if the interim court too easily prohibited publication, it would obstruct much of the transparency and effectiveness of independent agency's enforcement. Supervisory authorities have a public task to perform oversight and must be able to take and account for that responsibility. If the enforcement decision cannot be published during appeal procedures, which can take several years to complete

[84] Afdeling bestuursrechtspraak 10 November 2010, OPTA/ECS c.s. *Mediaforum* 2010-11/12, nr. 32. Translated for the purposes of this book.

in some countries, this will hinder the oversight performed by the agency and prevent competitors and consumers from becoming aware of the situation.

Commitment decisions

One of the ways to protect market competition, besides imposing a fine or initiating legal proceedings, is to issue a commitment decision.[85] Such a decision replaces the establishment that an infringement has occurred[86] and, in fact, aims to put an end to the—alleged—infringement of the concerned party. A commitment decision allows the party or parties to restructure their economic relationships and, in case the alleged infringement and therefore the commitment decision have an EU scope, to address or assuage the European Commission's concerns.[87] In the event of a material change in any of the facts, the Commission can decide to pursue further action and reopen the case if a party acts contrary to its commitments, or if the commitment decision was based on incomplete, false, or misleading information.[88] So, although there is no scope to impose a fine, issuing a commitment decision does not mean that no further proceedings can be initiated, be it on a national or the EU level.

Besides the alleged infringement being brought to an end, there are other positive sides to commitment decisions. They meet the need for a speedier and cheaper resolution of competition cases[89] as, by actively negotiating, the parties instantly address the main issue of anticompetitive conduct. Whereas legal proceedings can take a long time to complete, commitment decisions represent a fast solution in a dynamic and rapidly changing landscape. The active negotiations, in which the enterprise concerned can also propose its own solutions, place the responsibility on the enterprise to ensure it complies with the commitment made. This makes a commitment an effective way of changing an enterprise's behaviour.

[85] Following from Article 9 of Regulation 1/2003. Commitment decisions must be distinguished from settlements: in a settlement the parties concerned admit the infringement; it is an arrangement for past behaviour. In the case of a commitment, no infringement has actually been established and arrangements for the future are made between the agency and the parties concerned.

[86] It replaces a finding of an infringement with a finding that there are no longer grounds for action by the Commission without concluding whether there has been or still is an infringement.

[87] Y Svetiev, 'Private Law and the Visible Hand of EU Regulation' (2013) Working Paper for the Max Weber Programme, European University Institute.

[88] As laid down in Article 9(2) of Regulation 1/2003.

[89] H Schweitzer 'Commitment Decisions under Art. 9 of Regulation 1/2003: The Developing EC Practice and Case Law' (2008) Working Paper European University Institute, Law 2008/22.

Commitment decisions also provide legal certainty as they can be brought before a court.[90] The proportionality principle will then be of importance, given the ECJ's ruling in the *Alrosa* case[91] that the European Commission had to verify whether the decision addressed the competition concerns and whether the enterprise concerned had offered any less drastic solutions to deal with the problem adequately. The need for active negotiations, however, is one of the reasons why some scholars see potential problems in this enforcement tool.[92] The broad discretion allowed to the European Commission in EU competition cases may lead to its imposing commitments in cases where the law is unclear. The Commission may also use commitments to pursue other goals. Imposing commitments in such cases can then lead to legal precedents being created outside the ECJ's judicial control. At the same time, however, the *Alrosa* case clearly shows that the extent of the Commission's discretion is limited.

Self-regulatory oversight

Different terminology is used for the phenomenon whereby internal processes and systems are designed by a sector to ensure compliance with applicable rules and to detect and reduce risks. These systems are called 'self-regulatory oversight', 'meta-regulation', 'self-regulation', 'self-regulatory forms of governance', or 'self-oversight', with examples including certification systems by schools, standardization by the aviation industry, and the self-regulation of accountancy firms. The independent agencies control only the set-up and functioning of the self-regulatory system, but not the individual enterprises, or at least only incidentally. In this system of control, the main responsibility for oversight shifts from public authorities to the private sector. In fact, these private organizations in essence become 'surrogate regulators'.[93]

It follows from research that these kinds of self-regulatory systems will work only if all the following criteria are met. Firstly, there needs to be a high degree of self-regulatory capacity and authority in the relevant sector.

[90] Although parties to the commitment procedure normally do not have the option of appealing the decision in court, third parties adversely affected by the decision have the option of bringing the case before the court. See further: Schweitzer (n89).

[91] C-441/07 *Commission v Alrosa* [2010] OJ C234/3.

[92] Article 7 of the regulation states that if the European Commission finds there to be an infringement, it can impose any structural or behavioural remedies on an enterprise, which are proportionate to the infringement in order to bring it to an end.

[93] N Gunningham and D Sinclair, 'Designing Smart Regulation' (2004) OECD Global Forum on Sustainable Development, Paris <www.oecd.org/environment/environmentinemergingandtransitioneconomies/37719119.pdf> accessed 24 September 2014.

Secondly, risk-based assessment and detection must be possible. Thirdly, the industry should have a common interest in avoiding risks. Self-regulatory arrangements will not work if there are conflicting interests in the group as these arrangements assume that the group to be regulated is homogeneous. Lastly, objective control mechanisms and dispute-resolution procedures must be in place. If not, the system will be arbitrary and lead to discrimination. In many of the situations in which self-regulation has failed to work, some or all of these conditions were not met. The efforts needed to ensure fulfilment of these conditions are often underestimated in practice, with a resultant collapse in the system.

This system-based approach is all too easily seen as a cost-cutting exercise, where it is assumed that the independent agency's tasks can be reduced. What is often forgotten is that such an approach requires a different set of skills and expertise on the part of the agency, and that these skills will have to be developed. This in itself requires additional investments and a differently structured supervisory organization. Unless these initial investments are made, there will be insufficient control over the self-regulatory system. Enterprises themselves can also call in the regulatory authority by, for example, submitting a plan to integrate proposed measures into supervisory decisions. This procedure, which is also referred to as co-regulation or enforced self-regulation, offers certain clear benefits as it means that the industry endorses the measures, which can then be quickly implemented. Incorporating industry agreements into the regulatory agency's rules will also increase the agency's enforcement powers and allow measures to be introduced uniformly across the entire industry. Although this type of market-based governance does justice to the principles of equality and legal certainty, it may be disadvantageous to stakeholders who were not involved in the standardization process. The independent agency will consequently have to ensure that the standardization is not motivated by self-interest of a certain group and does not lead to discrimination.

Compliance programmes

Criminologists and organizational experts see in-company compliance programmes as an important means of encouraging compliance with rules, and of not only preventing breaches, but also quickly pinpointing any that do occur. Market and competition authorities should consequently encourage the introduction of compliance programmes in varying degrees of flexibility, ranging from non-binding agreements to detailed enforcement covenants. This could create scope for different monitoring and enforcement methods. Empirical studies in the environmental industry clearly show that although the presence of a compliance programme is no guarantee that environmental rules will be complied with, it is an important instrument in facilitating compliance. There is no reason why this experience could not be applied to market supervision, certainly if the market is in a more advanced stage of liberalization and most of the regulations have already been fleshed out. In my opinion, the drafting and use of compliance programmes should be actively promoted in practice, not only by taking account of their existence and effectiveness when imposing fines, but also by encouraging enterprises to implement such programmes. Supervision and enforcement policy should then be geared accordingly.

The previous Dutch competition authority NMa encouraged enterprises to draft their own compliance programmes and also advised trade organizations and individual enterprises on these programmes. At the NMa's instigation, the Dutch insurance industry, for example, drew up and implemented an industry-wide compliance scheme, the effects of which were monitored by the NMa. This was also actively done in the United Kingdom by the OFT, the predecessor of the CMA. The OFT provided ways for enterprises and their directors to review whether their business had truly embraced a culture of competition law compliance. It offered a four-stage methodology for enterprises to create a competition law compliance programme: the 'virtuous circle of effective competition law compliance culture', comprising risk identification, risk assessment, risk mitigation, and review.[94] This recognized that an effective compliance culture requires an unambiguous and top-down commitment to competition law compliance within the enterprise. The primary responsibility clearly lies with management at all levels of the organization. The compliance programme must be built around these four stages of risk identification, assessment, and mitigation, with internal procedures and measures being taken to identify and reduce risks. These will generally include appropriate policies and procedures, and appropriate training activities. Finally, there is the review stage, when the enterprise reviews all stages of the process to ensure there is still an unambiguous commitment to compliance throughout the organization.[95] The CMA, the new UK competition authority, is also seeking to perform compliance and awareness work, and to significantly broaden the reach of its compliance work.[96] It is committed to strengthening the compliance tools and techniques used to achieve a culture

[94] OFT, 'Drivers of Compliance and Non-Compliance with Competition Law' (2010) <https://www.gov.uk/government/publications/business-drivers-of-compliance-and-non-compliance-with-competition-law> accessed 27 June 2014.

[95] This virtuous circle can be found in the report from the OFT (n94).

[96] Speech A Chisholm, 'Achieving a Culture of Compliance' (2014) Speech Law Society Competition Section Annual Conference, London <https://www.gov.uk/government/speeches/achieving-a-culture-of-compliance> accessed 24 September 2014.

of compliance with competition and consumer law. In the case of the CMA, however, there will also be 'an appropriate mix of "soft measures" (such as encouraging measures within business to comply) and "tough measures" (such as sanctions) as appropriate'.[97] In the Netherlands, the new competition and market authority ACM also favours compliance programmes,[98] although it has not yet published any policy guidelines explaining its position, and nor does its Strategy Document mention any explicit plans to do so.

In any case, and as previously stated, the presence of a compliance programme should in my opinion be 'rewarded' by the promise of lower fines. If an enterprise commits a breach despite having a compliance programme, any fine will take account of the enterprise's compliance efforts. This practice is designed to encourage enterprises to accept their own responsibility. However, if the programme is simply 'window dressing', failure to comply with either the rules or the compliance programme could be seen as an aggravating circumstance and thus a good reason to impose a higher fine.

Advocacy

As stated in chapter 2, independent agencies clearly have an advocacy role, which the International Competition Network (ICN) defines as follows:

> Competition advocacy refers to those activities conducted by the competition authority related to the promotion of a competitive environment for economic activities by means of non-enforcement mechanisms, mainly through its relationships with other governmental entities and by increasing public awareness of the benefits of competition.[99]

ICN considers advocacy explicitly not to fall within the domain of enforcement. Although this is true in the strict sense of the meaning of (vertical) enforcement, advocacy clearly forms part of an agency's overall oversight strategy to prevent competition infringements from taking place and to ensure that competition is safeguarded in the future. In practice, advocacy activities mainly focus on ensuring that legislators and governments do not cause unfair competition, either through their legislation or activities. Fair competition should also form part of the mindset of local and central governmental bodies. According to the ICN, competition advocacy aims to encourage the elimination of regulations that distort market competition or impose

[97] ibid. [98] ICC speech C A Fonteijn (n79).

[99] ICN Advocacy Working Group, 'Advocacy and Competition Policy' (2002) ICN Conference Naples <http://www.internationalcompetitionnetwork.org/uploads/library/doc358.pdf> accessed 5 September 2014 p. 25.

barriers to entry. There is a clear link with enforcement practice, given that enforcement and advocacy are complementary, and enforcement actions contribute to the credibility and relevance of advocacy activities.[100]

Awareness can be created by training and presentation, but also by advising governmental bodies on competition and regulatory issues. In practice, it is important that market and competition authorities are consulted on these matters, for example on draft legislation, in a timely manner. Making use of these agencies' independent expertise can improve the substantive quality of the rules. The timing of consultations in the legislative and regulatory process is crucial if the advocacy role is to be performed effectively. Late consultation of such agencies could form an impediment to fulfilment of their advocacy mission.[101] Other instruments of advocacy include the publication of market or survey reports on certain sectors or industries, sending letters expressing specific concerns to parliament (highlighting regulatory concerns in legislation, for example), and annual reports.[102]

Advocacy is an intrinsically communicative activity, which should mean that communications and relationships with the media, but also the use of social media, are highly important activities for any independent agency. The importance of communication as a tool of advocacy, but also as a branding and enforcement tool, is often underestimated, but it is a technique and skill that agencies must be able to use appropriately. Jenny points to the risk that independence of agencies may have the effect that their relationship with government will suffer and therefore governments will lack the required expertise to take the advocacy role themselves.[103]

Enforcement Choices in the United Kingdom and the Netherlands

The following section elaborates on some choices the competition and market authorities in the United Kingdom and the Netherlands have made with regard to enforcement styles, and the tools and instruments best suited, in their view, to achieve optimal results given the circumstances and the time juncture. Taking the merged agencies of the Netherlands and United Kingdom introduced in chapter 4 to illustrate the balancing and effects of

[100] ICN report (n99) 75. [101] ibid 60.

[102] For a full overview, see: ICN Advocacy Working Group, 'Advocacy Toolkit. Part I: Advocacy Process and Tools' (2011); and ICN, 'Advocacy Toolkit. Part I: Advocacy Process and Tools' (2012).

[103] F Jenny, 'Competition Authorities. Independence and Advocacy' in D Sokol and I Lianos, *The Global Limits of Competition Law* (Palo Alto, Stanford University Press 2012).

the different enforcement methods, we can build on the factual knowledge and the historical background that has already been discussed.

Compliance approach

In 2006, the previous Dutch independent post and telecommunications authority OPTA, which merged into the ACM in April 2013, fined the Dutch telecommunications incumbent KPN for the illegal discounts it granted to large numbers of customers.[104] This was the biggest case OPTA had ever dealt with, and the practice of the incumbent was seen as a deliberate strategy to maintain its market position by unlawful means. The fine of 17 million euros was the highest ever imposed on KPN and, although the company initiated the filing of the case with OPTA, the scale of the discounts given and the specific discount policy applied meant that OPTA considered the case to be very serious and so imposed the high fine. Instead of just issuing the fine, OPTA also added two further elements by including a combination of deterrent and preventive elements in its sanctioning decision and, for those two reasons, reduced the fine imposed. Firstly, OPTA required KPN to initiate negotiations with its competitors in order to compensate them for the losses suffered as a result of KPN's unlawful discounts. OPTA took the agreement that KPN reached with its competitors into account as a mitigating factor when calculating the fine. Secondly, OPTA was also willing to take account of the fact that KPN agreed to set up a compliance programme to ensure that its behaviour would comply with telecommunications regulations in the future and to engage in a compliance culture at all layers of its organization. This commitment by KPN, as confirmed in the sanctioning decision, formed the legal basis for a new approach to compliance in the future, and enabled OPTA to take formal steps to ensure that KPN would perform the compliance actions required of it.

Clearly, OPTA's approach in the sanctioning decision combined vertical (deterrent) and horizontal (preventive) elements, laid down in an administrative decision. This not only provided legal certainty and transparency, but was also very effective in seeking to achieve direct results. The regulator took an active role in providing a basis for negotiating civil damages, which meant that costly litigation could be avoided and direct results could be shown to

[104] Besluit OPTA op grond van artikel 15.4 Telecommunicatiewet inhoudende het opleggen van een boete ter handhaving van het bepaalde in artikel 34, eerste lid onder d, 35, eerste lid en 38, eerste lid van het Besluit ONP huurlijnen en telefonie (Penalty decision of OPTA pursuant to Article 15.4 Dutch Telecommunications Act with reference to the sections 34, 1 sub d and 35, 1 and 38, 1 of the Decree on Leased Lines and Telephony).

have been achieved within a reasonable period of time. All the third parties concerned were able to participate and negotiate the civil damages with the incumbent, under the auspices of OPTA. By engaging the competitors in the sanctioning process, OPTA increased the accountability of the process and the final decision. At the same time, responsibility was shared between the market regulator and the supervised company to ensure that KPN put its house in order, while also giving OPTA the instruments it needed to control the compliance process. This innovative approach, combining the instrumental and safeguard dimensions of the LITER principles, contrasted with previous years, when OPTA had issued one sanctioning decision after another in what became a continual legal battle with the incumbent. At a certain point OPTA started questioning whether this *ex post* approach was actually producing the desired results and so made an explicit decision to set out on a new route by calling on KPN to account for its behaviour and discussing how it could improve its compliance.

This case was the trigger that forced the incumbent to make the investments needed to set up a sound compliance system and to roll out a training scheme for all its staff. OPTA closely tracked the compliance process and monitored the results. However, the skills, expertise, and mindset of agency staff required for monitoring purposes differs from those required in standard enforcement practice. An independent agency needs to be aware of this and to invest in its knowledge of compliance and monitoring systems. This requires both capacity and budget. Unless these skills and capacity are available the agency will not be able to provide adequate monitoring, and the compliance oversight strategy may then fail. Implementation of the compliance commitment is not a 'one-off' activity, but needs continual attention and effort to ensure that progress is made.

OPTA stated in its March 2008 publication on new perspectives in oversight and enforcement that it wanted its enforcement policy to devote more attention to preventing breaches of the law and other rules of conduct. It intended to achieve this by encouraging market players to develop their own compliance programmes and to implement and execute these within their own organizations, with support from OPTA in the form of 'compliance assistance'. If an enterprise managed to maintain its own compliance programme, OPTA would choose to exercise more remote supervision. However, that would apply only if there was no doubt that the compliance system was not merely 'window dressing', but a genuine corporate policy designed to achieve compliance with the regulation. This compliance assistance approach was also implemented in OPTA's penalty guidelines: if an infringement happened despite the presence of an effectively functioning compliance system, OPTA would regard that system as a mitigating factor when calculating the penalty.

As well as publishing its vision on enforcement, OPTA consulted with the market on the agreement (the 'KPN and OPTA Compliance Charter') that it was seeking to conclude with KPN and which was ultimately signed after the consultations. In this charter KPN and OPTA agreed how an effective compliance system should work, how it needed to be built, and how potential or actual infringements would be notified to OPTA. The aim of the charter was to create more transparency with regard to KPN's behaviour and to ensure that all potential or actual infringements were notified, thus resulting in preventive measures and creating a basis for discussion on how the telecommunications regulation should be interpreted. A system was introduced whereby KPN would notify all possible infringements from the past to ensure it started out with a clean sheet. OPTA would then investigate these cases and take the compliance system and charter into account in its sanctions. This new approach was certainly not intended to result in a policy whereby penalties would no longer be issued. OPTA made it clear that although it would still impose penalties, it would regard the charter as a mitigating factor. In other words, OPTA would take the efforts of KPN to cooperate and to set up the required compliance system into account when calculating any penalties. This approach obviously represented a challenge and put pressure on the relationship between the agency and the company in that it required an *ex ante* approach (i.e. encouraging compliance and building trust) to be reconciled with an *ex post* approach (i.e. investigating and sanctioning), and this required a sharp eye and critical approach to the process and progress.

OPTA's approach was heavily criticized by academics and KPN's competitors, who accused the agency of not being sufficiently transparent about what was going on and questioned whether such a charter was allowed under administrative law (i.e. was there a sufficient legal basis for it). The charter instrument was clearly not explicitly recognized in administrative law. At the same time, the fact that the enforcement principles were agreed and published meant that market parties (i.e. competitors) were able to follow the process, see the attempts to detect all possible infringements, and take appropriate preventive measures. A trade-off had to be made between transparency and confidentiality as KPN was prepared to notify possible infringements only if it could be guaranteed a certain level of confidentiality. This process gave OPTA better insight into the business of the incumbent and a better understanding of the market forces, while it was also fully aware of the risk of capture and, wherever possible, communicated about the steps taken.

OPTA's horizontal approach came under renewed pressure when OPTA discovered that KPN had frustrated a bidding process for a large telecommunications contract of the central Dutch government to the detriment of its competitors. This resulted in a new sanctioning decision and a record fine of around 30 million euros.[105] OPTA considered this behaviour not only to be a severe infringement, but also a reason to reconsider its compliance approach and to take a more strict view on enforcement. It consequently decided to subject KPN to increased monitoring and, despite the charter, decided that the fine should be increased because of the recidivism factor and the arrangements agreed in the charter. It subsequently imposed sanctions on KPN for various infringements of the Dutch Telecommunications Act. However, following an interim ruling by the administrative court, OPTA was initially not allowed to impose this penalty. This only became possible after the Court of Appeal issued its final judgement on 23 January 2014; in other words, two years after the original decision was taken. In 2014 the ACM and KPN added to and further clarified the charter.[106]

This case shows that investing in compliance can help prevent infringements, but that this cannot be fully guaranteed. The independent agency must therefore remain critical and alert and adapt its strategy when circumstances require. A compliance strategy must also be backed up by a sanctioning regime, putting supervised enterprises under continual pressure to perform. Transparency is required at all times so as to avoid any perception of capture and to ensure that the agency can be held accountable for its actions. Balancing the transparency interest, as required by market parties in general, with the confidentiality interest of the individual enterprise remains a delicate issue, with the principles of transparency and effectiveness clashing directly with the principle of legality. The independent agency should, in my opinion, be fully aware of the delicate nature of this aspect and ensure, whenever possible, that it gives priority to the transparency principle within the legal boundaries of the applicable regime.

Problem-solving approach

It was Sparrow's work that inspired the Dutch competition and market authorities NMa and OPTA, and the Dutch Consumer Authority (CA) to opt for problem-solving as one of their key strategic choices for ensuring mixed teams and cross-fertilization between their various departments when

[105] OPTA decision of 21 December 2011, TELEC 05/937 HRK <http://uitspraken.rechtspraak.nl/inziendocument?id=ECLI:NL:RBROT:2006:AV6379> accessed 11 September.

[106] 'Compliance Handvest KPN en ACM' <https://www.acm.nl/nl/publicaties/publicatie/13072/Vernieuwd-Compliance-Handvest-KPN-en-ACM/> accessed 28 July 2014.

they merged into the ACM.[107] The ACM's objective is to resolve market and consumer problems, which entails continually taking the context and market structure into consideration. Do consumers in a specific market, for example, behave actively or passively? Are there any barriers to switching? And is the market sufficiently transparent? In its Strategy Document the ACM consequently states that it will look at issues from a broader perspective and, instead of merely investigating the alleged violation, will also seek to determine the root cause of the market or consumer problem in question. One way to do this is by tackling harmful market developments from a broader angle, something the ACM should be quite capable of as it is a multifunctional agency with years of experience combining competition *and* market expertise.

In many cases the ACM will start by trying to establish whether unwanted market behaviour that has been identified is a symptom of a larger, underlying problem in the market. In this respect it will seek to take advantage of the fact that it has multidisciplinary teams with access to a wider variety of formal and informal instruments for tackling the particular market problem. Its solutions will be tailor-made. In addition to applying sanctions, the ACM can, whenever circumstances require, deploy instruments such as norm-transmitting discussions, commitment decisions, monitoring, and market scans. It can also make greater use of strategic communications aimed at increasing the willingness to comply as a means of resolving market problems. In order, however, to avoid any misconception that a problem-solving approach means an absence of sanctions, the ACM makes it very clear in its Strategy Document that the power to impose sanctions remains an important instrument in its toolkit. A fine imposed on an enterprise for violating the law can—in the ACM's view—be perfectly compatible with other types of instruments, such as an awareness campaign on the demand side of the market (i.e. consumer empowerment).

An example of such consumer empowerment was seen in the energy market, where the former Dutch competition authority, the NMa, launched a campaign to encourage consumers to switch supplier. In November 2012 it published a trend report on consumer confidence in the energy market.[108] This revealed that consumers could save up to 500 euros on their annual energy

[107] Sparrow, *The Regulatory Craft* and *The Character of Harms. Operational Challenges in Control* (n47).

[108] 'Working Group Report on Transparency in EU Retail Energy Markets' (2012) report prepared for the 5th Citizens' Energy Forum, 2012 <http://ec.europa.eu/energy/gas_electricity/doc/forum_citizen_energy/2012111314_citizen_forum_meeting_working_group_report.pdf> accessed 11 September 2014.

bills, as well as that 64% of consumers had never switched energy providers, even though the number of consumers willing to switch was reported to be at a record high. Around the time the trend report was released, *Consuwijzer* (the NMa, OPTA and CA website geared specifically towards consumers) decided to create an online 'switching coach' to help consumers compare energy companies' offers.

Another example is the ACM's Buma/Stemra case.[109] The ACM initiated a procedure against Buma/Stemra, the Dutch copyright collecting society, in response to a complaint alleging that the society was abusing its dominant position in music copyright management. Composers and songwriters need Buma/Stemra to collect royalties from renderings of their work on television or radio, but not always, for example, for renderings on the internet. At the time, Buma/Stemra operated an all-in-one package for copyright transfers. As composers and songwriters were not able to opt to transfer only parts of their copyright to Buma/Stemra, this package meant in practice that they had little choice and basically no opportunity to sell their lyrics or compositions online. They were tied for all their products to the Buma/Stemra collection management system. The procedure initiated by the ACM resulted in a commitment decision: Buma/Stemra agreed to offer composers and songwriters more options for managing their music copyrights and has since modified its copyright management system. Its system has become simpler, more flexible, and more accessible for composers and songwriters, who now have more choice as to which rights they want to transfer to Buma/Stemra. This new structure is likely to result in more ways to stream and download music being introduced. Composers and songwriters will thus benefit, as will listeners. Buma/Stemra uses various means to bring these new copyright management options to the attention of composers and songwriters, including information on its website and at music conferences. In addition, an online calculation tool is to be released to help composers and songwriters decide whether to transfer all or just part of their copyright to Buma/Stemra. A third party has been appointed to verify the implementation of the commitment and report to the ACM annually. This commitment decision immediately removes any anticompetitive concerns, while the opportunities and options available to composers, songwriters, and consumers have been increased.

As explained earlier, a commitment procedure offers the possibility for a case to be handled quickly, transparently, and as part of a sanction trajectory,

[109] The text on this case is based on the English version of the press release of ACM, published on the English-language version of ACM's website, and on the final commitment decision of 6 June 2014, available at <https://www.acm.nl/nl/publicaties/publicatie/13026/Definitief-toezeggingsbesluit-Buma-Stemra/> accessed 11 September 2013.

thus preventing further damage. This instrument gives both the independent agency and the enterprise involved an incentive to round off the case more quickly as the enterprise will avoid the possibility of lengthy proceedings and both parties will know within a relatively short period of time where they stand. In addition, a sanction is waived in return for giving the commitment. The enterprise accepts responsibility and comes up with a solution to the problem. This is an effective way for an independent agency to achieve rapid results, while also promoting the interests it represents.[110] In the case of Buma/Stemra the ACM combined the problem-solving approach with the legal instrument of a commitment: designing the solution of the problem pragmatically, while also ensuring legal certainty through transparency and effectiveness. By first consulting on the draft decision, the ACM was able to verify whether the solution intended to be opted for was acceptable to all parties concerned.

Enforced self-regulation

A variety of indicators prompted the OFT in late 2013 to launch a market-wide investigation into the children's online game industry.[111] This investigation gained empirical input through an analysis of thirty-eight freemium[112] online games and an official call for information. This call for information resulted in input from 200 parties, including 160 parents and fourty other stakeholders, such as the leading game developer associations. The OFT's efforts to gather input from all perspectives were crucial in enabling it to gain a detailed understanding of the interaction between consumer bias and

[110] The Court of First Instance pronounced an interesting judgement about the application framework of the European Commission for the usage of this instrument: General Court 11 July 2007, T-170/06, *Alrosa Company Limited v Commission*. According to this judgement, the European Commission is bound by the principle of proportionality while using this instrument. The voluntary character of the commitments does not discharge the Commission from taking this principle into account.

[111] The following text on the OFT cases on behavioural economics is (with permission) taken from and prepared by B Nunez, master student of Law and Economics at Utrecht University for his master thesis: 'The Application of Behavioural Economics by Regulators in the UK: A Theoretical and Practical Analysis' (2014).

[112] As the OFT states in its survey, 'freemium games can also be played online or downloaded for free, but incorporate the ability to make in-game purchases for advanced features or functionality, such as additional levels, in-game "currency" or the ability to speed up the game's progress.' OFT, 'Children's Online Games: A Survey of the Literature' (2014) paragraph 3.32 <https://assets.digital.cabinet-office.gov.uk/media/53330bf4ed915d6938000007/oft1518.pdf> accessed 24 September 2014.

observed business practices, as well as to understand whether those practices would harm consumers.

At a general level, the extremely high profits and growth rates recorded in the market sent a vague signal to the OFT that consumers may be being exploited. However, this information alone was not significant, given the relative youth of the industry and the fact that mobile phones are commonly used as a platform for the games. Instead, it was the insight that children represent a separate, especially vulnerable group of consumers that pointed to the potential existence of exploitive practices. The OFT drew on social psychology research[113] when assessing consumers in general and concluded that children represented a separable consumer segment that could be more susceptible to particular practices adopted by game developers. This insight was a major contribution to the OFT's eventual decision to intervene in the market.

The business practices specifically identified as troublesome were the use of aggressive or misleading in-game messages, the use of unclear pricing structures such as 'drip pricing', the specific timing of certain mandatory in-game payments, and the failure to ensure that the consumer was able to give fully-informed consent to all in-game purchases. The OFT correctly identified that aggressive[114] or misleading[115] messages asking or requiring players to make in-game purchases were an example of an industry practice that could exploit the vulnerability of young consumers. The potential for exploitation in this case was significant because game developers routinely used delivery methods that were especially persuasive to children, such as having a familiar in-game character deliver the commercial message.

In consultation with the industry and other stakeholders, the OFT drew up eight rules of conduct which set clear expectations against which the industry would be held to account by UK regulators. These eight rules are intended to prevent 'information overload' and are characterized by simplicity and clarity. They are short, avoid complicated legal terminology, and

[113] Research in the field reveals that it is particularly difficult for children of any age to recognize the commercial intent of 'embedded' advertising. Roeder's (1999) experiments demonstrate that children make only 'simple, expedient, and egocentric consumer decisions based on very limited information, usually a single perceptual dimension.'

[114] An example of the former is a message stating to the player: '[y]our seagull is hungry! Feed him ice cream or he will be unhappy.' Ice cream is then available within the in-game shop for real money, a fact that is not made expressly clear through a transition away from the game to a website.

[115] For instance, a game tells the players that they can finish a particular mission instantaneously by purchasing an in-game item for real money without informing them that the mission can also be completed simply by waiting a certain amount of time.

include examples of both compliant and infringing conduct. These rules are now being used all over the world as the standard of good practices for preventing the use of misleading and aggressive practices in online gaming sales.

If this case is examined in the light of the LITER principles, the OFT can be seen to have acted within a clear mandate granted by the UK Enterprise Act 2002. The OFT also complied with the principle of transparency during its investigation by entering into a series of ongoing dialogues with all significant stakeholders. As a result, the rules constitute an example of how behavioural economics can help independent agencies both to identify market issues and to design effective remedies. Finally, and most importantly, the OFT's use of behavioural economics proved effective because it resulted in the agency's creation of a set of industry best practice principles[116] that have had an immediate impact. The outcome of the case was very effective, therefore.

Conclusion

Enforcement is the most visible activity of and also what the outside world expects from an independent agency: oversight is its core business. At the same time, interventions have a major impact on the enterprises concerned and are therefore subject to scrutiny. There is a continual tension between the public interest in supervising activities on the one hand (i.e. preventing and detecting consumer harm) and the individual interest of the alleged infringer on the other hand (i.e. in lessening the burdens for the enterprise and the industry in general). The independent agency has to zigzag along this rocky terrain.

It is important in the light of the good agency or LITER principles that the independent agency can set its own enforcement agenda and choose the enforcement style, as well as the tools and instruments, it considers appropriate, while also following a fair process and complying with the proportionality principle. The agenda must be tailored around the agency's overall strategy, which must provide a clear mission and direction for allocating capacity and cases, and find the right balance within the enforcement portfolio of cases. It is important that the agency identifies real problems and does not focus solely on the legal requirements. This is because, in practice, risks do not necessarily

[116] In this case, the decision to opt for 'soft' enforcement may follow from the OFT's acknowledgement that platforms developers, such as Apple and Google, represent the key enforcement party in this market as it is they who directly control which gaming content is made available to consumers.

correlate with lawbreaking, but rather follow their own path. The dynamic environment of independent agencies requires discretion so as to ensure that the agency can adapt its enforcement strategy accordingly. Too formalistic an approach by both the legislator and the agency may result in the wrong or inappropriate action being taken.

6

Evaluation of Independent Agencies and Review by the Courts

Introduction

The final step in the decision-making process is the possibility of an appeal by interested parties who do not agree with the initial outcome of a case. Market and competition authorities' decisions can be challenged before national and, in some cases, European courts, and the possibility of a court review forms an essential element of the system by which independent agencies provide their oversight. The independence of these agencies has to be matched by a series of checks and balances, with the independent court playing a vital role in our democratic societies. Courts are a crucial participant in the debate on agencies' accountability as they ensure market parties' right to effective legal protection and hold agencies accountable for their actions. Since these agencies are funded, at least in part, by public money and perform public tasks, they need to account for their actions and behaviour by reporting on their activities and by allowing their decisions to be subjected to legal review, as well as by themselves reviewing or assessing their organizations and decision-making processes.

This chapter examines these review mechanisms in three stages. Firstly, the evaluation of independent agencies is examined on the basis of reports published by internal or external evaluation committees. Secondly, the case law on the review of independent agencies' decisions is analysed by taking a legal view of these decisions. Thirdly, the circumstances in which agencies can be held liable for their actions and behaviour are analysed. These aspects will be discussed in the light of the good agency or LITER principles—legality, independence, transparency, effectiveness, and responsibility—introduced and discussed in chapter 3. The purpose of these principles is to provide a framework for the design of independent agencies, their decision-making process, and the enforcement choices. In the first instance, therefore, the LITER principles operate at the level of the agencies themselves. However, since these principles should also influence the way evaluation committees and courts judge the decisions and behaviour of these agencies, at this second level too, the LITER principles play a role by providing a frame of reference and control.

Evaluations of independent agencies are not based on a legal analysis of cases, but instead provide insight into how an institution is functioning, how decision-making processes are managed, why decisions or interventions go wrong, and how independent agencies are performing in general. The main focus, therefore, is on process and organization. These evaluations can be done on a regular basis, without any need for a specific reason, or be case- or incident-driven if the outcome of a case was unsatisfactory. Such reports contain useful information that can be applied outside the context of a specific case and can be put into practice by other independent agencies. The focus in this chapter is on reports on different sectors in the Netherlands and the United Kingdom.

The second and third sections of this chapter adopt a legal approach by analysing the case law on court reviews of individual independent agencies' decisions or conduct, while also discussing the liability of agencies. The courts' tasks are complex owing to the economic and dynamic context in which agencies operate. Over the years independent agencies and national courts alike have adopted a more economic approach to the application and interpretation of economic regulations and competition law. A mix of economic and legal analyses is required within a legal context. Specialized market and competition authorities have the expertise and experience required for these economic analyses, and this raises the question as to what extent the courts should respect these agencies' margin of appreciation. What standard of proof should the courts require, and how should decisions be reviewed by the courts? How should a balance be found between safeguarding the right to effective legal protection on the one hand and an effective functioning of the national independent agencies on the other? These questions are dealt with in this chapter on the basis of national and European case law, with examples from the Netherlands and the United Kingdom used to illustrate the different issues at stake.

At the end of the chain is the liability of independent agencies. This chapter focuses on those situations where agencies have failed to enforce in cases where action was needed and where action taken by them, such as the publication of information on their website, has caused damage. Under which circumstances should such agencies be held liable? The third section of this chapter discusses these liability issues on the basis of tort law cases, wherein a Dutch or UK civil court examined the matter at hand.

Examining the negative side to arrive at a positive stand

Errors committed by independent agencies can be divided into 'type I' and 'type II' errors. A type I error (also referred to as a 'false negative' or 'under-inclusiveness') occurs when the agency fails to act in a timely or adequate manner in situations requiring intervention. These types of errors are mainly based on allegations that the independent agency did not take any action (for example, failed to see the risks), was too late in taking action, or chose the wrong remedy. Type II errors (also referred to as 'false positives' or 'over-inclusiveness') occur when an agency takes action in a situation that does not require intervention: if, for example, a competition authority prohibits a certain type of behaviour on the grounds of the abuse of a dominant position, even though pro-competitive effects are present. Most of the cases and reports examined in this chapter involve type I errors.

Focusing on these two types of errors has, however, certain inherent limitations. Taking the reports as a starting point for further research means the focus is almost exclusively on things that go wrong, thus giving a one-sided (negative) perspective of how independent agencies operate. In reality, many cases fall within the range of normal business activities and are performed satisfactorily. Moreover, evaluations of the enforcement practice of market and competition authorities are almost completely case-driven; a practice Kovacic refers to as the 'activity-oriented calculus'.[1] This approach completely ignores what Kovacic refers to as 'non-litigation activities': in other words, enforcement activities that do not lead to formal decisions or sanctions and so are not taken into account when assessing and evaluating an agency's work, even though these activities form an important part of its work and can produce effective results. Taking the reports and case law as the basis for the analysis enables us, however, to improve the decision-making processes and, therefore, the outcome of cases and the performance of these organizations in general.

Qualitative outcomes instead of quantitative outputs

This chapter, and indeed the book as a whole, adopts a qualitative approach and so disregards quantitative aspects of measurement. The measurement of outcomes and effects of independent agencies' interventions is still underdeveloped in practice, and is an aspect to which more attention should be

[1] W E Kovacic, 'Rating the Competition Agencies: What Constitutes Good Performance?' (2009) 16(4) George Mason Law Review 908.

paid. Performance indicators are still largely based on outputs rather than outcomes: in other words, on the number of cases, the number or total amount of penalties imposed, the number of notices issued, or the number of legal appeals lost by the agency. Calculations, however, clearly have their limitations. These numbers do not provide much information on the actual outcome of cases or the effect of independent agencies' interventions. Furthermore, they often fail to take account of anticipatory effects, such as the deterrence effects of interventions, or the positive effects of agencies' advocacy work. This book focuses on identifying qualitative criteria, based on the LITER principles of good agency behaviour.

Evaluation of Independent Agencies

Many, mostly external, evaluation reports have been published on financial institutions and financial market regulators in the years since the financial crisis started in 2007. These provide a useful and rich source of information on enforcement and on financial authorities' decision-making processes. Reports on other sectors have also been published, including a few on competition authorities, sometimes by the agencies themselves (internal reviews), and sometimes by external committees or national audit offices. All these reports, both on financial institutions and regulators and on other sectors, contain useful information that can be applied outside the context of the specific cases and be put into practice by other independent agencies. Moreover, they can be analysed from a broader perspective than just the evaluated sector, and can also be brought into the context of the LITER principles for other independent agencies: what lessons can be learned by these other independent agencies if these principles are applied to their situations?

Based on the publications in the Netherlands and the United Kingdom, the various types of reports can be categorized as follows:

1. Evaluation reports on a general level: mostly after a defined period of time.
2. Reports on organizational change and design: after a merger or separation.
3. Reports by external committees: mostly after an incident.
4. Internal reports by an independent agency: case evaluations.

The reports mentioned under 1. contain certain interesting aspects. Still, they are mostly very general in nature and do not provide much detailed information and instructions that can be applied by other agencies. Although the types of reports mentioned under 2. and 3. are less common than those in category 1., most reports discussed in this chapter fall into the third category and involve external committees, usually appointed by governments, investigating a certain case and making recommendations for improvements. These reports contain important lessons for agencies as they provide good insight into certain cases that have had severe consequences. They identify the risks more specifically, built around the circumstances of the case. Rather than discussing the recommendations one by one, this chapter takes these reports as a basis for discussing certain themes that are relevant in the context of the LITER or good agency principles. The reports have been selected at random, insofar as they are considered relevant for the purposes of this book. In some cases, the reports selected relate to independent agencies other than market regulators or competition authorities, but contain lessons of relevance to both types of independent agencies.

Institutional design

Since institutional design issues are central when setting up or merging independent agencies, reports discussing institutional design aspects can usually be found amongst those evaluating mergers or other forms of reorganizations. Mergers of independent agencies have not always been successful. Decisions to merge can be ill-considered and motivated by political grounds or a need to cut spending, or presented as an efficiency gain.

In the Netherlands, for example, it was decided to merge the Food and Consumer Product Safety Authority (VWA) with the General Inspectorate of the Dutch Ministry of Economic Affairs (AID) and the Plant Pathology Inspectorate of the Dutch Ministry of Agriculture (PD) to create the new Netherlands Food and Consumer Product Safety Authority (NVWA)[2] on 1 January 2012.[3] The idea behind the merger had been to introduce a risk-based approach throughout the organization and it had been forecast to reduce overall spending by 50 million euros through the introduction of new enforcement methods and efficiency savings from the combination of joint inspections, joint staff training, shared offices, and lower operating costs. The Netherlands Court of Audit stated in its subsequent report that the forecast savings of 50 million euros were not based on any evidence or in-depth research. The pros and cons of the merger had also not been investigated in advance; instead, the decision was taken essentially on the basis of general

[2] The *(Nederlandse) Voedsel- en Warenautoriteit* ((N)VWA), *Algemene Inspectiedienst* (AID), and *Plantenziektekundige Dienst* (PD).

[3] This analysis is based on the following report on the evaluation of this merger: Algemene Rekenkamer, 'Toezicht bij de Nederlandse Voedsel- en warenautoriteit na de fusie' (The Hague 2013).

considerations and presumptions, with the three organizations themselves believing that cost savings of no more than 12 million euros were feasible. In addition, the new risk-based enforcement strategy had not yet crystallized and was not yet being applied to its full extent. Although the intention had been to introduce a risk-based approach throughout the new organization, the previous experience of introducing such a system had been limited, and the fact that such an introduction would require a substantial investment in expertise and training, and also in identifying the differing profiles of the entities concerned, had been underestimated. Not only did the merger fail to achieve the target of 50 million euros of cost savings, but integration also failed to take place, and the quality of the enforcement in the various areas for which the NVWA was responsible was substantially lower than had been envisaged. In addition, there was no budget for realizing a joint IT network, and this meant that various joint projects, such as the sharing of expertise and knowledge, failed to get off the ground.

The Court of Audit concluded on a general level that before deciding to merge such organizations, governments needed to draw up a plan based on thorough research into the pros and cons and realistic calculations of budgets. Account also had to be taken of the crucial importance of a joint IT system, the investments required to introduce a new enforcement strategy, and housing issues. Moving three organizations into a single organizational structure cannot be done overnight; it requires investments and restructuring, as well as realistic calculations, so as to ensure that the new organization does not descend into chaos. As explained in chapter 4 on institutional design, putting three organizations under one roof does not automatically result in integration. The latter requires a fundamental and strategic approach, accompanied by the requisite investments if it is to succeed. In many cases these aspects, and what they entail, are underestimated, with the result that the effectiveness of the new organization is undermined. The independent agency can then no longer perform its tasks adequately.

Another interesting report on institutional design is the one published by the UK National Audit Office on the government's decision to reform the regulation of the British financial services sector. The subject matter of this report was not a merger, but instead a movement in the opposite direction: an existing agency was divided into two new organizations. In fact, as from April 2013 the UK Financial Services Authority (FSA) was replaced by the newly created Financial Conduct Authority (FCA) on the one hand and the Prudential Regulation Authority (PRA) on the other. The PRA was made responsible for prudential regulation of banks, building societies, insurers and credit unions, and major investment banks, while the FCA was made responsible for conduct regulation and for prudential regulation of enterprises not covered by the PRA. There are, however, numerous areas of overlap in the regulatory work of these two organizations, and they are legally required to coordinate their activities effectively.

In its report entitled *Regulating financial services*[4] the UK National Audit Office investigated the new plans and the start of the two new independent agencies. Although the implementation process was still underway, the National Audit Office made some interesting observations that may help any independent agency needing to split or build a new organization. In its report it welcomed and stressed the importance of the clear strategic approach set out by both organizations. Both new agencies had defined their objectives, based on the new financial regulation, and had structured their organizations around these goals, while also translating their statutory objectives into more specified and measurable operational aims. The National Audit Office received feedback from working-level supervisors that the changing approaches had had practical benefits in providing a clearer, separate focus and greater depth to prudential and conduct work, and encouraged earlier and more decisive regulatory intervention. This suggests that a separation of tasks (the coordination model, as discussed in chapter 4 of this book) will lead to greater focus and more dedication, at least in this case. However, in this particular case the coordination model also has certain inherent problems that need separate attention. The FCA and the PRA acknowledge that the regulators' respective prudential and conduct objectives can by their very nature conflict. They manage this conflict through formal coordination arrangements ('memoranda of understanding'), as well as by building on good day-to-day interaction, which the National Audit Office recognizes, while also observing that this is complex to achieve in practice. Although this is not made explicit in the National Audit Office's report, the process of coordinating the two organizations' activities could in my view prove to be a weak link in the chain of the new institutional setting.

In this case, it was clear to all stakeholders that operating two organizations would cost more than one: the splitting-up of the agency involved a substantial increase of almost 24% in total operating costs. This rise in costs was attributable to the recruitment of more front-line staff, additional IT costs, higher overheads in the form of management support and premises costs, and substantial additional regulatory costs resulting from the appointment of highly qualified and experienced professionals. It was assumed, however, that these additional costs would be offset by the potential benefits resulting from changing the regulatory approaches (specifically more judgement-based,

[4] National Audit Office, 'Regulating Financial Services' (London: 21 March 2014). The following paragraphs are based on this report.

forward-looking, and proactive regulation compared to the approaches previously adopted by the FSA); the new approaches are expected to effectively reduce the harm to consumers. At the same time, the UK National Audit Office pointed out that the arrangements for assessing economy, efficiency, and effectiveness (especially of the PRA) needed to be further qualified and that both agencies should refine the way they measured their performance. What the actual costs and benefits of these new institutional arrangements are has still, therefore, to be seen.

These reports make it clear that building the organization is an essential element of the process of establishing an effective agency. Investments in personnel, training, expertise, and information technology will be needed if the agency is to perform its tasks adequately. Supervising markets requires professional experts, equipped with the necessary tools and instruments, not only on paper (as laid down in legislation), but also in practice, and with the necessary funding and appropriate design. Focusing solely on costs creates the wrong incentives and runs the risk that the goals of regulation will fail to be achieved. The infrastructure consequently forms an essential building block for compliance with the LITER principles, and specifically with the principles of legality, independence, and effectiveness.

Process management

Once an institution has been built, the next question is how to process its decisions. Process management is a topic addressed in many of the evaluation reports. As in any big organization, choosing the right structure for independent agencies' decision-making process is a challenge. Given that the end product of the organization is the decision itself (rather than consumer products such as shoes or cars) and public interests are at stake, the independent agency must pay special attention to the internal process management leading up to an interim or final decision. Various reports show that delegating decision-making powers to lower levels in the organization can cause problems if control by senior management is insufficient. This was clearly the situation in, for example, the Dutch case of SNS Reaal, where the Dutch central bank (DNB) was responsible for oversight,[5] and in Project Condor, which involved the UK's former consumer and competition authority, the Office of Fair Trading (OFT).[6]

[5] R J Hoekstra and J Frijns, 'Het rapport van de evaluatiecommissie nationalisatie SNS Reaal' (Amsterdam 2014).

[6] Office of Fair Trading, 'Project Condor Board Review' (London, October 2010).

In its report on the collapse and subsequent nationalization of SNS Reaal, a Dutch conglomerate of banking and insurance activities, the evaluation committee observed that important decisions were taken and risk assessment made at a too low level within the central bank's organization, and that the board of the central bank had not been aware of these decisions at the time they were made. To put it differently, there was too great a distance between the central bank board and the various management layers, while the team responsible for supervising SNS Reaal based its assessments too much on information submitted by the bank–insurer itself. The team did not subject the information submitted to critical review, and insufficient weight was attributed to the related risks. The team gave permission for SNS Reaal to take over a property portfolio, and it was this that ultimately led to the financial institution's collapse in January 2013 and its subsequent rescue by the Dutch state.

Analysing the SNS Reaal case and reviewing its evaluation report, I cannot but remark that independent agency boards should clearly pay more attention to the risks involved in delegation. Although in many cases it is the agency's board that has formal powers to decide on cases, in practice these powers are often delegated to lower management levels within the organization. But it is nevertheless the board that should be responsible for the outcomes of cases and all decisions taken within the organization. This is because, in the event of errors, it is the board and the independent agency as such that will be held accountable (and, in some cases, liable) for wrong decisions. Boards should consequently review their delegation structures regularly and remain involved in all important cases being handled by the agency. It is essential for there to be sufficient expertise, experience, and knowledge at the level to which decisions are delegated, and it is at that level that the coordination of decisions within the agency must be guaranteed for consistent and expert risk assessment to be ensured. In the case of SNS Reaal, the macroeconomic expertise on real estate available within the central bank did not fall within the expertise of the team supervising SNS Reaal, and while such expertise was certainly required for a proper, microlevel assessment of the risks involved in SNS Reaal's property portfolio, team members also failed to ask colleagues from the macroeconomic department for advice. As a consequence, the central bank's real estate expertise was not used for microprudential oversight of individual financial institutions' activities in this area.

In the OFT's Project Condor, too, which related to the collapse of the criminal trial in *R v Burns and Others*, it was clear that the case team was inexperienced and senior management was insufficiently involved.[7] This

[7] The following description of the case is based on the Appendix to the OFT report (n6) 9.

case arose following an investigation by the OFT into alleged price-fixing of fuel surcharges on long-haul passenger flights by British Airways and Virgin Atlantic Airways. Project Condor was a criminal investigation under the British Enterprise Act 2002 and was directed at the individuals believed to have been involved in the alleged cartel. It resulted in four men being charged in August 2008 and in the start of a criminal trial in April 2010. On 10 May 2010, however, the OFT decided not to offer any evidence after the discovery of a large volume of electronic material that neither the OFT nor the defendants had previously been able to review. In view of the quantity of material, the court's rulings on disclosure, and the timing of witness hearings, the OFT accepted that it would be potentially unfair to continue the trial. The defendants were consequently acquitted.

In its internal report the OFT referred to the critical importance of communicating, identifying, and managing risks, especially in important and challenging cases. Risks need to be systematically and regularly reassessed and reported to the senior level. The OFT stated that there should have been greater involvement and challenge from senior management in the Condor case, as well as from other parts of the agency with an interest in the issues arising.

Analysis of these reports also made it very clear to me that IT problems can often arise and can create substantial risks for the independent agency. These problems relate not only to the functioning of the IT systems as such (which can represent a major obstacle for efficient integration in a merger process), but also to the safety of systems (collection and storage of big, mostly confidential data) and the control of forensic data gathering (electronic evidence). In the Condor case, for example, the inadequate handling of evidence and management of forensic information technology was the main reason why the OFT decided to withdraw the case and consequently incur substantial reputational damage. The UK National Audit Office's report on financial regulation also states that the regulatory agencies did not yet fully comprehend their inventories of regulatory data collection and ought to gain a better understanding of what data are held and needed. Independent agencies can be severely compromised if data are lost or security incidents occur. There can also be severe consequences if information is accessed without authorization. Information technology, and security and forensic systems, must consequently be subject to in-depth scrutiny by the independent agency. Otherwise the latter may be exposed not only to the risk of having to pay compensation for damage caused, but also to the risk of a major case failure.

It follows from these reports that process management forms an essential part of an agency's organization, and that neglecting this aspect can have severe consequences for the agency's effectiveness. The agency's independence can also be at risk if there is insufficient expertise available at the decision-making level within the organization. The quality of the agency's decisions depends on this expertise and on the quality of its process management; the latter is also, therefore, a crucial element for implementing the good agency principles.

Decision-making process

The decision-making process must be robust, efficient, and fair. Not only because of the legal requirements imposed in administrative law, but also because these three elements are essential ingredients in determining the final quality of the decisions. The LITER or good agency principles require an effective and transparent decision-making process. However, things can go wrong during this process. Although reference could of course be made to legal mistakes, the emphasis in this section is on the behaviour of the independent agency itself during the process. The reports examined regard the following behaviour as representing a potential threat to the decision-making process: (i) postponing behaviour; (ii) the problem of tunnel vision; and (iii) high staff turnover. Each of these types of behaviour can significantly influence the quality of the decision-making.

Postponing behaviour

The committee in the SNS Reaal evaluation report referred explicitly to the dangers inherent in the postponing behaviour displayed by the oversight authority. Although an independent agency may wish to intervene and indeed be justified in doing so in law, it may nevertheless decide not to intervene in order to avoid possible adverse consequences.[8] Agencies have a tendency to take a too rosy view of risks and to postpone taking action for fear of damaging their reputation. Their hope is that the problems will resolve themselves and that there will be no need to intervene in the market. Intervening too early can have major adverse consequences, while an agency that intervenes too late may be seen as not performing its preventive work properly.[9] The agency may therefore postpone taking a decision. The committee recommends a strict approach, especially when things are going well, so as to avoid having to intervene when it is too late or a situation in which intervention is no longer a surprise.[10] Objective parameters should be used to determine in advance when an independent agency should intervene.[11] The

[8] SNS Reaal report (n5) 264. [9] ibid 265.

[10] Interview with Hoekstra and Frijns in *NRC Handelsblad* (15/16 February 2014) E2–3.

[11] SNS Reaal report (n5) 265.

agency should in any event act and follow through promptly, and have the courage to take what the committee referred to as 'prompt corrective action' whenever required. The Scheltema report published in the wake of the DSB case[12]—in which the smaller Dutch DSB Bank could not be rescued and was declared insolvent in October 2009—also identified this as an important lesson for independent agencies: all too often, agencies have continued to discuss issues with supervisees in an attempt to find solutions, but at a certain point enough is enough and the agency will need to intervene in order to avoid the situation escalating even further. It follows from this latter report that the Dutch central bank did not take prompt corrective action in response to the financial difficulties encountered by DSB Bank. Instead the oversight authority continued discussing matters with the bank's board for too long and seeking to apply 'soft', informal measures to resolve the various problems, while also, according to the Scheltema Committee, demonstrating too much good faith and failing to act sufficiently stringently. The solutions finally identified came too late as, by then, it was no longer possible to rescue the bank.

Another timing issue occurs if a case drags on and the team continues working on it despite the evidence being anything but clear-cut. Not only do risks need to be reassessed from time to time to see whether the risk environment has changed since the initial assessment, but so, too, should the robustness of the evidence be examined from time to time. The Condor report recommended establishing a steering group in major cases so as to strengthen both the internal and external challenge and quality assurance. Clear 'stop/go' decision points to assess the risks and evidence of the case, as well as more formalized reporting stages for the board or executive committees, also need to be introduced during the decision-making process. A system where senior managers are assessed on the amount or number of penalties issued creates the wrong internal incentives and is, in my opinion, unacceptable.

Tunnel vision

Another danger during the decision-making process is the risk that the team handling the case will develop tunnel vision. The legal department or another special review team should, therefore, arrange for a fresh pair of eyes to review the process. As mentioned in chapter 4, the UK Competition & Markets Authority (CMA) gets the panel members to scrutinize competition cases so as to enhance the quality of decisions and the decision-making process. The OFT's internal report in the Condor

[12] 'Rapport van de Commissie Onderzoek DSB Bank' (The Hague 2010).

case recommended that some form of steering group should be set up in high-profile cases so that the factors contributing to the decision could be subjected to critical challenge. Outside council is not regarded by the OFT as a 'fresh pair of eyes'. These 'devil's advocate evaluations' can also form a remedy against capture, as discussed in chapter 3. The evaluation committee in the SNS Reaal case refers to this phenomenon as 'regulatory forbearance', whereby the agency is consciously or unconsciously influenced by the supervisee. Processes to prevent such tunnel vision need to be in place, either in the form of 'devil's advocate' teams or consultations. It is important in any case for information used to be double-checked and for evidence to be gathered through several channels.

High staff turnover rate

Allocations of resources also need to be closely monitored. Fights for capacity may break out between divisions, and the importance of the respective cases may be over- or underestimated. The FSA's internal report on the Northern Rock case[13] mentioned this rivalry as a complicating factor in the process of supervising that particular institution. Owing to understaffing and a lack of the required expertise within the team, Northern Rock's risk profile was not appropriately assessed. The risks arising from the increasing risk profile of Northern Rock's business were not effectively pursued by the team performing the oversight. The continuity of the team handling the case was also seen as an issue requiring special attention. A high staff turnover rate is in any event a risk that must be recognized and monitored as staff changes can have severe consequences for the quality and continuity of the team handling the case. A lack of senior, experienced staff can cause problems in terms of quality. Financial resources must consequently be available to ensure that the agency can recruit highly skilled people as and when they are needed. However, constraints on budgets and government recruitment may form significant impediments when an agency is seeking to develop and expand its skilled capacity. Understaffing and a lack of qualified personnel will clearly have an adverse influence on the effectiveness and independence of an agency as they will mean it has insufficient resources to take on the right cases or to bring cases to a satisfactory conclusion. This is made very clear in the Netherlands Court of Audit's evaluation of the Netherlands Food and Consumer Product Safety Authority.

[13] FSA Internal Audit Division, 'The Supervision of Northern Rock: a Lessons Learned Review' (London 2008).

Professionalism

Lack of expertise was also a problem in the SNS Reaal case, where the Dutch central bank's supervisory team essentially based its observations and conclusions on the information provided by SNS Reaal itself. A striking aspect, in addition to the excessively rosy and over-optimistic picture painted by this information, was the number of experts that both the central bank and the Ministry of Finance brought in from outside during the overall evaluation process. The two organizations appear to have had too little in-house expertise to evaluate the situation for themselves. The specialists brought in from outside were also used to get difficult decisions taken. The risk then, however, is that the supervising organization itself will be insufficiently able to form an opinion of its own, will have no overall view of the issue, and will be unable to learn from past mistakes. This was also the problem in the Condor case, where a lack of sufficient internal expertise on criminal litigation and the gathering of evidence meant the OFT was heavily reliant on external council to provide quality assurance. As discussed in chapter 3, independent oversight of complex institutions and dynamic markets requires investments in supervisory infrastructure. The case of the Netherlands Food and Consumer Product Safety Authority discussed earlier in this chapter also clearly demonstrates how budget cuts can result in the new organization being unable to invest in the infrastructure, training, and personnel it needs.[14] In its report on financial regulation the UK National Audit Office recognized the importance of expertise and knowledge in any professional organization. If inadequate, '[t]his could undermine industry confidence in the regulators, poses a risk that knowledge be lost within organisations and impacts on the regulators' capacity to carry out their functions'.[15]

Adequate training is therefore crucial. Expert capacity must be built throughout the organization. The focus should be not only on building expertise, but also on training professional, political, and societal skills. Independent agencies' staff additionally need to develop the skills needed to communicate with and understand the complex landscape around them, and to learn how to anticipate political pressure and deal with stakeholders' varying interests. In my experience, these skills are often underestimated and underdeveloped because of the focus being mainly on the content of

[14] This was also the case with DNB in the SNS Reaal case. In an interview one of the investigators of the SNS Reaal case, Mr Hoekstra, mentioned that as a result of all the drastic cuttings there is insufficient expertise and experience available at the market and competition authorities: *Elsevier* (22 February 2014) 32–34.

[15] SNS Reaal report (n5) Conclusion 9.

decisions and less on the consequences of a decision for the outside world. An agency's professionalism forms an important building block because having a good reputation for expertise will contribute both to the agency's authority and to its independence.

Agency culture

An independent agency's internal culture constitutes another important element in stakeholders' acceptance of and respect for the agency. If the agency requires supervisees to comply with a regulatory regime, this requirement will be respected only if the agency itself complies with the rules and ethical standards. Internal compliance with rules on conflicts of interest, financial procedures, or risk and safety management is essential. The internal culture of the independent agency must be fully oriented towards compliance, with the agency setting the right example to its supervisees. As discussed in chapter 3, the integrity of the agency and its staff is a prerequisite for its independence and authority. Otherwise the agency's reputation will immediately be damaged and its authority eroded.

An example of this happening can be seen in the case of the Dutch Healthcare Authority (NZa). A whistleblower sent a file to a national newspaper, claiming that the NZa's internal procedures were not being followed, and that this was giving rise to various safety and financial issues. The material presented clearly showed that members of the independent agency's board had made trips paid (at least in part) by healthcare companies supervised by the NZa and that non-compliance with IT protocols meant that the confidentiality of information on supervised enterprises and patients could not be guaranteed. In addition, the agency's internal accounting rules were not always followed, while there were also indications that the Minister of Health had intervened in an individual enforcement case and disregarded the agency's independence. This scandal led to the resignation of both board members and the launch of a full investigation into the matter.[16] This series of incidents caused substantial damage to the NZa's authority, not only because of the failure to comply with internal rules, but also because of the perceived regulatory capture arising from these activities. By not showing the right example, the NZa lost its authority. The evaluation committee concluded that essential elements required to protect confidential information were not available at the agency and that the agency's integrity and compliance culture was inadequate. It explicitly stated that it was the agency's responsibility to

[16] H Borstlap, P F M van der Meer Mohr and L J E Smits, 'Rapport van de Onderzoekscommissie intern functioneren NZa' (2014).

ensure it had effective employment policies in place and that the board and management had to demonstrate leadership in ensuring that personnel could develop the necessary qualities and professional standards. These should include not only output-related aspects, but also attention to the aspects of human interest needed to ensure appropriate personnel development within the organization. The LITER principle of responsibility clearly plays an important role here.

Although the evaluation committee in the NZa case did not conclude that the responsible minister had intervened in individual decisions of the agency, it made it clear that the relationship between the agency and the ministry was too close and endangered the independent position of the former. The committee also advised changing the governance structure of the independent agency and installing a supervisory board so as to introduce a greater degree of countervailing powers.

Since rules and safeguards are put in place in order to prevent capture, not complying with these rules indicates the independent agency is—at least in danger of—being captured, and is infringing the principle of independence, one of the LITER principles. In the case of the US Minerals Management Service (MMS), the capture problems identified as a result of the Deepwater Horizon oil rig fire in April 2010 ultimately led to the complete disbanding of the MMS. Lunches, sporting events, hunting and fishing trips, and all kinds of other events were paid for by the oil industry, thus creating cosy relationships with the industry that MMS was supposed to oversee. Although this applied only to small numbers of MMS staff, the accusations of capture led to the collapse of the entire institution.[17] Rules on internal compliance and conflicts of interest, transparency on outside employment, internal disclosure forms, and publication of expenses (such as dining and travel costs) all help to avoid actual or perceived conflicts of interest and capture. The agency and its staff must obey these rules in order to gain and maintain the agency's authority.

Many of these problems can be avoided if the agency is transparent on these issues by, for example, publishing a register of board members' outside employment, investment, and other interests. Transparency is an important instrument for counteracting any suspicion or perception of capture. As one of the LITER principles, transparency is also essential for the agency's

[17] For a very interesting study of this case, see: C Carrigan, 'Captured by Disaster? Reinterpreting Regulatory Behavior in Shadow of the Gulf Oil Spill' in D Carpenter and D Moss (eds), *Preventing Regulatory Capture. Special Interest Influence and How to Limit it* (New York: Cambridge University Press 2014) 239. Carrigan shows that although capture was present, in fact there were other problems which should have led to other solutions instead of abolishing MMS as a whole.

authority and can be improved by agencies opting to publish self-evaluation reports. It is notable that so far only a few agencies (such as those responsible for compiling the Northern Rock and Condor reports) have published their internal evaluation of a case. Publication of such reports emphasizes the agency's openness—a core value of most agencies—and should be seen as a sign of strength and as evidence that an independent agency is willing to learn from past mistakes and to improve its procedures and processes. However, potential claims and liability risks, a topic discussed in the section on liability in this chapter, form an impediment to agencies seeking to demonstrate their openness. Although independent agencies are generally very reluctant to share their experience with the outside world, these types of publications demonstrate the greater transparency inherent in the good agency or LITER principles.[18]

Enforcement

One particularly compelling topic when analysing evaluation reports is the fact that some agencies try to resolve matters through more informal channels, with the risk that any corrective action taken is too late (see, for example, the previously discussed cases of the Dutch financial sector players SNS Reaal and DSB Bank). Such postponing behaviour is evident in many of the evaluation reports mentioned in this chapter. In the case of DSB Bank, for example, it was acknowledged that the supervisee was not an average bank with a longstanding reputation, but instead a young, aggressive bank with a completely different background from others in the banking sector. DSB Bank was not 'playing the game' according to the conventional rules of the banking sector. The approach adopted by the Dutch central bank in an effort to persuade DSB Bank to change its behaviour was not appropriate. What was needed was a stronger and stricter style of enforcement. By the time the central bank took those measures, however, it was too late.[19] According to the committees evaluating the various cases discussed, the independent agencies should have acted more boldly, which may seem to suggest that more horizontal enforcement strategies would not be preferable. In my opinion, this would be the wrong conclusion to draw: these horizontal approaches can be

[18] Transparency was also recognized as an important principle in the NMa's 2007 general evaluation report: 'Toezicht op mededinging door de NMa' Parliamentary Papers II, Vol 31 055 No 2.

[19] A complicating factor in cases of supervision of financial institutions is the risk of a bank run. See for the discussion of this specific characteristic: M Aelen, *Beginselen van goed markttoezicht, Gedefinieerd, verklaard en uitgewerkt voor het toezicht op de financiële markten* (dissertation, Utrecht University, the Hague: Boom Juridische Uitgevers 2014).

effective, even though there is always a risk that supervisees will be unwilling to cooperate and may need a different approach, or that the circumstances of the case may change and a quick change of strategy by the agency will be required. Informal interventions or discussions can under certain circumstances also produce quicker results.

As discussed in chapter 5, horizontal approaches, such as self-regulatory oversight, contain the risk of capture or of undue influence being exercised. Trust in self-enforcement by the industry can come into conflict with the necessary critical attitude, required in specific cases to investigate possible infringements.[20] There is a fine line between collaboration with the industry (in order, for example, to develop standard codes) and capture. It is in the industry's interests to seek to influence the agency so that the standards set are as favourable as possible. The agency needs, therefore, to remain critical and also to use different sources of information to verify the input provided and the outcome of the process. A cooperative regulatory style requires careful monitoring[21] and, as the Netherlands Court of Audit's report on the NVWA shows, substantial resources. The Netherlands Court of Audit stated that the introduction of what is referred to as 'system supervision' cannot be seen as a reason to cut budgets. On the contrary, it requires investment in staff training, the screening of supervised enterprises, and the setting-up of new supervisory systems, as also discussed in chapter 5 of this book.

In the Dutch Icesave report of 2009 the investigators pointed out that the opposite approach in the supervisory practice, an overly legalistic and formal approach to oversight, can cause the agency to become paralysed. In this case the Dutch central bank did not take sufficient action to safeguard the savings held at the Dutch branch of the Icelandic bank Landsbanki. The central bank interpreted its powers strictly and formalistically, as a result of which it was unwilling to take a sufficient degree of action. According to the evaluation committee, this approach was 'defensible, but too strict and too cautious'. Here we can see a direct clash between the

[20] This risk was identified in the general evaluation report of OPTA: Berenschot, Kwink Groep, and TNO, 'Evaluatie OPTA' (2009).

[21] See in that context also the Deepwater Horizon oil rig fire as discussed by C Carrigan (n17). A clear-cut case is also the Dutch case on the fire in the area of Rotterdam. It was established that the joint environmental protection agency for the Rijnmond area DCMR did not take appropriate action although it was fully aware of the problems. It postponed strict enforcement too long. See the judgement of the Dutch civil court: *Brouwer, Janssen/Gemeente Rotterdam* 26 May 2004 ECLI: NL:RBROT:2004:AR2320 <http://uitspraken.rechtspraak.nl/inziendocument?id=ECLI:NL:RBROT:2004:AR2320> accessed 26 September 2014.

legality and effectiveness principles: the legal approach leads to non-intervention, even though the problem exists and intervention is needed, while society demands intervention, even though the legal powers enabling such intervention may not yet be available. The Dutch central bank was criticized for this attitude, and this criticism resulted in a new vision of oversight, involving a more proactive and intrusive attitude to enforcement, being formulated.[22]

As discussed in chapter 5, a risk-based approach as a possible enforcement strategy of an agency requires the proper identification and categorization of risks, and staff need to be allocated accordingly. Risk profiling is a difficult and time-consuming task, while risks can also change over time, and care must be taken to ensure that supervisees do not fall under the radar. Two reports regarding oversight of the financial sector in the Netherlands and the United Kingdom illustrate these dangers of the risk-based approach. The FSA's self-evaluation of its handling of the Northern Rock case pointed out that some of the key elements of the risk framework were not being used as intended, partly because of inappropriate prioritizations and resourcing capacity issues. Individual supervisees were checked only in response to signals or alerts, rather than on the basis of effective mechanisms or regular monitoring. As in the case of the Dutch central bank and the Dutch bank-insurer SNS Reaal, there was insufficient understanding of Northern Rock's business model. A risk-based approach is sensible only if the risks can be identified and are fully understood. The National Audit Office also highlighted this risk in its report on the new institutional design of financial oversight in the United Kingdom.

Conclusion

It can be concluded from the evaluation reports examined that, as far as the LITER principles are concerned, the focus in these reports is almost entirely on agencies' operational effectiveness and to some degree on independence and transparency. The responsibility principle is clearly also at stake. Any failure by the agency's internal culture to reflect the appropriate standards of integrity and professionalism will put the reputation of

[22] See for the report: A J C de Moor-van Vugt, C E du Perron, and P J Krop, 'De bevoegdheden van De Nederlandsche Bank inzake Icesave' (2009) Report commissioned by the Dutch Ministry of Economic Affairs, University of Amsterdam <http://www.dnb.nl/binaries/Rapport%20DNB-Icesave_tcm46-228434.pdf> accessed 26 September 2014.

the agency at risk, and this can have severe consequences for its authority. Failing to set the right example will automatically have an adverse impact on the authority of the agency. It is also crucial for the agency to demonstrate that it is behaving independently and avoiding any perception of bias or partiality. This not only means independence from market parties, but also independence in the agency's relationship with the responsible minister and ministry.

It can be said that if the process management, the infrastructure of the organization (including IT), and the capacity and quality of staff are inadequate, this may have severe consequences for the decision-making process and the outcome of cases. Obvious as this may be, it is one of the most difficult aspects involved in overseeing enterprises in practice. These reports contrast with the mostly legal and economic literature, where the focus is mainly on the interpretation of the regulation, the content of decisions, and the enforcement instruments. It should be emphasized that the importance of the organizational issues surrounding the legal and economic decision-making processes should not be overlooked. A combination of organizational, professional, and economic skills needs, therefore, to be available within these agencies in order to ensure that independent agencies can comply with the good agency or LITER principles.

Independent agencies should be learning organizations, investing in and experimenting with innovations, learning from experience, and taking any prompt corrective action required. Analysing internal risks should be a standard aspect of their day-to-day work so as to ensure oversight of internal processes, compliance issues, and safety measures. Given the current focus on budget cuts and public spending, it should also be realized that adequate resources need to be available in order to ensure the independent agencies can perform as they should. The risk in a one-sided focus on budget cuts is that not only will the agency fail to function properly, but that also the market this agency is overseeing will function less well too, with consequences for the whole or significant parts of the economy.

Decision-making does not just involve applying rules correctly; it is also a matter of knowing how to get things done, with professional teams operating in a dynamic environment. Although the evaluation committees examine the agencies with the benefit of hindsight, their reports provide interesting and important lessons for all independent agencies. This also applies to general evaluations of agencies (i.e. where there is no specific scandal or incident), and where the LITER principles of good agency behaviour can provide a solid framework for evaluating and investigating whether the agency is performing its tasks and functions accordingly.

Review by the Courts

This section discusses how market and competition authorities' decisions should be reviewed by courts. The primary question is how courts should look at those decisions and which standards they should apply when reviewing decisions. What are the considerations determining whether to conduct an intense or lighter review?

These questions must be answered both in relation to the roles of the independent agencies and the courts themselves, and with regard to the institutional design of the specific agency. As discussed in chapter 4, there is an important link between the institutional design of the independent agency and review by the courts. Depending on the design chosen for the decision-making process (i.e. a separated or integrated model, see chapter 4), courts may decide to conduct a more comprehensive review or adopt a more light-touch approach. The type of decision is also of importance. For sanctioning (*ex post*) decisions, a full review is required because of the fundamental rights involved, whereas a different type of review could be possible for *ex ante* decisions (such as merger decisions or market assessments).

This section analyses these aspects within the framework of the LITER or good agency principles. This analysis does not seek to provide a full, extensive overview of judicial review (that topic would justify a book of its own), but instead discusses the main, universal aspects of the subject as far as relevant in the context of the LITER principles for market and competition authorities, with examples of case law from the European courts, the Netherlands, and the United Kingdom taken to illustrate the various issues.

Different standards of review

The standard of review relates to the nature and extent of the investigation to be undertaken by the court when facing an appeal concerning an agency's decision.[23] What are, in principle, the possible standards of review? Although different countries use different terminology, a general distinction can be made, at least in theory, between a marginal review and a full review on the merits of the case. In practice, however, this distinction is not always easy to draw.

[23] I S Forrester, 'A Bush in Need of Pruning: the Luxuriant Growth of Light Judicial Review' in C Ehlerman and M Marquis (eds), *European Competition Law Annual 2009: Evaluation of Evidence and its Judicial Review in Competition Cases* (Oxford and Portland: Hart Publishing 2010) 407.

Marginal review

A marginal review is also referred to as a 'light-touch review', 'limited review', or 'deferential review'. In this case the standard of review is limited only to review in relation to alleged or manifest errors of appraisal or analysis. The independent agency is allowed a degree of appreciation or margin of discretion. However, the courts closely examine matters of law, procedure, and facts for this standard of review, too. It will test, for example, whether the principle of legality has been followed by checking the legal basis of the decision, whether the decision has been sufficiently reasoned and based on the correct facts, and whether the intervention meets the proportionality test. Not only must the court establish whether the evidence put forward by the agency is factually accurate, reliable, and consistent, but also whether that evidence contains all the relevant data to be taken into consideration in appraising the situation. This means that the interpretation of the law, the procedures followed, and the factual findings are also fully reviewed in the event of a marginal review.

The review is limited as far as the complex assessment of non-legal, notably economic and scientific, evidence by the independent agency is concerned. The court will also be reluctant to interfere in cases where explicit discretion has been given to the agency. This applies in the case, for example, of prioritization decisions (see chapter 5), where independent agencies in most jurisdictions have a wide margin of discretion when deciding whether to pursue an investigation. This judicial review is also prescribed in, for example, the UK legislation on appeals to the Competition Appeal Tribunal (CAT) relating to CMA merger and market investigations.

Full review on the merits

The standard set for a full review on the merits is also referred to as an 'intense review', 'comprehensive review', or 'full jurisdiction' (from the French administrative law concept of *recours de pleine juridiction*). The court may deal fully with a decision in these cases and has the power to scrutinize details of decisions in a profound and rigorous manner. The court can form its own view on whether the decision was right, even if different options are possible within a range of reasonable choices. The court will not be reluctant to allow its judgement to replace the choices made by the independent agency. Sanctioning cases are an example of situations in which this full review should be followed as—in accordance with the requirements of fundamental rights—the European and national courts in European countries need to be able to exercise unlimited jurisdiction in such cases.

Courts' role in the light of the LITER principles

What should the courts' role be in relation to the review of independent agencies' decisions? The approach to the standard of review varies, depending on how this role is perceived. The more roles and functions are assigned to the court, the more intensely the court should monitor decisions by independent agencies.

Geradin and Petit consider three perspectives on the role of the courts in reviewing the decisions.[24] They distinguish (i) a lawyer's standpoint, (ii) an economist's standpoint, and (iii) a political scientist's standpoint. From the lawyer's standpoint the court's role is to safeguard universal values, such as fundamental rights and the general principles of law. It is a 'rights-based' approach, where appeals to courts are a means to protect fundamental rights. In contrast to this rights-based approach, economists adopt an outcome perspective on judicial review. As they see it, the purpose of the review is to promote economic welfare by eliminating decisional errors and setting normative standards. From a political scientist's standpoint meanwhile, judicial review is necessary in order to counterbalance agencies' independence. Review by an independent court is needed in order to restore the institutional balance, while the independent court can also correct for the risk of capture or political bias. The appeal system improves independent agencies' accountability as it forces them to give sufficient reasons for their decisions, and these can then be verified by the courts through judicial review. These perspectives can be translated into the good agency principles (i.e. legality, independence, transparency, effectiveness, and responsibility), which follow the same lines of argument.

The legal rights-based (or safeguard) approach is closely related to the legality principle, the letter 'L' in LITER, which ensures that agencies' legal powers are subject to controls and the legal rights of supervisees protected. Effective legal protection through high standards of judicial review should clearly be available as this is a fundamental right. Taken solely from a legal perspective, the court's role is therefore of paramount importance and must not be restricted. Fundamental rights must be protected and monitoring is needed in order to correct errors by independent agencies. Decisions by these agencies can also interfere with property rights or result in severe measures and penalties, and so require full scrutiny by the courts.

[24] D Geradin and N Petit, 'Judicial Review in European Union Competition Law' in M Merola and J Derenne (eds), *The Role of the Court of Justice of the European Union in Competition Law Cases* (Bruges: College of Europe, Global Competition Law Centre 2012) 24–31.

There are also good arguments, on the other hand, for limiting judicial review. These arguments are on the interface between the legality and the independence principles. Firstly, and as dicussed in chapter 3, independent agencies need to have certain discretionary powers, as part of the legal madate assigned to them. Topics in the field of regulation and competition can be complex and require specialized expertise (cf. the independence principle), which the courts may lack. Complex assessments of economic and technical issues must therefore be provided by the expert agency. The independent agency has been set up specifically for its expertise and experience, and so its views should be challenged only in very specific circumstances as the administrative body is better placed to perform these tasks than the court.[25] Agencies must also be able to take the dynamic environments in which they operate into account, and this requires discretionary powers too. If choices made by independent agencies are reasonable and appropriate, and reliable methodologies have been used, interventions by a court may not be straightforward. Replacing the agency's decision by the court's own views may in itself distort competition if these judgements come at a time when market conditions may already have changed. These arguments consequently point more in favour of a light-touch review by the courts.

EU law provides an additional argument in favour of a more restrained review. Although Article 263 of the Treaty on the Functioning of the European Union (TFEU) gives the European Court of Justice (ECJ) unlimited jurisdiction on specific questions relating to the imposition of fines under Article 31 of Council Regulation 1/2003, the court exercises a form of self-constraint. This approach is justified by the principle of institutional balance,[26] with the self-constraint being based on the idea that the power of economic analysis is granted to the European Commission as the institution best placed to investigate complex economic problems and access technical expertise.[27] The rules on the division of powers between the European Commission and the EU judicature are fundamental to the Union's institutional system.[28] The court must not become a competition authority by

[25] R Nazzini, 'Administrative Enforcement, Judicial Review and Fundamental Rights in EU Competition Law: A Comparative Contextual-Functionalistic Perspective' (2012) 49(3) Common Market Law Review 971, 1000.

[26] See for example Geradin and Petit (n24) 79–80; and J Laguna de Paz, 'Understanding the Limits of Judicial Review in European Competition Law' (2014) 2(1) Journal of Antitrust Enforcement 203, 217.

[27] Geradin and Petit (n24) 80.

[28] See the Advocate Generale in his conclusion in the *Tetra Laval* case: Case C-12/03P *Commission of the European Communities v Tetra Laval BV* [2005] ECR I-987, paragraph 89.

examining the merits of the European Commission's complex economic assessments or by substituting its own point of view for that of the administrative body.[29] These arguments point to a more limited review by national and European courts.

Judicial review nevertheless constitutes a corrective mechanism for all kinds of biases that independent agencies may demonstrate.[30] This clearly correlates with the LITER principle of independence. Agency officials may be too much oriented towards achieving results, thus leading to a pro-enforcement bias.[31] Independence and impartiality should be the leading principles for decision-makers. As bias risks may occur, it is up to the court to provide a fresh pair of eyes and to ensure objectivity, bearing in mind the procedural safeguards and legal protection against agency interventions, particularly in the case of decisions involving sanctions.

The accountability argument of political scientists accords with the LITER principles, and specifically with the principles of transparency and legality. Judicial review is an accountability instrument to counterbalance the independence of the agency. It serves 'good governance purposes'.[32] The courts also need to check whether sufficient reasons have been given for the decision and whether the remedies in place accord with the proportionality principle.

Economists have argued that judicial review can contribute to reducing type I decisional errors.[33] According to this argument, and when seen from an economic point of view, the review system contributes to the effectiveness of the supervisory system in accordance with the LITER principle of effectiveness. There is also a clear link between the effectiveness principle and the legality principle. The ECJ developed the principle of effective judicial protection on the basis of the European principle of effectiveness. This implies that individuals should be able in the national courts to enforce all rights conferred on them by EU law.[34] An effective system of legal protection must, therefore, be available. The European effectiveness principle may also include

[29] J Laguna de Paz (n26).

[30] W Wils, 'The Combination of the Investigative and Prosecutorial Function and the Adjudicative Function in EC Antitrust Enforcement: A Legal and Economic Analysis' (2004) 27(2) World Competition 201.

[31] Geradin and Petit (n24) 38.

[32] Geradin and Petit (n24) 30. They point out, however, that political scientists remain divided over the effectiveness of this instrument, as market and competition authorities may anticipate these corrections by the courts and judges might also pursue selfish motives or be influenced by behavioural biases.

[33] Discussed by Geradin and Petit (n24) 26–27.

[34] J H Jans, R de Lange, S Prechal, and R J G M Widdershoven, *Europeanisation of Public Law* (Groningen: Europa Law Publishing 2007).

rules on evidence, such as the burden of proof. If the national administrative rules on evidence are too strict (from the perspective of the individual seeking to enforce rights) or the standards on judicial control insufficient, this could undermine the rights of effective judicial protection. In this respect, the European principles of effectiveness and effective judicial protection can influence national rules on proof and evidence and the scope of the judicial review.[35]

All these arguments suggest that a form of intense judicial review of independent agency decisions is required. However, an 'overkill' of judicial protection can frustrate the effectiveness of the supervisory system and lead to ineffective market control. There are consequently two sides to the LITER principle of effectiveness: the effectiveness of the supervisory system, and the effectiveness of judicial protection. These two sides of the coin mirror the two dimensions (instrumental and safeguard) of the LITER principles, as discussed in chapter 3. The intensity of the judicial protection demanded can vary, depending on which dimension receives more attention. As the literature on judicial review demonstrates, lawyers litigating in European and national courts will be more likely to argue for a stricter and more intense review by the courts,[36] whereas the plea from the agencies' perspective will be for greater discretion and a lighter regime.[37] The right balance obviously needs to be found between effective oversight on the one hand and effective legal protection on the other, while respecting the independence of both the agency and the court.

Lastly, the courts clearly have a role to play with regard to the responsibility principle. It is up to them to check whether the independent agencies are acting within the legal mandate they have been granted, as well as whether their performance accords with the tasks and roles assigned to them pursuant to the goals of the legislation and regulations. By reviewing the performance of these tasks, the courts fulfil their responsibility to provide effective judicial protection.

[35] A Gerbrandy, 'Case C-8/08, *T-Mobile Netherlands BV, KPN Mobile NV, Orange Nederland NV, Vodafone Libertel NV v Raad van bestuur van de Nederlandse Mededingingsautoriteit, Judgment of the Court* (Third Chamber) of 4 June 2009' (2010) 47(4) Competition Law Review 1199. In this casenote Gerbrandy explains the tension between the national procedural autonomy principle and the requirements for effective legal protection in the light of the T-Mobile case and the uncertainties which remain in relation to national procedural rules on evidence.

[36] For example I Forrester, 'Due Process in EC Competition Cases: a Distinguished Institution with Flawed Procedures' (2009) 34(6) European Law Review 817; and I Forrester (n23).

[37] Wils (n30).

Institutional design of enforcement

There is also another element to be considered. As mentioned earlier in this chapter, there is a clear link between independent agencies' chosen institutional design and the consequences of this for the required judicial review. The various options for the institutional design are discussed in chapter 4. In the coordination model, the investigative and decision-making tasks are performed by two different institutions: in other words, there is a complete *institutional* separation between the two functions. In the integrated model there is only a *functional* separation, where different functions have been created and separated from each other within the same institution. This can be done either by a lighter regime, with a 'Chinese wall' between the two teams, or by a stricter regime, with two different bodies or divisions within the same institution being responsible for prosecution and decision-making. There is also a third option, where there is no functional division or separation whatsoever and the same person or institution is responsible both for prosecution and for the decision on the infringement and any possible sanctions. This applies in the case, for example, of the European Commission.

An inadequate enforcement structure means a clearly greater risk of bias, and stronger judicial control will then be needed.[38] The more safeguards and precautions the agency takes during the decision-making process to avoid pro-enforcement bias, the less need there will be for an intense review (from the perspective of the independence principle).[39] Here, the protection of fundamental rights plays a crucial role. In the *Menarini* case (discussed in chapter 4) the European Court of Human Rights (ECtHR) established that a system of functional separation was in accordance with Article 6 of the European Convention of Human Rights (ECHR), providing decisions can be appealed to an independent court with 'full jurisdiction'. Although the court did not specify what it meant by 'full jurisdiction', this will in any event involve a review on the merits of the case rather than a marginal

[38] See Geradin and Petit (n24) 39–42 and R Nazzini (n25).

[39] The same argument could be followed for example in case there is an independent, internal review procedure followed before an appeal can be initiated before an independent court. This was for example the case in the Netherlands, where an advisory objection procedure had to be followed. See on this procedure: J Jans and A Outhuijse, 'Advisory Objection Procedures in The Netherlands: a Case Study on Their Usefulness in Dutch Competition Law' in S Comtois and K Graaf, *On Judicial and Quasi-Judicial Independence* (The Hague: Eleven International Publishing 2013) 450–96. This procedure is no longer obligatory under the new legislation, which came into force on 1 August 2014: 'Wijziging van de Instellingswet Autoriteit Consument en Markt en enige andere wetten in verband met de stroomlijning van het door de Autoriteit Consument en Markt te houden markttoezicht' (*Stroomlijningswet*) <http://www.eerstekamer.nl/behandeling/20140703/publicatie_wet/document3/f=/vjl4b3is9wzg.pdf> accessed 15 September 2014.

review. It is not yet clear whether this also requires a comprehensive review of complex economic and technical issues, but it should include at least the examination of all questions of law and fact. From the *Tsfayo* and *Bryan* cases considered by the ECtHR it would seem to follow that a more limited review is justified if the issues to be determined require 'a measure of professional knowledge or experience and the exercise of administrative discretion pursuant to wider policy aims'.[40] If, however, the two cases are taken together, this would seem possible only if the administrative authority complies with the requirements for independence and impartiality, and this should mean in my view (although not specified by the court) at least some form of functional separation.[41]

It follows from the above three examples that a marginal review can be considered sufficient in all cases involving a separation model. A full review of the law and the facts is required in the case of an integrated model, whereas a more limited review is allowed in cases involving complicated assessments that demand a higher degree of discretion, although it is admittedly not exactly clear how far such a review should go. A light-touch review is in any event not allowed in situations in which there is no (internal or external) separation at all.[42] In the event of a non-punitive decision (in regulatory market decisions, for example, or *ex ante* merger decisions), Article 6 ECHR does not apply; a marginal review is then acceptable (from a fundamental rights perspective, that is).

Standards of proof and economic evidence

An issue related to, but distinct from the standard of review is the standard of proof.[43] This standard reflects the degree to which an independent agency's decision must be convincing in establishing its case: does the agency need to

[40] *Tsfayo v United Kingdom* (2009) 48 EHRR 18, paragraph 46; and *Bryan v United Kingdom* (1995) 19178/91.

[41] See for this interpretation: R Nazzini (n25) 998. For a different view, see: W Wils, 'The Increased Level of EU Antitrust Fines, Judicial Review and the European Convention on Human Rights', (2013) 33(1) World Competition 5, 24. Wils claims that the judicial review can be limited to a control of manifest errors in all cases where the issues require a measure of professional knowledge or experience and the exercise of discretion.

[42] This last point has been made very clear by Nazzini in relation to the decisions of the European Commission and the review by the European Courts. As there is no separation installed by the Commission, a full review should be done by the Courts, which is in his view (and others) currently not the case: R Nazzini (n25).

[43] This paragraph is based on and partly taken from: A T Ottow, 'Observations on Economic Proof in Economic Cases' in O Essens, A Gerbrandy, and S A C M Lavrijssen (eds), *National Courts and the Standard of Review in Competition Law and Economic Regulation* (Groningen: Europa Law Publishing 2009) 39.

prove, for example, that the existence of the infringement is 'beyond reasonable doubt', on the 'balance of probabilities', or in accordance with some other standard?[44] Various standards of proof are used, and courts are not always consistent in the terminology they use or apply, nor in what these standards exactly mean.[45] The standard of review looks at how courts have to verify decisions. Despite this theoretical distinction between the two standards, however, these concepts are so closely linked that they have become almost 'inseparable'.[46] Court reviews will consequently fluctuate, depending on the underlying standard of proof required: the higher the burden of proof resting on the agency, the more intense the review will be, and the more it will focus on the facts and context of the case.

This fluctuation is illustrated by the clear tendency towards applying competition law and sector-specific regulation in the years from around 2003 onwards.[47] A strict legalistic application of the rules is no longer considered sufficient and 'rules for the sake of rules' are consequently less accepted. Instead, independent agencies have been under increasing pressure to take sufficient account of the economic reality and the impact their decisions may have on the market when considering competition and regulatory cases.[48] They are being urged to ensure a more economic approach, taking the economic context into account and analysing the effect on competition of the behaviour concerned and they have to give sound economic reasons for their interventions.

Any adverse or positive effects on the market need to be proven, particularly if the intervention includes sanctions or fines imposed by the independent agency.[49] It is argued, for example, that the agency has to prove that there is an adverse effect on the market if it wants to establish a prohibited restriction on competition and that automatic application of the prohibition is no longer acceptable. This shift from a legalistic (i.e. formal) approach to a more economic effect-based approach requires a balancing act in most competition and regulation cases,[50] with due weight being given to both procompetitive

[44] I Forrester (n23).

[45] B Vesterdorf, 'Standard of Proof in Merger Cases: Reflections in the Light of Recent Case Law of the Community Courts' (2005) 1(1) European Competition Journal 25.

[46] ibid 8.

[47] J Bourgeois and D Waelbroeck, *Ten Years of Effects-Based Approach in EU Competition Law. State of Play and Perspectives* (Bruges: College of Europe, Global Competition Law Centre 2013).

[48] L Y J M Parret, 'Sense and Nonsense of Rules on Proof in Cartel Cases: How to Reconcile a More Economic-Based Approach to Competition Law with More Attention for Rules on Proof' (2008) 4(1) European Competition Journal 169.

[49] L Y J M Parret (n48).

[50] R Van den Bergh and P D Camesasca, *European Competition Law and Economics. A Comparative Perspective* (Antwerp: Intersentia 2001) 70.

and anticompetitive effects. 'Black and white' prohibitions have become less common and a more dynamic approach has come to the forefront, with the agency having to demonstrate this balancing act and the positive results of its intervention.

This economic approach has consequences for independent agencies as they now have to devote more attention to the economic proof of their reasoning, and to substantiate their case with sufficient economic evidence, in order to demonstrate the effects they claim the case has or will have on the market. This raises the standard of proof. It is not only a matter of providing more economic assessments; these assessments must also be substantiated by sufficient facts. The theory of harm has to be substantiated by and applied to the facts (it is in the end all about the facts). As mentioned earlier, the standard of judicial review cannot be studied in isolation from issues relating to evidence, and the rules on the standard and burden of proof.

The intensity of the review has immediate consequences for the evidence required to substantiate allegations. Decisions based solely on form or economic analysis will not be upheld in court as the latter will subject these decisions to critical review and demand more actual proof to justify interventions by the European Commission or national market and competition authorities. In the case, for example, of an infringement of Article 101(1) TFEU, the burden of proof, according to ECJ case law, is on the independent agency alleging the infringement.[51] The ECJ has held that for the European Commission to establish a breach, 'sufficiently precise and coherent proof' must be produced.[52] The economic-based approach stresses a need for more economic analysis and, therefore, a need for more use of economic evidence. It requires the restrictive effects of the agreement to be weighed against the economic benefits and efficiencies created by the agreement. This automatically sets a higher standard for and imposes a higher burden of economic proof on independent agencies.

This may result in what is referred to as the 'proof paradox':[53] intervention by competition or market authorities is considered necessary, but a (too) strict approach towards rules on evidence can result in insufficient enforcement of the competition or market rules.[54] This in turn can lead to

[51] See also Article 2 of Regulation 1/2003.

[52] Joined cases 29/83 and 30/83 *Compagnie Royale Asturienne des Mines SA and Rheinzink GmbH v Commission of the European Communities* [1984] ECR 1679.

[53] See also L Y J M Parret (n48).

[54] See also: D M B Gerard, 'The Effects-Based Approach under the Article 101 TFEU and its Paradoxes: Modernization at War With Itself?' in J Bourgeois and D Waelbroeck, *Ten Years of Effects-Based Approach in EU Competition Law. State of Play and Perspectives* (Bruges: College of Europe, Global Competition Law Centre 2013) 32–34. Gerard identifies the drop in enforcement activity and the increase in enforcement and justification costs as paradoxes, although he argues

ineffective market control. How can the right balance be found between the need for sufficient economic proof and the need for effective oversight and regulation of the market? Which specific rules on proof should be developed to reconcile the need for a more economic approach with the need for effective market regulation? A more economic approach in competition law and regulatory cases requires more economic-based evidence and can consequently lead to a more critical approach by European and national courts analysing decisions taken by independent agencies. As the analysis in the following section shows, the focus on economic evidence in economic cases has resulted in a more intense judicial review, at least in national regulatory and competition cases.

Review by the courts in practice

It could be concluded from analyses of case law of the European courts and courts in the Netherlands and the United Kingdom that courts apply a fairly comprehensive review, both in punitive decisions and in regulatory cases. They closely examine matters of law, fact, and procedure. A certain margin of appreciation is allowed in some, but not all, cases involving a complex assessment of non-legal issues, notably with regard to economic or scientific evidence. However, there are many examples of national courts requiring independent agencies to provide substantial factual and economic evidence in substantiation of their cases.

Competition cases

The standard case in which the ECJ set out its formula for reviewing competition decisions by the European Commission is the *Tetra Laval* case.[55] Here the ECJ stated that proof of anticompetitive conglomerate effects of a merger of the kind notified called for a precise examination, supported by convincing evidence, of the circumstances allegedly producing those effects. The ECJ considered that:

> Whilst the Court recognizes that the Commission has a margin of discretion with regard to economic matters, that does not mean that the Community Courts must refrain from reviewing the Commission's interpretation of information of an economic nature. Not only must the Community Courts, inter alia, establish whether the evidence relied on is factually accurate, reliable and consistent but also whether that evidence contains all the information which must be taken into account in

that the EU Court of Justice remains rather conservative in its approach and mainly follows an object-based approach.

[55] Case C-12/03P *Commission of the European Communities v Tetra Laval BV* [2005] ECR I-987.

order to assess a complex situation and whether it is capable of substantiating the conclusions drawn from it. Such a review is all the more necessary in the case of a prospective analysis required when examining a planned merger with conglomerate effect.[56]

Although this consideration was made in a merger case (involving an *ex ante* assessment by the European Commission rather than a penalty decision), this judgement is seen as a landmark case, in which the ECJ clearly focused more on the effects required to be proven by the European Commission and the evidence to be produced to substantiate those effects.[57] Analysing this standard of review shows that the ECJ did more than just a marginal review. Although some margin of discretion is available, the test applied is quite substantive. The court in the *Tetra Laval* case conducted a detailed examination of the European Commission's decision. Where the competition authority's assessment is based on conclusions drawn from primary facts, more limited discretion is allowed, while a greater margin is permitted in cases involving pure economic assessments.[58] In practice, however, the distinction between the review of factual findings and the appraisal of an economic nature (what do economists contribute?) will not always be easy to draw. In the famous *Microsoft* case the European General Court (EGC)[59] also followed this standard, although it attracted criticism for in reality undertaking only a limited review of the decision.[60]

The same review criteria as in *Tetra Laval* were used by the Dutch Trade and Industry Appeals Tribunal (CBb)[61] in the *Nuon/Reliant* merger case,[62] where the CBb annulled the decision of the former Dutch competition

[56] See paragraph 39 of the judgement.

[57] Later followed by the judgement of the General Court in the case of an abuse of dominant position by Microsoft: Case T-201/04 *Microsoft v Commission*, judgement of 17 September 2007 [2007] ECR II-3601, at paragraph 89. The General Court has since repeated this formulation in several article 102 cases, notably in the case *AstraZeneca*: Case T-321/05 *AstraZeneca v Commission*, judgement of 1 July 2010 [2010] ECR II-02805; and similarly under the EU merger regulation the Case T-210/01 *General Electric v Commission*, judgement of 14 December 2005, [2005] ECR II-5575. However, in the *Intel* case (on rebates), the General Court has followed clearly an object-based approach, without looking into the effects: Case T-286/09 12 June 2014, not yet published. This object-based approach is clearly confirmed by the ECJ in Case C-67/13 P *Groupement de Cartes bancaires v Commission,* 11 September 2014, not yet published.

[58] B Vesterdorf (n45) 22.

[59] A constituent court of the ECJ since the Lisbon Treaty became effective on 1 December 2009. Previously, it was known as the European Court of First Instance.

[60] *Microsoft v Commission* (n57) paragraphs 88–89. See also D Edward, 'Quality Control of Competition Decisions' in M Bulterman et al (eds), *Views of European Law from the Mountain* (Liber Amicorum Piet Jan Slot Kluwer Law International 2009).

[61] The Dutch CBb is a specialized administrative court which rules on appeals in competition law cases amongst other things.

[62] CBb, 28 November 2006, AWB 05/440, *Nuon/Reliant*, LJN: AZ3274.

authority NMa. The appeals tribunal found that the NMa had used too abstract a methodology to substantiate its findings on the market and should provide more factual evidence to specify the circumstances of the market concerned and the possible effects that the merger may have on the position of the relevant enterprises.

In cases involving the abuse of a dominant position the Dutch competition courts also seem to adopt a more economic approach, which results in the evidence produced by the national competition authority being subject to critical review. In the case of *CRV Holding BV*,[63] for example, the Court of First Instance in Rotterdam required the NMa to investigate both the demand side of the relevant market and whether it was difficult for other parties to make competitive offers. Instead of simply accepting that a discount can in principle lead to protection of the market, the court required the NMa to present proof that such results actually occurred (i.e. to demonstrate the actual effects on competitors). The theoretical and mathematical proof produced by the NMa was considered insufficient by the court.[64]

In cartel cases, too, the CBb[65] has followed the standard set in *Tetra Laval*. The standard applied in the *T-Mobile* case, for example, was very similar to that used in *Tetra Laval*[66] in that the CBb carefully reviewed the NMa's decision and concluded that the latter had failed to demonstrate that the mobile operators were engaged in a concerted practice with regard to the conditions and prices of prepaid connections. This was also done in, for example, the case involving a cartel between flour companies, in which the CBb carefully examined the facts and the evidence presented of the alleged cartel.[67]

UK law explicitly states the need for a full review of the case on its merits.[68] In practice, too, the CAT intensively scrutinizes decisions (previously taken by the OFT) in cartel cases. An example of this is the *Tobacco* case, where the appeals tribunal intensively scrutinized the facts of the case and concluded that the factual evidence put before the court did not support its economic analysis of the tobacco product sale agreements at stake.[69] The

[63] CBb, 4 juli 2007, MEDED 05/3911-STRN, *CRV Holding BV*, LJN: BA9164.

[64] This case eventually went to appeal, with CRV Holding filing for appeal on 5 July 2007. See *CRV Holding NMa*, LJN BN9947.

[65] In competition cases an appeal can be made in two instances: to the specialized District Court of Rotterdam and after that first appeal to the highest administrative court in competition and regulation cases, the CBb, established in The Hague.

[66] See CBb, 12 August 2010,AWB 06/657, 06/660 and 06/661, *T-Mobile et al*, LJN BN3895.

[67] Rechtbank Rotterdam, ECLI:NL:RBROT:2014:5822

[68] See M Smith 'Standards of Review and Appeal in Cases Before the Competition Appeal Tribunal' (2012) 3 Competition Law 169.

[69] See the joint cases: (1) *Imperial Tobacco Group plc* (2) *Imperial Tobacco Limited v Office of Fair Trading*, Case No. 1160/1/1/10 <http://www.catribunal.org.uk/237-6574/1160-1-1-10-1-Imperial-Tobacco-Group-plc-2-Imperial-Tobacco-Limited.html> accessed 26 September 2014.

CAT heard witnesses (including twenty days of witness testimony under cross-examination), thus allowing the possibility of different interpretations of the facts. During the course of the proceedings it became clear that the evidence presented by the OFT did not support the novel analysis and theory of harm on which the OFT had based its final decision to fine the companies. This case illustrates how extensively the CAT examines the facts.[70] The standard of proof applied by the CAT is based on the balance of probabilities. Any doubt as to whether a point is established on the balance of probabilities must, in the CAT's view, operate to the advantage of the enterprise alleged to have infringed the competition rules.[71] The more innovative or controversial the theory of harm used in the decision is, the more critically the CAT will analyse the reasoning applied by the competition authority. Comparing the CAT's review with the review by the ECJ and the EGC, it must be concluded that the CAT conducts a fuller review on the merits of the case.

Market regulation cases

A similar tendency can be seen in market regulation cases, where independent agencies have the right to intervene in specific markets, including telecommuniations, energy, and transport. Economic proof plays an increasingly important role in these cases. These agencies are expected to apply the regulation effectively in order to ensure a level playing field in the sector concerned. How to measure regulatory effects is, however, a complicated matter. Regulatory bodies need, for example, to make reliable estimates of the efficiency potential of their intervention, to calculate the efficient level of costs, and to measure the gains in terms of consumer prosperity. An illustrative example in this respect is the Dutch mobile phone case,[72] where the CBb required OPTA, the former Dutch independent post and telecommunications authority, to provide sufficient evidence ('careful study and sound argumentation') that its intervention in mobile termination rates resulted in benefits for end users and positive societal effects. The appeals tribunal ruled that OPTA had not assessed these effects sufficiently, while also considering that the obligations imposed had far-reaching consequences and needed a more in-depth study in order to prevent infringement of the principle of legal certainty.

The prospective nature of the analysis that market regulators have to conduct when examining the market structure and the positions of the relevant

[70] For another case where the CAT has done so: CAT 20 December 2012 *Tesco v OFT*, Case No. 1188/1/1/11.

[71] *Tesco* case (n70) paragraph 88.

[72] CBb, 29 August 2006, AWB 05/903 and 05/921-05/931, *Dutch mobile* case, LJN: AY7997.

market players constitutes a complicating factor.[73] They have to make a forward-looking analysis that takes account of the dynamics of the market throughout the regulatory period (normally three years). The question arises as to whether this prospective character has legal consequences for the standard of proof. These cases involve the imposition of *ex ante* regulation and contrast with *ex post* interventions, where independent agencies draw conclusions on the basis of past behaviour. As seen in the section cited from the ECJ judgement in the *Tetra Laval* case, the ECJ takes the view that the prospective aspect of the decision should result in the decision being subject to a more intense review.[74]

The CAT also conducts a full review on the merits in regulatory cases and subjects the substance of the decision to scrutiny:

> However, this is an appeal on the merits and the Tribunal is not concerned solely with whether the 2007 Statement [a decision of OFCOM being appealed under section 192] is adequately reasoned but also whether those reasons are correct. This Tribunal accepts the point made by H3G in their reply on the SMP [significant market power] and Appropriate Remedy issues that it is a specialist court designed to be able to scrutinise the detail of regulatory decisions in a profound and rigorous manner. The question of the Tribunal is not whether the decision to impose a price control was within the range of reasonable responses but whether the decision was the right one.[75]

In cases, however, where there are a number of different approaches to a dispute, all of which can be regarded as legitimate and appropriate, the CAT will 'be slow to overturn a decision',[76] while still conducting a review of the decision on its merits. If there is no single 'right answer', and particularly if the independent agency is seeking to articulate policy preferences compliant with its statutory duties, the CAT will not interfere. The same approach was used in the *Tele2* case in the Netherlands, where the CBb ruled that the methodology followed by the Netherlands Authority for Consumers & Markets (ACM, succeeded OPTA in telecoms oversight; see chapter 4) was reasonable, although different options or deviations from this methodology were possible.[77]

[73] A T Ottow, *Telecommunicatietoezicht. De invloed van het Europese en Nederlandse bestuurs(proces)recht* (dissertation, University of Amsterdam, The Hague: SDU 2006) 232–51.

[74] The national courts are in principle not obliged to follow the same standard of review as the Court of Justice, as established in the *Tetra Laval* case (n55).

[75] *T-Mobile, BT, Hutchinson 3G, Cable & Wireless and others v OFCOM*, Case Nos. 1089/3/3/07, 1090/3/3/07, 1091/3/3/07, 1092/3/3/07, [2008] CAT 12, at paragraph 82.

[76] See the cases: No. 1046/2/4/04 [2008] CAT 31, [2009] CompAR 28, at paragraph 72 and *BT v OFCOM*, Case No. 1151/3/3/10 [2011] CAT 24, at paragraph 230.

[77] CBb 17 July 2014, *Tele2 v ACM*, Case 13/459, ECLI:NL:CBB:2014:285.

A specific, but not insignificant detail in the case of communications is the special requirement imposed by Article 4 of the EU Communications Framework Directive.[78] This article was adopted in accordance with the ECJ principle of effective judicial protection and stipulates various minimum requirements for the right to appeal against national independent agencies' decisions. It has consequences for the intensity of the judicial review, requiring that 'the merits of the case are duly taken into account'. This means that a limited judicial review is insufficient. Case law of the Court of Rotterdam and the CBb regarding decisions by the Dutch telecoms regulator at the time (OPTA, now ACM), indicates that despite the existence of discretionary powers, strict requirements apply to evidence to be submitted and to the grounds underlying decisions. Such judicial reviews cannot, therefore, be regarded as limited. The judicial review applied in such cases would appear to meet the requirements of Article 4 of the Framework Directive. A full review by the CAT on the merits of the case can consequently be regarded as being in accordance with the requirements of Article 4.[79]

Conclusion

The ongoing trends and developments in judicial review raise the question of whether the focus on economic proof and the heavier burden of proof still allow independent agencies to produce results that lead to more efficient and dynamic markets. It has been argued that an independent agency should have a wide margin of discretion to decide on complex economic matters.[80] The essential function of evidence is to establish convincingly the merits of an argument or a decision in general. The question, however, is what the requisite standard of review and the standard of proof should be in order to provide the agency on the one hand with sufficient flexibility to assess

[78] Directive 2009/140/EC of the European Parliament and of the Council of 25 November 2009 amending Directives 2002/21/EC on a common regulatory framework for electronic communications networks and services, 2002/19/EC on access to, and interconnection of, electronic communications networks and associated facilities, and 2002/20/EC on the authorisation of electronic communications networks and services [2009] OJ L337/68; see also: A T Ottow, *Telecommunicatietoezicht* (n73).

[79] As established by the CAT in the case: Supreme Court of Judicature Court of Appeal (Civil Division) on appeal from the CAT, *T-Mobile (UK) v Ofcom*, 12 December 2008, Case Nos. C1/2008/2257, 2257 (A) and 2258. See for a critical analysis of the consultation of the Department for Business, Innovation & Skills (BIS) on streamlining regulatory and competition appeals, where it is questioned whether the full review should stay: J Aitken and R Romney, 'Quis Custodiet ipsos Custodes? Do Proposed Reforms Risk Undermining Confidence in UK Competition and Communications Appeals?' (2013) 4 Competition Law 389.

[80] A T Ottow, *Telecommunicatietoezicht* (n73) 97–111.

and establish the required competitive conditions in the relevant market (cf. principle of effectiveness), but on the other hand to create a sufficient legal protection against the decision of the agency (cf. principle of legality). Should the standard of proof be 'convincing', 'not incomprehensible', or 'beyond any reasonable doubt'? These differing criteria reflect the different views on the position of independent agencies and the intensity of the judicial review of their decisions.

While the ECJ recognized in the *Tetra Laval* case that the European Commission has a margin of discretion with regard to economic matters, that does not mean that courts must wholly refrain from reviewing market and competition authorities' interpretation of information of an economic nature. In my view, the standard set by the ECJ in *Tetra Laval* adequately balances the interests of effective judicial protection on the one hand and effective oversight on the other hand. Market and competition authorities must be given some leeway and discretion to make the necessary technical assessment, while still continuing to take their policy objectives into account. At the same time their analysis must be critically checked against law and the facts. Not only must courts establish inter alia whether the evidence relied on is factually accurate, reliable, and consistent, but they must also determine whether that evidence contains all the information to be taken into account when assessing complex situations, and decide whether this evidence can substantiate the conclusions drawn from it. According to the ECJ, such a review is all the more necessary in the case of a prospective analysis. In recent years both the ECJ and the EGC have shown little reluctance to subject relatively complex legal and economic assessments in merger cases to review.[81] In this respect, the ECJ's *Tetra Laval* judgement, in which it sanctioned a remarkably intense review and the subsequent overturning of a European Commission merger decision by the EGC (at the time acting as the European Court of First Instance), can be seen as illustrative. Although intense, this EGC review was significantly less intense than the reviews on the merits the CAT is used to do. Many decisions in cases that have come before the CAT have, however, been annulled on the grounds of insufficent evidence. It would nevertheless seem sensible to require such a review on the facts to be conducted in all cases.

As Laguna de Paz[82] correctly points out, a court is not a competition or market authority: it can make many choices, none of which may be wrong.

[81] For an overview of the case law, see for example B Vesterdorf (n45). He is of the opinion that the Court of Justice has done this in all cases and that there is no real change in its case law over the recent years. See also: D Bailey, 'Standard of Judicial Review Under Articles 101 and 102 TFEU' in M Merola and J Derenne (n24) 103.

[82] J Laguna de Paz (n26).

The assessment of complex and technical matters can have different outcomes, none of which is right or wrong. This degree of margin must be allowed to independent agencies, while also leaving courts scope to demonstrate any manifest error of assessment. By doing so, the courts fulfil their duty to provide the necessary checks and balances, thus counterbalancing the independence of the market and competition authorities, while at the same time respecting the function and role of these independent agencies.

Liability of Independent Agencies

This section makes some comments and discusses case law on the liability of independent agencies. Its aim is not to examine all the legal aspects of liability, but rather to identify certain situations in which the actions or behaviour of independent agencies should give rise to liability. These are not situations in which decisions by agencies are annulled by administrative courts, as discussed in the previous section. Instead the focus is on those special cases where factual actions, such as the publication of information, or the agency's inactivity, may result in loss or damage for third parties. In most countries the basis for this liability is tort law, whereby the civil court has to examine the matter. These liability issues are discussed here in relation to the LITER principles and on the basis of cases from the Netherlands and the United Kingdom.

Grounds for liability

For liability to be established on the basis of tort law, the following elements essentially need to be present: (i) a breach of the independent agency's duty of care to the claimant; (ii) negligence by the independent agency; and (iii) the claimant's suffering of actual damage as a result of that negligence. This section discusses only the issue of negligence by the independent agency, as the key element in the agency's behaviour. Negligence constitutes the failure by an institution to act in the way that a comparable institution, displaying a normal degree of care, would act in the same circumstances. There are two different types of negligence: nonfeasance and misfeasance. Nonfeasance means neglecting a situation by omitting to take action required. Failure by an independent agency to act may constitute negligence and thus give rise to liability.[83]

[83] C van Dam, *Liability of Regulators* (British Institute of International and Competition Law, Report commissioned by the Research and Documentation Centre of the Netherlands Ministry of Justice 2006).

Misfeasance on the other hand means acting wrongfully,[84] for example by making a false or incorrect public announcement.

Negligence: nonfeasance

The *Vie d'Or* case[85] is the standard case in the Netherlands with regard to the first category of negligence. In this liability case it was claimed that the Dutch Insurance Chamber, the administrative authority previously responsible for supervising insurance companies, had failed to perform its statutory task as a supervising agency by failing to appoint a silent administrator in good time, despite the severe financial difficulties being suffered by the insurance company concerned. The court established a series of criteria for determining whether failure to perform a discretionary task could give rise to liability:

> The Insurance Chamber enjoys considerable policy freedom and discretion in performing its oversight and deciding whether to use the statutory powers that it has been granted in this respect. [...] This policy freedom and discretion means the court should adopt a restrained approach to reviewing decisions. What is at stake is not whether, in retrospect, a different decision would have been better, or whether this could have prevented a third party suffering damage as a result of the insurance company's ultimate collapse, but rather whether the Insurance Chamber was reasonable in arriving at its decision in the prevailing circumstances and given the knowledge available at the time [...].[86]

The court explicitly stated that the financial market authority needed to weigh the interests of the individual policyholders against the general public interest ('societal interests') and that the measures to be taken had to be effective and proportionate.[87] If discretionary powers were involved, the court would only review the case marginally and liability would be established only if the chamber failed to act 'in a reasonable way'. Although the court took all facts into consideration, it also emphasized that the mere

[84] H W R Wade and C Forsyth, *Administrative Law* (9th edn, Oxford: Oxford University Press 2004).

[85] *Vie d'Or* case, LJN AP0151

[86] Translated from the Dutch original taken from *Vie d'Or* (n85) paragraph 7.2.

[87] The court also refers to what it calls the 'supervisory dilemma', which is a specific problem for financial market authorities. This dilemma is that 'the supervisory authority has to find a balance between conflicting interests, which are intrinsically connected with the basic objectives of prudential regulation: on the one hand, maintaining the safety and soundness of financial institutions and the financial system as a whole; on the other hand, protecting the depositors and other creditors of financial institutions'. This quote is from M Tison, 'Challenging the Prudential Supervisor: Liability versus (Regulatory) Immunity' (2004) Gent University, Financial Law Institute Working Paper Series, WP 2003-04 2004.

existence of a negative outcome could not be the sole reason for holding an institution liable.

Negligence: misfeasance

Two cases from the United Kingdom can be mentioned in relation to misfeasance. Both concern the failure to supervise a bank effectively. Third parties claimed that the Bank of England's Banking Supervision Department acted in bad faith when issuing a licence to a specific financial institution as it should have known that the financial position of that institution did not justify such a licence. In *Three Rivers District Council v Bank of England*[88] it was ruled that misfeasance could be established if two factors could be proven: the supervising authority's knowledge of the unlawfulness of its actions, and the supervising authority's awareness of the consequences of its actions. With regard to the first factor, it had to be established that the financial market authority had actual knowledge of the unlawfulness or demonstrated 'reckless indifference' to the lawfulness or otherwise of its actions. The same test applied with regard to the awareness of the consequences, and the financial market authority had to have had knowledge of or demonstrated reckless indifference to the possible consequences.[89] The 'bad faith' criterion was also considered to be proven by the elements of the tort (i.e. knowledge of unlawfulness and its consequences), with no requirement for specific dishonesty. In this case the court considered there to be no negligence on the part of the Bank of England.

Another case on misfeasance is that of *Davis v Radcliffe*,[90] in which several claimants argued that the damage they suffered (in the form of lost deposits following the revoking of a bank's licence) was caused by the supervising authority's negligence or the breach of its statutory duty. The court considered that the tasks of the financial market authority were laid down in law and were typical of modern government, and that those laws established some degree of protection for third parties. However, it was not only the interests of the third parties (in this case, the customers and creditors of the bank), but also, in this specific case, the future of the financial services sector that had to be considered. Any competing interests had to be carefully weighed and balanced against the background of the public interest. The

[88] *Three Rivers District Council and others v Governor and Company of the Bank of England* [2000] 2 WLR 1220

[89] The court claimed that 'reasonable foreseeability', i.e. inadvertent recklessness, was not enough to establish the supervising authority had in fact been acting recklessly with regard to the possible consequences. There needed to be a subjective sense of awareness with regard to the supervising authority's reckless behaviour.

[90] *Davis v Radcliffe* [1990] 1 WLR 821.

court emphasized that decisions taken by such supervising authorities, where they were required to take the public interest into account, could not be based on a duty of care in favour of a particular group. The court ultimately ruled that there was no reasonable cause of action based on negligence by the financial market authority and no breach of a statutory duty.[91]

Two Dutch cases relating to misfeasance concern the issue of a press release (*Accel Group v NMa*)[92] and publication of information on a website (*KPN Telecom v OPTA).*[93] In the *Accel Group* case, the NMa issued a statement of objection claiming that four companies had made price-fixing arrangements and exchanged commercially sensitive information. The NMa issued a press release based on this statement of objection (which did not constitute the final decision in the case). As the Accel Group did not receive the press release until shortly before publication, it did not have any time to comment on the text. The companies affected subsequently claimed in court that they had suffered damage both from the statement of objection and from the press release. The court first established that the press release was based solely on suspicions, without the companies having had any chance to respond prior to publication, thus putting the presumption of innocence in jeopardy. The supervisees should have had the opportunity to rectify any inconsistencies or to respond to the NMa's allegations. The NMa should consequently have notified the supervisees in advance of the forthcoming press release and given them the chance to comment on the draft. The text of the press release should also have taken into account that 'the public' would have interpreted the text as if the infringement had already been established in a final decision by the competition authority, which was clearly not the case. The court thus concluded, given both the contents and timing of the press release, that the statement was unlawful.

In the *KPN Telecom v OPTA* case,[94] OPTA published factually incorrect statements about KPN Telecom (specifically an incorrect comparison of prices) on its website. Even though the court stressed that not all incorrect statements published by a government institution were unlawful, this could be the case under certain circumstances. An important factor to be considered is that publication of prices will be taken seriously by consumers if this is done by a specialized agency entrusted with supervising the telecommunications market. In view of its reputation and independence, consumers

[91] See for restricted liability in the Netherlands: *Wet aansprakelijkheidsbeperking DNB en AFM en bonusverbod staatsgesteunde ondernemingen* <http://wetten.overheid.nl/BWBR0031680/geldigheidsdatum_26-09-2014> accessed 26 September 2014.

[92] *Accel group v NMa*, 24 February 2005, ECLI:NL:GHSGR:2005:AS9694.

[93] *KPN Telecom v OPTA*, 14 April 2005, ECLI:NL:GHSGR:2005:AT3883.

[94] ibid.

will take more notice of information published by the independent agency than of information published by the enterprise. The civil court considered the following:

> The issue here concerns statements by an autonomous administrative authority that, in view of its name and the way it presents itself externally, will be regarded by the public as an independent government body and also as 'authoritative'. The public will consequently assign greater weight to and be more likely to trust statements/information published by OPTA than statements made by a commercial enterprise.[95]

The independent agency—in this case, OPTA—consequently needed to act very cautiously when publishing factual information on its website or providing information to consumers. The authority that the agency is perceived to have is, therefore, an important aspect.

The LITER Principles in the Context of Liability

How can the liability of independent agencies be evaluated in the light of the good agency principles? It follows from case law that courts are generally reluctant to hold such agencies liable. This is understandable, given that the agency must be free to perform its tasks, and that these can involve dilemmas and risks, as well as the need to weigh different interests against each other. As discussed, trade-offs will in practice be required, and this means that not all interests can be served to an equal degree. The risk of being held liable could make an agency afraid to take action or to expose itself to risk, thus resulting either in no enforcement or in a highly cautious or defensive independent agency. The legality principle protects the independent agency against unforeseen consequences in this respect. Although there is a general duty of care, a breach of this duty will generally lead to liability only if the independent agency acts recklessly or behaves unreasonably. At the same time the risk of being held liable can also act as an incentive for agencies to behave carefully. Being exposed to this risk may have a certain deterrent effect and, from that perspective, be seen as an effective tool for keeping the agency sharp.[96] Liability, however, may lead to extra costs for society and these may outweigh the benefits for the party concerned. In the light of their legal mandate and duties, and their independence, the courts clearly play an important role in terms of the monitoring of independent

[95] Translated from the Dutch original taken from *KPN Telecom v OPTA* (n93) paragraph 18.

[96] I Giesen, 'Regulating Regulators Through Liability. The Case for Applying Normal Tort Rules to Supervisors' (2006) 2(1) Utrecht Law Review 8.

agencies. As discussed earlier, review by the courts is an important countervailing power for controlling agencies' independence in a democratic society. Having their actions subject to court review means that these agencies can be held accountable for their actions and omissions and that cases will come out into the open. This function will be lost, however, if agencies are completely excluded from liability.

Although liability could be sufficient to ensure that independent agencies behave responsibly and provide more transparency on their performance,[97] the courts are right, in my view, also to take account of the discretionary powers of and the dilemmas facing these agencies. Their societal responsibility is key in this respect. Courts recognize that institutions entrusted with this kind of responsibility face a difficult task in seeking to serve the public interest and have to weigh different interests against each other. However, this responsibility also means that the public will assign greater weight to and be more likely to trust statements and information published by the agency. The special position these agencies have in society means they consequently have to take extra care when publishing information and must ensure that it is correct and not misleading. Supervising agencies are vested with this responsibility to society or, coined in a more or less familiar phrase, with 'good agency social responsibility'.

Conclusion

Set off against the framework of the LITER principles, evaluations, assessments, and reviews of agency decisions by committees and courts play a decisive role in ensuring that the work of independent agencies testifies to good agency behaviour. Evaluations by committees and reviews by the courts are of significant importance to guarantee independent agencies do their jobs transparently. These agencies have to account for their actions, interventions, and behaviour, not only so as to provide lessons for the future, but also to ensure that they act carefully and give sufficient reasoning for their decisions. The scrutinizing of independent agencies is a healthy mechanism that not only creates countervailing powers, but also strengthens the legitimacy of these institutions. When reviewing agencies' actions, account must be taken of the special functions and roles that they have as a result of their independent position in society. There are two sides to this special

[97] E Hüpkes, M Quintyn, and M W Taylor, 'Accountability Arrangements for Financial Sector Regulators' (2006) 39 International Monetary Fund Economic Issues series.

position: on the one hand agencies must be allowed some degree of discretion and it must be realized that they have to weigh different interests against each other, while on the other hand an agency's position entails a degree of authority that creates more responsibility and, therefore, in some cases can lead to liability.

7

Conclusions and Recommendations

Introduction

In reality, there is no such thing as a model agency. Circumstances are never ideal, while powers assigned to an agency are never complete, conflicts of interest occur, trade-offs have to be made, and budgets and capacity are never sufficient. This, however, is the environment in which market, competition, and consumer authorities have to operate and, with these limitations in mind, the environment in which they have to strive to optimize their performance, taking account of the good agency or LITER principles: the principles of legality (L), independence (I), transparency (T), effectiveness (E), and responsibility (R).

In doing so, they need support and assistance from legislators and policymakers to create the right framework in the form of clear regulatory and competition goals and values, the required legal mandate, and the optimal institutional structure; or, in a mantric order of things: goals, values, mandate, structure. Stakeholders such as supervised enterprises, third parties, stakeholders' associations, consumers, and the courts will monitor the activities of and interventions by independent agencies critically. And rightly so, since these organizations and individuals hold up a mirror to the agency and serve as a countervailing power. An agency's independence should not be taken for granted: in a democratic society, it must be counterbalanced by accountability and controls in order to create the correct institutional balance.

However, stakeholders' expectations also need to be realistic. Oversight is not a panacea for all ills. Although compliance behaviour can and must be encouraged by independent agencies, it also has to be acknowledged that this is a shared responsibility. Enterprises and consumers need to accept their responsibilities and to share the burden of regulation and compliance by taking measures of their own to prevent harm or damage and avoid high-risk behaviour. Agencies for their part need to set the right example by devising and operating internal ethical codes of conduct, demonstrating their compliance with integrity standards, and avoiding conflicts of interest or capture of the organization itself.

What can independent agencies do to adhere to the LITER or good agency principles? This chapter summarizes the key issues that, in my view, form the basic ingredients for success. The most important recommendations in the book are briefly reiterated here to create a check list for agencies, legislators, governments, policymakers, and courts.

Key Issues for Independent Agencies

The red thread in the life of an independent agency is the continual need to balance different interests and demands (public versus private) and different goals (short-term versus long-term), while combining carefulness with effectiveness (procedural fairness versus efficiency) and selecting the appropriate enforcement strategy (cooperation versus repression). In my opinion, the need to balance rights and obligations, weighing the safeguard and instrumental dimensions of the LITER principles, constitutes the biggest challenge in the day-to-day life of an agency. An agency following the LITER principles will have to adapt these principles to suit the role that is at play. This book identifies five different roles in this respect: the advisory, advocacy, reflective, preventive, and repressive roles:

1. *Advisory role*: advising the government, other agencies, the general public, and enterprises being supervised.
2. *Advocacy role*: educating the general public and government to create a sound regulatory and competition culture, and good practices.
3. *Reflective role*: timely reflecting on risks and problems in markets and society, with proposals for solutions and measures.
4. *Preventive role*: preventing harm and infringements as the key to ensuring that rules achieve their goals.
5. *Repressive role*: ensuring that rules are complied with and that any infringements are punished.

Each of these roles requires a different set of skills and experience and may require adherence to different aspects of the LITER principles. Some principles will come more to the forefront than others, depending on the role and the circumstances at the time. An agency consequently has to have the flexibility to switch, where necessary, from one role to another, and to combine functions and skills.

Independence is key

To gain authority and achieve impartial outcomes, an agency must ensure not only that it has *de jure* independence, but also that its behaviour assures it of *de facto* independence. It is up to agencies themselves to ensure they retain their independence. This requires rules and procedures on integrity so as to prevent capture and inappropriate or unethical activity. Integrity must be high on the agenda of any agency's board, with the board members themselves practising transparency by compiling, for example, a board members' affiliation register. This can be ensured through procedures on compliance, as well as by setting rules for dealing with conflicts of interest, budgetary expenditure, reimbursement of expenses, travel costs, and so on. Agencies need to set the right example and create respect and, by doing so, gain authority. Failing to gain or losing this authority will have severe consequences, even if all the requisite statutory powers, budgets, and instruments are in place. The organization will then fail to function properly. Although it is vital to be able to show that all the structures required to prevent such failure are present, no organization can entirely exclude the possibility of an incident or form of misbehaviour. Personal and (IT!) system integrity should therefore be a top priority.

In addition to internal ethics, it is also vital to have measures preventing capture in place. Staff rotating in flexible teams and organizing a fresh pair of expert eyes can improve impartiality and prevent the development of tunnel vision or bias. Although it is understandable for agencies to focus on achieving results—enforcement is, after all, their core business and what society expects from them—agencies can easily be blamed for pro-enforcement bias if they are too much results-oriented. Their decisions must instead be balanced and take account of all relevant facts and the evidence presented. Straightforward as this may seem, facts can in practice be interpreted in a narrow, one-dimensional way, while important facts may be overlooked or omitted. Indeed, most cases that come before courts and are lost, are unsuccessful because of insufficient evidence.

Independence does not mean working from an ivory tower. Instead it requires openness, and sharing and receiving ideas and information with and from others, through all kinds of stakeholder participation and consultation. As a result, an agency does take decisions on its own account, but these decisions are well informed. In addition, independence requires a sense of political sensitivity and an understanding of the governmental environment, as well as good working relationships with ministers and their staff. The advocacy and advisory roles will have much more impact if the independent agency knows what is going on at a governmental level and is asked for advice at timely moments. Investing in these government relationships is consequently essential for agencies, while each side also has to respect the other side's position and ensure it safeguards its own independence.

Define the strategy

Defining the independent agency's strategy creates focus and ensures that its long-term goals are made visible. If well prepared, a strategy reflects the values and principles that the agency itself, its staff, and the society it belongs to hold dear. Such a strategy clearly has an effect both internally and externally and gives the agency an identity. It also creates an opportunity to send out clear messages on both competition and regulation. As well as providing clarity on the organization's core business, the strategy also serves as a tool for communicating this message.

Identifying the central objectives and the steps needed to implement these objectives will provide the organization with a clear vision and encourage delivery along those lines. This is especially true for multifunctional agencies combining different fields (i.e. competition with consumer and/or regulatory tasks). An important condition for an independent agency to become more than just the sum of its constituent parts is for it to have a comprehensive strategic vision of its core identity. This vision should colour the regulatory and competition philosophy, both internally and externally, and create opportunities for cross-sector synergies. Formulating this strategy is consequently a key element of the integration process and the focus of a multifunctional agency, while also being an important way to prevent silos and to encourage cross-fertilization within the agency.

By setting out its strategy and making choices clear, an independent agency can manage expectations, as formulating its strategy means making and communicating choices concerning the agency's behaviour and performance, and the outputs and outcomes it aims for. During this process the agency needs to consult stakeholders and create a sense of internal commitment at all levels. A bottom-up approach should be used to develop the strategy, which should be inspired by experts in the field and interested parties who need to comply with the rules and understand the problems and risks in the relevant markets.

Enforcement choices

It is important for independent agencies to have a balanced portfolio of cases, reflecting different levels of risk appetite. The selection of cases should answer to strategic enforcement choices, which in turn should be driven by the agency's overall strategy. The agency will therefore have to take account of the various tasks assigned to it and to allocate its capacity and budget accordingly. This requires flexible budgets, a project-based approach, and dynamic allocation of resources. Opting solely for smaller, easier cases will not demonstrate great overall effectiveness on the part of the agency. Multifunctional agencies in particular run the risk of choosing cases that will have the greatest political impact (consumer cases, for example) or the highest branding effects for the agency. Although agency branding is a legitimate practice, short-term media or political issues should be counterbalanced by strategically chosen issues that arrange for more long-term and fundamental solutions that serve larger target groups in society.

Prioritization is unavoidable and constitutes, by clearly stating choices, another method for the agency to manage expectations. It should in any event be clear, in view of the independence principle, that the agency itself must set its own priorities and select the cases it considers appropriate in the light of its overall strategy. Prioritization guidelines should be published in order to satisfy the legality and transparency principles; these guidelines should contain objective and general criteria that market and competition authorities can use as the basis for selecting their enforcement cases. Strategic planning is an import aspect of the prioritization process. Agencies must realize that the longer a case continues, the more difficult it is to decide that there is insufficient evidence to establish an infringement. Agencies should build in safeguards and introduce 'milestone moments' for 'stop/go' decisions. It is necessary to review planning and prioritization processes regularly and to harness counteracting safeguards in order to avoid allocating capacity to weak cases that cannot meet the required standards of proof.

Choosing the appropriate methods of enforcement is one of the most difficult tasks facing independent agencies, and is a daily struggle. Conflicting aims in the underlying regulations may also form an impediment to making the right enforcement choices. Various tools and instruments are available, and their effectiveness is not always conclusive. Although certain enforcement trends can be identified, these change over time, and choices made are greatly influenced by views on and in society and on the different roles that agencies, enterprises, and consumers should play in achieving compliance and reducing risks. Situations are never 'black and white'; instead, different combinations and choices have to be made in different circumstances. Approaches to oversight and the instruments considered most appropriate are in most cases complementary and need not be seen as mutually exclusive. Agencies should therefore attempt to find the right mix of instruments or, as I put it, perform customized enforcement.

In my opinion, it is important for an agency to take on an active role and to look for innovative, effective solutions to ensure compliance with the law and to achieve the goals of the legislation. In that search the agency has to respect the legal boundaries of its powers, and to set fair and transparent procedures. Whatever approach the agency adopts, it must be careful not to become tied to a choice for a specific form of enforcement. Indeed, problems and risks change over time, and flexibility is therefore needed from agencies, legislators, and policymakers. This in turn requires agencies to remain alert at all times and to subject any choices they make to critical examination. Enforcement also means more than just waiting for complaints or whistleblowers. Independent agencies need to take a proactive stand and to be alert to the need for initiative at all times. Participation of consumers and consumer associations, whether through social media or otherwise, and their involvement in setting the agenda and in identifying key issues will help ensure the necessary input from society.

Enforcement practice should not focus only on individual cases, but should also examine markets and the root causes of problems, and consider how these can be resolved. Agencies should not concentrate too much on their own statutory powers; instead they should also seek to involve other areas of expertise in order genuinely to resolve problems or, at least, to draw attention to the matter should their own powers fall short. Issues and problems need to be looked at from a broader perspective, following a more hybrid approach and, if necessary, coordinated with other agencies or institutions at a national, European, or even international level. Such complex issues for which different and more hybrid expert teams should be formed, call for separate steering groups. Enforcement should go hand in hand with a compliance strategy, whereby enterprises and governments are encouraged by the independent agency to ensure compliance with regulatory and competition rules.

As enforcement by independent agencies can have severe implications (in the form of sanctions) for supervised enterprises, special attention needs to be paid to the procedural fairness of the decision-making process and the proportionality of any sanctions. A delicate issue in this respect is the 'all-in-one-hand' system existing in many countries (including the Netherlands and the United Kingdom, as well as within the EU market and competition institutional framework), where the tasks of investigation, prosecution, and the imposition of sanctions are all in the hands of a single institution. This combination can result in prosecutorial bias. However, a complete separation between the investigation, prosecution, and sanctioning processes is not, in my view, the preferred option for remedying this risk. Such a strict separation will create extra costs and duplicate work, whereas it is possible to find solutions within a single, integrated organization.

It is crucial for the first-instance decision-making process to comply with the principles of legality, independence, and transparency, which can all be structured within the same agency. I regard the 'Chinese walls' models used in the Netherlands and the United Kingdom as satisfactory institutional-design options, even though they provide only minimal guarantees and safeguards. These agencies have to be sufficiently transparent so as to show that there is no interference between the two teams, and that their decision-making processes are governed by clear sets of rules. In my view however, the French example provides the best guarantees against bias within an integrated model, with a clear distinction being made between the two phases of investigating and sanctioning, and offering sufficient legal safeguards.

Invest in professionalism

Agencies must invest appropriate amounts in personnel, training, expertise, and information technology if they are to perform their tasks adequately. Overseeing markets requires professional expertise, with continuing professional development (CPD) being essential.

To create the right culture and professionalism within the organization, agencies could consider establishing an academy, either on a stand-alone basis or in conjunction with other agencies or educational institutes such as universities. An academy can take on responsibility for in-house training of staff, and for building relationships with fellow agencies and the academic world. Professional courses should be set up to provide education and training in skills and expertise for staff at all levels and of every degree of experience. These programmes will improve the organization's professionalism and that of its staff. This way an academy can play an important role in implementing the organization's strategy through education and training, and by ensuring a uniform style of enforcement and cooperation between and across departments. This in turn will result in better performance and increased independence, and thus improve the outcome of the agency's work.

Risk assessment

It is essential for risks to be identified, communicated, and managed, especially in important and challenging cases. Risks must be systematically and regularly reassessed, and reported to senior and executive management levels.

A specific issue relating to risks is the extent to which the board's decision-making powers can and should be delegated to lower levels of the organization. Delegation of decision-making processes is a delicate issue. In many cases it is the agency's board that has the formal powers to decide on cases. In practice, however, these powers are often delegated to other management levels of the organization, with the board remaining responsible for the outcome of the case and all decisions taken internally. In the event of errors, therefore, it is the board, and the agency as such, that can be held accountable (and, in some cases, liable) for decisions that prove to be wrong or for inappropriate action. Delegation of powers can give rise to risks if the expertise or experience at the delegated level is insufficient, and this aspect of risk needs to receive more attention from agency boards. It is essential for there to be sufficient expertise, experience, and knowledge at the delegated level, with the coordination of decisions within the organization guaranteed so as to ensure consistent and expert risk assessment.

In my opinion, boards should be kept informed of and responsible for all important issues facing the organization, and actively involved in the organization's most important decisions. This is because delegation has its limits and can create too great a distance between the board, senior management, and the rest of the organization. It is one of the major challenges for the board and senior management to delegate decision-making powers properly and to the right level for the job. Boards should therefore review and, where necessary, revise their delegation structures regularly, and assess whether powers have been delegated to the right level within the organization. There needs to be great commitment from the board and senior management, as well as from other parts of the organization with an interest in the issues arising. Procedures to safeguard these aspects must consequently be in place.

The reports discussed in the previous chapters make it clear that information technology frequently causes problems and can create substantial risks for an agency. These problems relate not only to the functioning of the IT systems as such (which can be a major obstacle to efficient integration in an agency merger process), but also to the safety of the systems (collection and storage of big, mostly confidential, data) and the gathering of forensic data (electronic evidence). Good detection and follow-up systems to detect developments in markets are indispensable in this respect and require substantial investments in forensic systems, data collection, and data research. The need for investments in information technology is often underestimated or even neglected, but IT can form a bottleneck in enforcement cases.

Agency mergers

In the specific case of agency mergers, special attention should be given to various institutional design aspects. Simply bringing agencies under a single, new roof will not automatically result in integration and greater efficiency. There is a risk that the previously separate agencies will operate as silos in the new organization and that cross-fertilization will be inadequate. Mergers undertaken with the sole aim of reducing costs, but without a clear vision on how to improve synergy and effectiveness, face a high risk of failure. A new design seeking integration on the basis of a clear vision and strategy is therefore necessary in order to provide focus and avoid rivalry between the different departments. The board's leadership is an important driving force in ensuring that a new entity comes into existence and shares its expertise so as to identify new, innovative solutions and opportunities.

Key Issues for Legislators, Governments, and Policymakers

Legislators, but also governments and policymakers clearly need to create the right environment to ensure that an independent agency can perform its tasks and roles adequately. It is not only the legal framework, with sufficient powers and instruments, that is essential; the agency also needs to be supported by the right regulatory and competition environment and culture. There is clearly a tension here between the independence of the agency, obliging the legislator and government to observe a certain distance, and the need to exercise some form of control over this agency and thus ensure, within a democratic society, that it can be held accountable for its actions. In my opinion, the emphasis needs to be on the forms of accountability and on the development of various accountability mechanisms, instead of on limiting the agency's powers or its independence. The ingredients—independence and sufficient powers—are necessary if such agencies are to function effectively and attain the goals of their oversight. The recipe for achieving this is to practise transparency, one of the fundamental good agency or LITER principles.

Broad legal mandate and clear policy goals

Nowadays, agencies have to perform their duties in a constantly changing, highly dynamic environment, with many new technological and other developments in an increasingly globalized world. In a rapidly changing environment, driven by technological developments and global challenges, such as the energy and environmental crises, it is essential for these agencies' legal powers, their tool box, and the procedures in place to be adequate in order to ensure an effective response to these rapid changes and developments.

The legislator has the responsibility to provide the expert agency with sufficiently flexible powers so that the latter can adapt its enforcement approach to the circumstances of the case and, if new or unexpected problems arise, can intervene or take any action required, based on its legal mandate. This inevitably demands a margin of discretion for the agency, which can only be granted after an agency's tasks and functions have been clearly defined. The legislative process is too slow to keep pace with these developments and to change in response to each and every case. In addition, the legislator cannot possibly foresee every single problem that can potentially occur in the future, as a result of which a broad mandate to take action—within the aims of the legislation—must be provided. Government too has to clearly state what its policies aim for, so the agency can take responsive action and adapt its approaches in line with these policy goals. On the other hand, this discretion also requires the agency to provide clarity—based, for example, on guidelines—on how it will act in specific circumstances. This means an agency will have to ensure as much transparency and predictability as possible.

Support regulatory and competition culture

Fair competition should form part of the legislators', governments', and policymakers' mindset, both at local and central level. Legislators, governments, and policymakers at all levels need to support the independent agency so that it can perform the roles and functions assigned to it by the legislator. In too many cases, independent agencies are seen as standing in the way of new legislation's implementation instead of as an expert able to provide input of significant importance. In order for an agency to perform its roles and functions and provide significant input, a clear regulatory and competition policy and culture are required, in which each party's roles and tasks are respected.

The independent agency clearly has an advocacy role to play in informing the government of any situations in which fair competition is at stake. The purpose of the agency's advocacy is to encourage the elimination of regulations that distort market competition or impose barriers to entry. The exchange of expertise and information between the government and agencies is an important tool in ensuring that this advocacy can take place, and in preventing governments from engaging in anticompetitive behaviour. The timing of consultations in the legislative and regulatory process is crucial if the advocacy role is to be performed effectively.

Respect the agency's independence

Government bodies must respect the independence granted to the agency. Independence does not mean a total absence of control or monitoring. Rather it means following certain rules to ensure that no undue influence occurs and that the independent agency is able to take decisions impartially, based on its legal mandate and taking account of the aims of the legislation and the specific circumstances of the case; in other words, balancing the different interests at stake. Which accountability mechanisms can governments use to achieve an acceptable level of control?

The basic rule is that the government has to refrain from interfering in individual cases. However, the responsible minister or government can issue general policy guidelines in order to create a framework for the independent agency. These guidelines should not be labelled 'general' if, in reality, they relate to an individual case.

The fact that the government can appoint and dismiss members of the agency's board is a very important instrument of control and can influence the scope of an agency's independence. Procedures behind closed doors, or not governed by clear sets of rules, do not accord with the LITER principles of independence and transparency. Politically motivated appointments are consequently not in line with these principles. The appointment process should rather be clear and transparent. Board appointments must therefore be based on objective, qualitative criteria so as to ensure members' impartiality and expertise.

If a legislator wishes to establish greater board accountability, it has several instruments available. These include appointing a supervisory board with the power to subject strategic decisions of the agency (on, for example, integrity procedures or financial issues) to verification or to monitor the quality of the organization. A board with such powers can operate as a buffer between the responsible minister, the government, and the independent agency. This institutional framework will provide the right balance between sufficient control over the agency on the one hand and the independence structure on the other hand. Members of the supervisory board should be appointed on the basis of their independence and expertise, once again with clear rules governing the appointment process and for dealing with conflicts of interest. An alternative is to appoint non-executive experts to the board, and for these experts then to serve as a countervailing power within the single-tier board.

Another important instrument from an accountability perspective is the publication of annual reports and regular (internal and external) evaluations, as well as public hearings before parliamentary committees, at which the independent agency accounts to parliament for its activities and effectiveness. In my opinion, this form of accountability is a necessary link in the accountability chain in that it ensures that the agency is sufficiently open towards parliament, while also creating a direct relationship between the agency and parliament, without the interference of the responsible minister.

An agency must have an adequate budget and sufficient numbers of appropriately qualified personnel if it is to be independent. A *de jure* independent agency without sufficient budgetary or human resources is, in reality, toothless. By limiting an agency's staffing or funding, a government or ministry can indirectly seek to limit the agency's powers. In that sense, having sufficient budgetary and human resources forms a buffer against undue influence. This does not mean the agency should be given a blank cheque. Governments obviously have to set and monitor agency budgets and expenditure so as to ensure that financial rules and boundaries are respected and the agency spends its money responsibly. An agency also needs to be able to allocate its budgetary and other resources independently so that it is free to decide which cases to take on, and to attract high-quality personnel able to deliver the required outcomes.

Key Issues for the Courts

Court reviews of decisions by independent agencies form the final link in the accountability chain. The court's role is of paramount importance and must not be restricted. Effective legal protection clearly needs to be available in the form of high standards of judicial review as this is a fundamental human right. Judicial review constitutes a corrective mechanism for all kinds of biases that independent agencies may demonstrate. There is always a risk of bias, and it is up to the court to provide a fresh pair of eyes and to ensure objectivity. This, however, requires specialized courts able to deal with complex technical and economic issues in the fields of regulation and competition law. If legal protection is to be effective, appeal procedures must also be dealt with within a reasonable period of time so as to ensure an acceptable degree of certainty in today's rapidly changing environments.

Full review on the merits

As concerns the standard of review adopted by the court, the choice between a marginal or a full review is only relevant when reviewing decisions made by agencies functioning in a model with separated prosecuting and sanctioning powers. In all other cases, and specifically if the agency operates an integrated model, a full review on the merits is preferable. A full review on the merits is in any case desirable in order to counterbalance the independence of agencies and the extensive powers granted to them.

A full or comprehensive review means that the court will deal fully with a decision and has the power to scrutinize details of decisions profoundly and rigorously. This applies not only to the interpretation of the law and the facts, but also to other aspects of the decision, specifically with regard to sanctions. However, an overkill of judicial legal protection can ultimately frustrate the effectiveness of the supervisory system and lead to ineffective market control. The independent agency must, therefore, be allowed a margin of discretion, especially in the event of complex economic and technical matters. While this margin must be available to the independent agencies, courts must also be allowed scope to demonstrate any manifest error of judgement. In doing so, the courts will fulfil their duty to provide the necessary checks and balances, thus counterbalancing the agency's independence, while at the same time respecting the latter's specific functions and roles.

Rules on evidence

There is clearly a proof paradox. Intervention by independent agencies is considered necessary to attain the goals of the rules that have been put in place, and the agencies have to gather evidence to substantiate their interventions for courts to be able to review the agencies' decisions. However, applying too strict approach an to evidence can result in insufficient enforcement of the applicable rules. This in turn can lead to insufficient market control and inadequate protection of consumers. The rules on evidence must therefore set reasonable standards and enable independent agencies to use the margin of discretion they have been given and thus to attain the goals of regulation, competition, and consumer law.

Agency liability

Concerns about the liability of independent agencies can have a deterrent effect on the agency: the mere risk of being held liable can create an incentive to act carefully or, to put it differently, behave responsibly. However, there is another side to this coin. The possibility of liability can also lead to an excessively defensive strategy on oversight: the independent agency could devote too much attention to avoiding liability claims instead of focusing on performing its tasks. This dilemma can be resolved by limiting liability to situations in which the agency failed to act reasonably, taking into account the tasks entrusted to the agency and its permitted margins of discretion. Courts should recognize that institutions entrusted with this kind of responsibility face a difficult task in seeking to serve the public interest, while also having to weigh different interests against each other. Although agencies have a general duty of care, a breach of this duty should result in liability only if the agency is found to have acted recklessly or behaved unreasonably.

* * *

The LITER principles of legality, independence, transparency, effectiveness, and responsibility offer a versatile framework to structure and evaluate an independent agency's functioning. Both the agencies themselves and the institutions and stakeholders they have to respond to can use these guidelines of good agency behaviour to align the agencies' governance, behaviour, performance, and outcomes. Although the weight conferred on each of the principles and each of their subvalues will differ according to the specific circumstances at hand, and different trade-offs will have to be made on each occasion, these LITER or good agency principles may serve as a source of inspiration and perhaps even a mantra to be repeated over and over again.

ANNEX 1

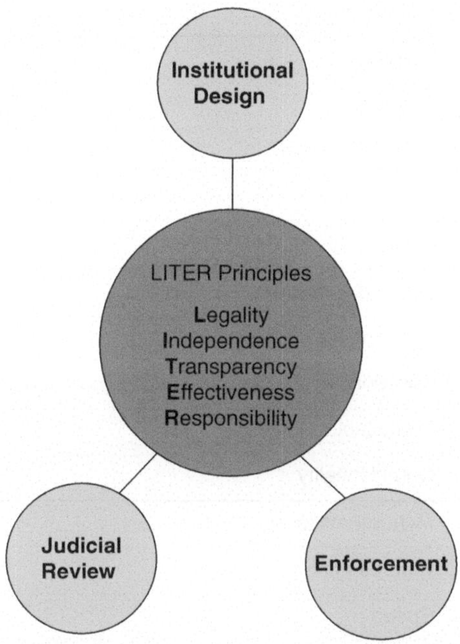

Figure 1 LITER principles' influence on the fabric of independent agencies

ANNEX 2

Legality	Legal mandate
	Fairness/Fair procedure
	Carefulness
	Proportionality
	Sufficient reasoning
	Human rights
Independence	Integrity
	Expertise
	Professionalism
	Objectivity
	Impartiality
Transparency	Open/accessible
	Accountable
	Participation
	Predictable
	Confidentiality
Effectiveness	Instruments/tools
	Enforcement
	Speed
	Efficiency
	Flexibility
	Prioritization
Responsibility	Trust
	Cooperation
	Social responsibility
	Compliance

Figure 2 LITER principles of good agency behaviour

ANNEX 3

Tables accompanying chapter 2

Table 2.1 Different types of multifunctional agencies in various countries

Country	Agency	Functions	Since
Brazil	CADE	Single function (competition)	1962
Chile	FNE	Single function (competition)	1973
China	NDRC	Single function (competition)	2008
India	CCI	Single function (competition)	2003
Japan	JFTC	Single function (competition)	1947
Germany	BNetzA	Multisector regulation	2006
Luxembourg	ILR	Multisector regulation	2000
Denmark	KFST	Competition & consumer protection	2010
Finland	KKV	Competition & consumer protection	2013
France	DGCCRF	Competition & consumer protection	1985
US	FTC	Competition & consumer protection	1914
UK	CMA	Competition & consumer protection	2014
New Zealand	NZCC	Competition & consumer protection	1986
Spain	CNMC	Competition & multisector regulation	2013
Netherlands	NMa	Competition & multisector regulation	1998
Netherlands	ACM	Competition, consumer protection & regulation	2013
Australia	ACCC	Competition, consumer protection & regulation	1995

Table 2.2 European networks of national agencies before and after 1 January 2011

Areas	2010	2011
Consumer protection	Consumer Protection Cooperation network (CPC)	Consumer Protection Cooperation network (CPC)
Competition law	European Competition Network (ECN)	European Competition Network (ECN)
Communications	European Regulators Group for Communications Networks and Services (ERG)	Body of European Regulators for Electronic Communications (BEREC)
Energy	European Energy Regulators Group (ERGEG)	Agency for the Cooperation of Energy Regulators (ACER)
Banking	Committee of European Banking Supervisors (CEBS)	European Banking Authority (EBA)
Securities	Committee of European Securities Regulators (CESR)	European Securities and Markets Authority (ESMA)
Insurance/pensions	Committee of European Insurance and Occupational Pensions Supervisors (CEIOPS)	European Insurance and Occupational Pensions Authority (EIOPA)

ANNEX 4

Organization charts accompanying chapter 4

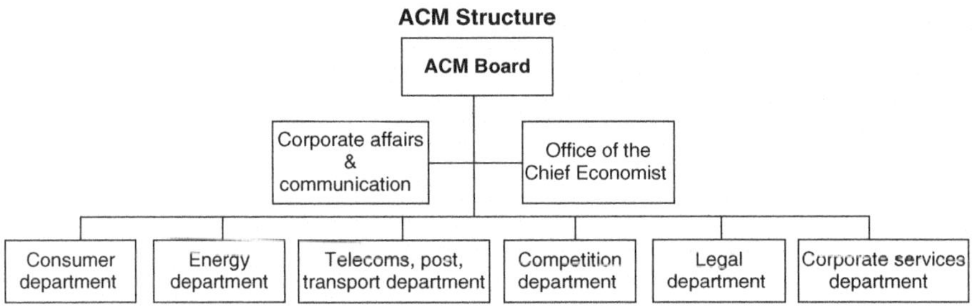

Figure 3 ACM's organizational structure

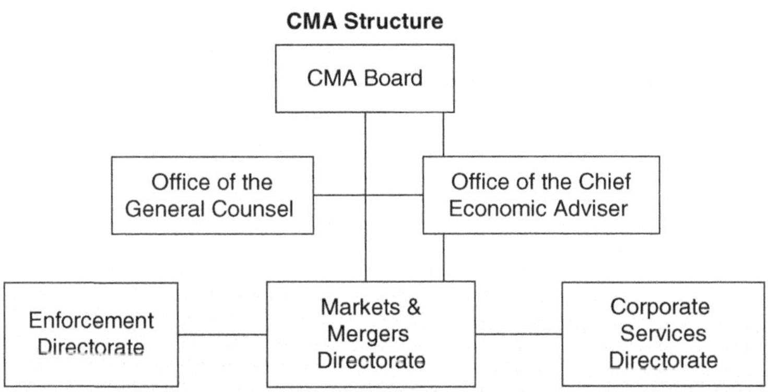

Figure 4 CMA's organizational structure

References

Accetto M and Zleptnig S, 'The Principle of Effectiveness: Rethinking its Role in Community Law' (2005) 11(3) European Public Law 375

Addink H, 'Principles of Good Governance, Lessons from Administrative Law' in D M Curtin and R Wessel (eds), *Good Governance and the European Union. Reflections on concepts, institutions and substance* (Antwerp—Oxford—New York: Intersentia 2005) 21

Addink H, *Goed Bestuur* (The Hague: Boom Juridische Uitgevers 2010)

Aelen M, *Beginselen van goed markttoezicht. Gedefinieerd, verklaard en uitgewerkt voor het toezicht op de financiële markten* (dissertation, Utrecht University, The Hague: Boom Juridische Uitgevers 2014)

Aitken J and Lamb T, 'What the New Competition and Markets Authority Means for the UK Market' [2012] International Financial Law Review

Aitken J and Romney R, 'Quis Custodiet ipsos Custodes? Do Proposed Reforms Risk Undermining Confidence in UK Competition and Communications Appeals?' (2013) 4 Competition Law 389

Andenas M and H-Y Chiu I, *The Foundations and Future of Financial Regulation: Governance for Responsibility* (London and New York: Routledge 2013)

Aubert C, Rey P and Kovavic W E, 'The Impact of Leniency and Whistle-Blowing Programs on Cartels' (2006) 24 International Journal of Industrial Organization 1241

Ayres I and Braithwaite J, *Responsive Regulation: Transcending the Deregulation Debate* (New York: Oxford University Press 1992)

Baarsma B, 'Ontwikkelingen in het mededingingstoezicht. Essay in het kader van het WRR-project Toekomst van toezicht' (2012) SEO Economisch Onderzoek, commissioned by the Wetenschappelijke Raad voor het Regeringsbeleid

Bailey D, 'Standard of Judicial Review under Articles 101 and 102 TFEU' in Merola M and Derenne J (eds), *The Role of the Court of Justice of the European Union in Competition Law Cases* (Bruges: College of Europe, Global Competition Law Centre 2012) 103

Baldwin R and Black J, 'Really Responsive Regulation' (2005) LSE Law, Society and Economy Working Papers

Baldwin R, Cave M, and Lodge M, *Understanding Regulation. Theory, Strategy, and Practice* (2nd edn, Oxford: Oxford University Press 2012)

Barkow R, 'Insulating Agencies: Avoid Capture Through Institutional Design' (2010) 89 Texas Law Review 15

Bator F M, 'The Anatomy of Market Failure' (1958) 72(3) Quarterly Journal of Economics 351

Becker T E, 'Integrity in Organizations: Beyond Honesty and Conscientiousness' (1998) 23(1) Academy of Management Review 154

Bennet M et al, 'What Does Behavioral Economics Mean for Competition Policy' (2010) 6 Competition Policy International Journal

Biber E, 'Too Many Things to Do: How to Deal with the Dysfunctions of Multiple-Goal Agencies' (2009) 33(1) Harvard Environmental Law Review 62

Bisset K and Thomas L, 'Lenciency Program: A New Tool in Competition Policy to Deter Cartel Activity in Procurement Auctions' (2004) 17 European Journal of Law and Economics 5

Black J, 'Managing Discretion' (2001) ARLC Conference Paper on Penalties: Policy, Principles and Practice in Government Regulation

Black J, 'The Emergence of the Risk-Based Regulation and the New Public Risk Management in the United Kingdom', (2005) 3 Public Law 19

Black J, 'Constructing and Contesting Legitimacy and Accountability in Polycentric Regulatory Regimes' (2008) LSE Legal Studies Working Paper No. 2/2008

Borstlap H, van der Meer Mohr P F M, and Smits L J E, 'Rapport van de Onderzoekscommissie intern functioneren NZa' (2014)

Botta M and Svetlicinii A, 'The Right of Fair Trial in Competition Law Proceedings: Quo Vadis the Courts of the New EU Member States?' (2014) Centre for Antitrust and Regulatory Studies, University of Warsaw 9th ASCOLA Conference on Procedural Fairness in Competition Proceedings

Bourgeois J and Waelbroeck D, *Ten Years of Effects-Based Approach in EU Competition Law. State of Play and Perspectives* (Bruges: College of Europe, Global Competition Law Centre 2013)

Bovens M, 'Analysing and Assessing Accountability: A Conceptual Framework' (2007) 13(4) European Law Journal 450

Bovens M, 'Two Concepts of Accountability: Accountability as a Virtue and as a Mechanism' (2010) 33 (5) West European Politics 946

Bovens M, Schillemans T, and 't Hart P, 'Does Public Accountability Work? An Assessment Tool' (2008) 86(1) Public Administration 225

Buccirossi P et al, 'Deterrence in Competition Law' (2009) Discussion Paper no. 285, Governance and the Efficiency of Economic Systems

Bulterman M et al. (eds), *Views of European Law from the Mountain* (Liber Amicorum Piet Jan Slot Kluwer Law International 2009)

Busuioc M, *The Accountability of European Agencies. Legal Provisions and Ongoing Practices* (dissertation, Utrecht University, Delft: Uitgeverij Eburon 2010)

Callies G and Renner M, 'Between Law and Social Norms: the Evolution of Global Governance' (2009) 22 Ratio Juris 260

Carpenter D, 'The Evolution of National Bureaucracy in the United States' in Aberbach J D and Peterson M (eds), *Institutions of American Democracy: The Executive Branch* (Oxford: Oxford University Press 2005) 41

Carpenter D, *Reputation and Power: Organizational Image and Pharmaceutical Regulation at the FDA* (Princeton: Princeton UP 2010)

Carrigan C, 'Captured by Disaster? Reinterpreting Regulatory Behavior in Shadow of the Gulf Oil Spill' in D Carpenter and D Moss (eds), *Preventing Regulatory Capture. Special Interest Influence and How to Limit it* (New York: Cambridge University Press 2014) 239

Cave M and Stern J, *Competition and Regulatory Policy and Institutional Design for Scotland* (2013) The David Hume Institute, Research paper No. 11/2013

Chetty D, Njisane Y, Mbikiwa M, and Martin C, '"Knowledge is Power". The Role of Market Inquiries in Assessing the State of Competition and Facilitating Ex Ante Regulation of Markets' (2014) Eighth Annual Competition Law, Economics and Policy Conference

Chisholm D, 'Problem-Solving and Institutional Design' (1995) 5 Journal of Public Administration Research and Theory: T-Part 451

Christensen T and Lægreid P (eds), *Autonomy and Regulation: Coping with Agencies in the Modern State* (Cheltenham: Edward Elgar 2006)

Clarke J, 'The Increasing Criminalization of Economic Law: a Competition Law Perspective' (2012) 19(1) Journal of Financial Crime 76

Connor J M, *Price-Fixing Overcharges: Legal and Economic Evidence* (2005) Staff Paper No. 04-17, Purdue University

Cseres K J, 'The Impact of Consumer Protection on Competition and Competition Law; The Case of Deregulated Markets' (2006) Amsterdam Center for Law & Economics Working Paper No. 2006-05

Cseres K J, 'The Controversies of the Consumer Welfare Standard' (2007) 3(2) Competition Law Review 121

Cseres K J, 'Competition and Consumer Policies; Starting Points for Better Convergence' (2009) Amsterdam Center for Law & Economics Working Paper No. 2009-06

Cseres K J, 'Integrate or Separate—Institutional Design for the Enforcement of Competition Law and Consumer Law' (2013) Amsterdam Law School Legal Studies Research Paper No 2013-03

Currie D, 'The new CMA: How Will it Promote Competition?' (2013) Beesley lecture 7 November 2013

Currie D, 'The Case for the British Model of Independent Regulation 30 years on' (2014) The Currie Lecture, Cass Business School, London

Curtin D M, ''Delegation to EU Non-Majoritarian Agencies and Emerging Practices of Public Accountability'' in D Geradin et al, *Regulation Through Agencies in the EU. A New Paradigm of European Governance* (Cheltenham: Edward Elgar 2005)

Curtin D M, 'Positioning Accountability in European Governance: An Introduction' (2010) 33 (5) West European Politics 929

Curtin D M and Dekker I, 'Good Governance: The Concept and its Application by the European Union' in Curtin D M and Wessel A R (red), *Good Governance and the European Union: Reflections on Concepts, Institutions and Substance* (Antwerp: Intersentia 2005)

Das U S and Quintyn M, 'Financial Crisis Prevention and Crisis Management—the Role of Regulatory Governance' in R E Litan, M Pomerleano, and V Sundararajan (eds), *Financial Sector Governance: The Roles of the Public and Private Sectors* (Washington, D.C.: Brookings Institution Press 2002) 163

de Bruijn H, ten Heuvelhof E, and Koopmans M, *Law Enforcement. The Game Between Inspectors and Inspectees* (Boca Raton, Florida: Universal Publishers 2007)

de Moor-van Vugt A J C, du Perron C E, and Krop P J, 'De bevoegdheden van De Nederlandsche Bank inzake Icesave' (2009) Report commissioned by the Dutch Ministry of Economic Affairs, University of Amsterdam

Deva S, 'Guiding Principles on Business and Human Rights: Implications for Companies' (2012) 9 (2) European Company Law 101

de Visser M, *Network-Based Governance in EC Law. The Example of EC Competition and EC Communications Law* (Oxford: Hart Publishing Ltd 2009)

Donaldson L, *The Contingency Theory of Organizations* (Thousand Oaks CA, London, New Delhi: Sage 2001)

Donnelly J, 'Publication Review "The General Principles of EU Law" by Tridimas' (2010) 32 Dublin University Law Journal 401

Duina F, 'Explaining Legal Implementation in the European Union' (1997) 25 International Journal of the Sociology of Law 155

Ebbers R, 'Nieuwe Big Brother' (2012) 19 VNO NCW Forum 24

Etienne J, 'Ambiguity and Relational Signals in Regulator-Regulatee Relationships' (2013) 7 Regulation & Governance 33

Ferran E, 'Understanding the New Institutional Architecture of EU Financial Market Supervision' in Ferrarini G, Hopt K J, and Wymeersch E (eds) *Rethinking Financial Regulation and Supervision in Times of Crisis* (Oxford: Oxford University Press 2012)

First H, Fox E, and Hemli D, 'Procedural and Institutional Norms in Antitrust Enforcement: The US System' (2012) NYU Law and Economics Research Paper No 12-18

Fonteijn C A, 'De toezichthouder is onafhankelijk, maar "noblesse oblige"' (2011) 2(3) Tijdschrift voor Toezicht 64

Fonteijn C A and Ottow A T, 'Independence of Competition Authorities. Independence in Heart, Mind and Law' in D Arts et al (eds), *Mundi et Europae Civis: Liber Amicorum Jacques Steenbergen* (Brussels: Larcier 2014) 405

Forrester I S, 'Due Process in EC Competition Cases: a Distinguished Institution with Flawed Procedures' (2009) 34(6) European Law Review 817

Forrester I S, 'A Bush in Need of Pruning: the Luxuriant Growth of Light Judicial Review' in C Ehlerman and M Marquis (eds), *European Competition Law Annual 2009: Evaluation of Evidence and its Judicial Review in Competition Cases* (Oxford and Portland: Hart Publishing 2010) 407

Fox E M, 'Antitrust and Institutions: Design and Change' (2010) 41 Loyola University of Chicago Law Journal 473

Fox E M and Trebilcock M J, 'The Design of Competition Law Institutions and the Global Convergence of Process Norms: The GAL Competition' (2012) NYU Law and Economics Research Paper No 12-20

Fox E M and Trebilcock M J (eds), *The Design of Competition Law Institutions. Global Norms, Local Choices* (Oxford: Oxford University Press 2013)

Freeman P, 'The Competition and Markets Authority: Can the Whole Be Greater Than the Sum of its Parts?' (2013) 1(1) Journal of Antitrust Enforcement 4

Freiberg A, *The Tools of Regulation* (Sydney: Federation Press 2010)

Geradin D, 'Institutional Aspects of EU Regulatory Reforms in the Telecommunications Sector: An Analysis of the Role of National Regulatory Authorities' (2000) 1 Journal of Network Industries 5

Geradin D,'The Opening of State Monopolies to Competition: Main Issues of the Liberalization Process' in D Geradin (ed), *The Liberalization of State Monopolies in the European Union and Beyond* (Deventer: Kluwer Law International 2000) 181

Geradin D,'Antitrust Compliance Programmes and Optimal Antitrust Enforcement: A Reply to Wouter Wils' (2013) 1(1) Journal of Antitrust Enforcement 325

Geradin D, Layne-Farrar A, and Petit N, *EU Competition Law and Economics* (Oxford: Oxford University Press 2012)

Geradin D and Petit N, 'The Development of Agencies at EU and National Levels: Conceptual Analysis and Proposals for Reform' (2004) Jean Monnet Working Paper 01-04

Geradin D, and Petit N, 'Judicial Review in European Competition Law' in Merola M and Derenne J (eds), *The Role of the Court of Justice of the European Union in Competition Law Cases* (Bruges: College of Europe, Global Competition Law Centre 2012) 21

Gerard D M B, 'The Effects-Based Approach Under the Article 101 TFEU and its Paradoxes: Modernization at War with Itself?' in J Bourgeois and D Waelbroeck, *Ten Years of Effects-Based Approach in EU Competition Law. State of Play and Perspectives* (Bruges: College of Europe, Global Competition Law Centre 2013)

Gersen J, 'Overlapping and Underlapping Jurisdiction in Administrative Law' (2007) Public Law & Legal Theory Working Papers No. 161

Giesen I, 'Regulating Regulators Through Liability. The Case for Applying Normal Tort Rules to Supervisors' (2006) 2(1) Utrecht Law Review 8

Gilardi F, 'Policy Credibility and Delegation to Independent Regulatory Agencies; a Comparative Analysis' (2002) 6 Journal of European Public Policy 873

Gilardi F, 'The Formal Independence of Regulators: A Comparison of 17 Countries and 7 Sectors' (2005) 11(4) Swiss Political Science Review 139

Gilardi F, 'The Same, But Different: Central Banks, Regulatory Agencies and the Politics of Delegation to Independent Authorities' (2007) 5(3) Comparative European Politics 303

Groenleer M, *The Autonomy of European Union Agencies. A Comparative Study of Institutional Development* (Delft: Uitgeverij Eburon 2009)

Gunningham N and Grabosky P, *Smart Regulation* (Oxford: Clarendon Press 1998)

Gunningham N and Sinclair D, 'Designing Smart Regulation' (2004) OECD Global Forum on Sustainable Development, Paris

Hampton P, *Reducing Administrative Burdens: Effective Inspection and Enforcement* (HM Treasury, London 2005)

Hancher L and Moran M, 'Organizing Regulatory Space' in Hancher L and Moran M (eds), *Capitalism, Culture and Economic Regulation* (Oxford: Clarendon Press 1989)

Hanretty C and Koop C, 'Comparing Regulatory Agencies: Report on the Results of a Worldwide Survey' (2009) European University Institute Working Paper RSCAS 2009/63 19

Hanretty C et al, 'Independence, Accountability and Perceived Quality of Regulators, a CERRE Study' (2012) Brussels: Centre on Regulation in Europe

Hart H L A, *The Concept of Law* (2nd edn, Oxford: Clarendon Press 1994)

Hellingman K and Mortelmans K J M, *Economisch publiekrecht. Rechtswaarborgen en rechtsinstrumenten* (Deventer: Kluwer 1989)

Hertig G, 'Regulatory Competition for EU Financial Services' (2000) 3(2) Journal of International Economic Law 349

Hoekstra R J and Frijns J, 'Het rapport van de evaluatiecommissie nationalisatie SNS Reaal' (Amsterdam 2014)

Huffman M, 'Bridging the Divide Theories for Integrating Competition Law and Consumer Protection' (2010) 6(1) European Competition Journal 7

Hukopian G, 'Criminalisation of EU Competition Law Enforcement—A Possibility after Lisbon?' (2010) 7(1) The Competition Law Review 157

Hüpkes E, Quintyn M, and Taylor M W, 'Accountability Arrangements for Financial Sector Regulators' (2006) 39 International Monetary Fund Economic Issues series

Hwang S and Satchell S, 'Tracking Error: Ex-Ante versus Ex-Post Measures' (2001) Financial Econometrics Centre Working Papers Series WP01-15

Hyman D A and Kovacic W E, 'Enforcing Competition Law: Benefits and Costs of a Multi-Purpose Agency' [forthcoming]

Hyman D A and Kovacic W E, 'Competition Agencies with Complex Policy Portfolios; Divide or Conquer?' (2013) George Washington University Law Faculty Publications & Other Works, Paper 631

Hyman D A and Kovacic W E, 'Institutional Design, Agency Life Cycle, and the Goals of Competition Law' (2013) 81 Fordham Law Review 2163

International Competition Network, 'Advocacy and Competition Policy' (Report prepared by the Advocacy Working Group, presented at the first ICN's conference in Naples, Italy, 2002)

Jans J H and Outhuijse A, 'Advisory Objection Procedures in The Netherlands: a Case Study on their Usefulness in Dutch Competition Law' in Comtois S and de Graaf K, *On Judicial and Quasi-Judicial Independence* (The Hague: Eleven International Publishing 2013)

Jans J H, de Lange R, Prechal S, and Widdershoven R J G M, *Europeanisation of Public Law* (Groningen: Europa Law Publishing 2007)

Jenny F, 'Competition Authorities. Independence and Advocacy' in D Sokol and I Lianos, *The Global Limits of Competition Law* (Palo Alto: Stanford University Press 2012)

Johanssen K, 'Regulatory Independence in Theory and Practice—a Survey of Independent Energy Regulators in Eight European Countries' (2003 AKF Forlaget)

Johnston A, 'ISO 26000: Guiding Companies to Sustainability Through Social Responsibility?' (2012) 8 (2) European Company Law 110
Johnstone R, 'Putting the Regulated Back into Regulation' (1999) 26 Journal of Law and Society 378
Jordana J and Levi-Faur D, 'The Politics of Regulation in the Age of Governance' in Jordana J and Levi-Faur D (eds), *The Politics of Regulation* (Cheltenham: Edward Elgar 2004) 1
Kalbfleish P, 'The Assessment of Interest in Competition Law: A Balancing Act' in Monti M et al (eds), *Economic Law and Justice in Times of Globalization—Festschrift for Carl Baudenbacher* (Baden-Baden: Nomos Verlagsgesellschaft 2007) 455
Karpoff J M and Lott J R, 'The Reputational Penalty Firms Bear from Committing Criminal Fraud' (1993) 36 Journal of Law and Economics 757
Karpoff J M et al, *The Cost to Firms of Cooking the Books* (Washington, D.C.: University of Washington 2006)
Kovacic W E, 'Competition Policy, Consumer Protection and Economic Disadvantage' (2008) 25 Washington University Journal of Law and Policy 101
Kovacic W E, 'Rating the Competition Agencies: What Constitutes Good Performance?' (2009) 16(4) George Mason Law Review 906
Kovacic W E, and Hyman D A, 'Competition Agency Design: What's on the Menu?' (2013) 8 European Competition Journal 527
Laffont J and Martimort D, 'Separation of Regulators Against Collusive Behaviour' (1999) 30(2) RAND Journal of Economics 232
Laguna de Paz J, 'Understanding the Limits of Judicial Review in European Competition Law' (2014) 2(1) Journal of Antitrust Enforcement 203
Larouche P, *Competition Law and Regulation in European Telecommunications* (Oxford: Hart Publishing Ltd 2000)
Larsen A, Pedersen L H, Sørensen E M, and Olsen O J, 'Independent Regulatory Authorities in European Electricity Markets' (2006) 34 Energy Policy 2858
Lassèrre B, 'The New French Competition Authority: Mission, Priorities and Strategies for the Coming Five Years' (Paris: Autorité de la Concurrence 2009)
Lavrijssen S A C M, *Onafhankelijke mededingingstoezichthouders, regulerende bevoegdheden en de waarborgen voor good governance* (dissertation, Tilburg University, The Hague: Boom Juridische Uitgevers 2006)
Lavrijssen S A C M, 'More Intensive Judicial Review in Competition Law and Economic Regulation in the Netherlands: Vice or Virtue' in Essens O, Gerbrandy A, and Lavrijssen S A C M (eds), *National Courts and the Standard of Review in Competition Law and Economic Regulation* (Groningen: Europa Law Publishing 2009) 173
Lavrijssen S A C M and Ottow A T, 'The Legality of Independent Regulatory Authorities' in Besselink L, Pennings F, and Prechal S, *The Eclipse of Legality in Europe* (Deventer: Kluwer International 2010)
Lavrijssen S A C M and Ottow A T, 'Independent Supervisory Authorities: A Fragile Concept' (2012) 39(4) Legal Issues of Economic Integration 419

Lenaerts K and Gutiérrez-Fons J A, 'The Constitutional Allocation of Powers and General Principles of EU Law' (2010) 47 Common Market Law Review 1629

Lugard P, (ed), *The International Competition Network at Ten. Origins, Accomplishments and Aspirations* (Antwerp: Intersentia 2011)

Macrory R, 'Regulatory Justice: Making Sanctions Effective—Final Report' (2006) Cabinet Office

Maggetti M, 'De Facto Independence After Delegation: A Fuzzy-Set Analysis' (2007) 1(4) Regulation & Governance 271

Majone G, 'Controlling Regulatory Bureaucracies: Lessons from the American Experience' (1993) European University Institute Working Papers No. 93/3

Majone G, *Regulating Europe* (London: Routledge 1996)

Majone G, 'The Regulatory State and its Legitimacy Problems' (1999) 22(1) West European Politics 1

Majone G, 'The Credibility Crisis of Community Regulation' (2000) 2 Journal of Common Market Studies 273

Marsden P, 'Checks and Balances: European Competition Law and the Rule of Law' (2009) 22(1) The Antitrust Marathon: Antitrust and the Rule of Law 51

Mashaw J L, 'Accountability and Institutional Design: Some Thoughts on the Grammar of Governance' (2007) Yale Law School Research Paper No 116

Mendeloff J, 'Overcoming Barriers to Better Regulation' (1993) 18 Law and Social Inquiry 711

Moloney N, 'EU Financial Market Regulation after the Global Financial Crisis: "More Europe" or More Risks?' (2010) 47 Common Market Law Review 1317

Monti G, 'Independence, Interdependence and Legitimacy: the EU Commission, National Authorities and the European Competition Network' (2014) EUI Department of Law Research Paper No. 2014/01

Motta M and Polo M, 'Leniency Programs and Cartel Prosecution' (2003) 21 International Journal of Industrial Organization 347

Nazzini R, 'Administrative Enforcement, Judicial Review and Fundamental Rights in EU Competition Law: a Comparative Contextual-Functionalistic Perspective' (2012) 49 Common Market Law Review 971

Nunez B, 'The Application of Behavioural Economics by Regulators in the UK: a Theoretical and Practical Analysis' (masters thesis, Utrecht University, 2014)

O'Connell A, 'The Architecture of Smart Intelligence: Structuring and Overseeing Agencies in the Post-9/11 World' (2006) 94 California Law Review 1655

Ogus A I, *Regulation: Legal Form and Economic Theory* (Clarendon Press Clarendon Law Series 1994)

Ottow A T, 'Europeanization of the Supervision of Competitive Markets' (2002) 18(1) European Public Law 191

Ottow A T, *Telecommunicatietoezicht. De invloed van het Europese en Nederlandse bestuurs(proces)recht* (dissertation, University of Amsterdam, The Hague: SDU 2006)

Ottow A T, *Mastering the Market? Exploring New Forms of Market Supervision* (inaugural lecture, 18 September 2008, University of Utrecht, The Hague: Boom Juridische Uitgevers 2009)

Ottow A T, 'Observations on Economic Proof in Economic Cases' in Essens O, Gerbrandy A, and Lavrijssen S A C M (eds), *National Courts and the Standard of Review in Competition Law and Economic Regulation* (Groningen: Europa Law Publishing 2009) 39

Ottow A T, 'Developing a Common Framework for Good Performances by Agencies' in Lugard P (ed), *The International Competition Network at Ten. Origins, Accomplishments and Aspirations* (Antwerp: Intersentia 2011) 251

Ottow A T, 'The Different Levels of Protection of National Supervisors' Independence in the European Landscape' in Comtois S and de Graaf K (eds), *On Judicial and Quasi-Judicial Independence* (Netherlands Institute for Law and Governance Series 7, The Hague: Boom Juridische Uitgevers 2013) 139

Ottow A T, 'Erosion or Innovation?: The Institutional Design of Competition Agencies—A Dutch Case Study' (2014) 2(1) Journal of Antitrust Enforcement 25

Ottow A T, 'The New European Supervisory Architecture of the Financial Markets' in Everson M, Monda C, and Vos E (eds), *EU Agencies in—and—the External Relations of the EU* (The Hague: Wolters Kluwer Law & Business 2014) 123

Ottow A T and Aelen M, 'Commission v Federal Republic of Germany' (2010) 11(6) European Human Rights Cases 679

Ottow A T and Svetiev Y, 'Institutional Innovation in Financial Supervision in the Interstices Between Public and Private Law' (2014) European Regulatory Private Law and Financial Services Third Annual Workshop, European University Institute, Florence

Owens J B, 'Have We No Shame?: Thoughts on Shaming "White Collar" Criminals, and the Federal Sentencing Guidelines' (2000) 49(5) American University Law Review 1047

Parret L Y J M, 'Sense and Nonsense of Rules on Proof in Cartel Cases: How to Reconcile a More Economic-Based Approach to Competition Law with More Attention for Rules on Proof' (2008) 4(1) European Competition Journal 169

Pierson P, 'The Limits of Design: Explaining Institutional Origins and Change' (2000) 13(4) Governance 475

Pollit C and Bouckaert G, *Public Management Reform: a Comparative Analysis* (2nd ed, Oxford: Oxford University Press 2004)

Pollit C, Caulfield J, Smullen J A, and Talbot C, *Agencies: How Governments Do Things Through Semi-Autonomous Organizations* (Basingstoke: Palgrave MacMillan 2004)

Porat A, 'Ex-Post Right, Ex-Ante Wrong' (2014) 89(3) Notre Dame Law Review 1209

Prechal S, *Directives in EC Law* (Oxford: EC Law Library 2005)

Prechal S and De Leeuw M E, 'Transparency: a General Principle of EU law?' in Bernitz U et al, *General Principles of EC Law in a Process of Development* (Alphen aan den Rijn: Kluwer Law International 2008)

Prosser T, *The Limits of Competition Law. Markets and Public Services* (Oxford: Oxford University Press 2004)

Prosser T, *The Regulatory Enterprise. Government, Regulation and Legitimacy* (Oxford: Oxford University Press 2010)

Quintyn M, 'Independent Agencies: More Than a Cheap Copy of Independent Central Banks?' (2009) 20 Constitutional Political Economy 267

Quintyn M and Taylor M W, 'Robust Regulators and Their Political Masters: Independence and Accountability in Theory' in Masciandaro D and Quintyn M (eds), *Designing Financial Supervision Institutions: Independence, Accountability and Governance* (Cheltenham, UK: Edward Elgar 2007) 3

Reindl A P, 'How Strong is the Case for Criminal Sanctions in Cartel Cases?' in Cseres K J et al, *Criminalization of Competition Law Enforcement, Economic and Legal Implications for the EU Member States* (Cheltenham: Edward Elgar Publishing Limited 2006)

Ritter J, *The Strange Case of Non-Ministerial Departments* (London: Institute for Government, 2013)

Sabel C F and Zeitlin J H, 'Learning from Difference: The New Architecture of Experimentalist Governance in the EU' in Sabel C F and Zeitlin J H, *Experimentalist Governance in the European Union: Towards a New Architecture* (Oxford: Oxford University Press 2010).

Sabel C F and Zeitlin J H, 'Experimentalist Governance' in Sabel C F and Zeitlin J H, *Experimentalist Governance in the European Union: Towards a New Architecture* (Oxford: Oxford University Press 2010)

Scholten M, *The Political Accountability of EU Agencies: Learning from the US Experience* (dissertation, Maastricht: Datawyse/Universitaire Pers Maastricht 2014)

Schultz W, Valcke P, and Irion K, *The Independence of the Media and its Regulatory Agencies* (Bristol/Chicago: Intellect, 2013)

Schweitzer H, 'Commitment Decisions under Art. 9 of Regulation 1/2003: The Developing EC Practice and Case Law' (2008) Working Paper European University Institute, Law 2008/22

Scordamaglia-Tousis A, *EU Cartel Enforcement. Reconciling Effective Public Enforcement with Fundamental Rights* (International Competition Law Series, volume 54, The Hague: Wolters Kluwer Law & Business 2013)

Sepúlveda M M et al, *Human Rights Reference Handbook* (5th edn, Reykjavik: Icelandic Human Rights Centre 2010)

Slater D, Thomas S, and Waelbroeck D, 'Competition Law Proceedings Before the European Commission and the Right to a Fair Trial: No Need for Reform?' The Global Competition Law Centre Working Papers Series GCLC Working Paper 04/08

Smith M 'Standards of Review and Appeal in Cases Before the Competition Appeal Tribunal' (2012) 3 Competition Law 169

Smits R, 'The European Competition Network: Selected Aspects' in (2005) 32(2) Legal Issues of Economic Integration 175

Sparrow M K, *The Regulatory Craft* (Washington D.C.: Brookings Institution Press 2000)

Sparrow M K, *The Character of Harms. Operational Challenges in Control* (Cambridge: Cambridge University Press 2008)

Svetiev Y, 'Networked Competition Governance in the EU: Delegation, Decentralization or Experimentalist Architecture?' in Sabel C F and Zeitlin J H, *Experimentalist Governance in the European Union: Towards a New Architecture* (Oxford: Oxford University Press 2010)

Svetiev Y, 'Private Law and the Visible Hand of EU Regulation' (2013) Working paper for the Max Weber Programme, European University Institute

Talbot T, 'The Agency Idea: Sometimes Old, Sometimes New, Sometimes Borrowed, Sometimes Untrue' in Pollitt C and Talbot C (eds), *Unbundled Government: a Critical Analysis of the Global Trend to Agencies, Quangos and Contractualisation* (London and New York: Routledge 2004) 3

Thaler R H and Sunstein C R, *Nudge. Improving Decisions about Health, Wealth and Happiness* (New York: Penguin Books 2008)

Thatcher M, 'Regulation after Delegation: Independent Regulatory Agencies in Europe' (2002) 9(6) Journal of European Public Policy 954

Thatcher M, 'The Third Force? Independent Regulatory Agencies and Elected Politicians in Europe' (2005) 18(3) Governance 347

Thatcher M and Coen D, 'Reshaping European Regulatory Space: An Evolutionary Analysis' (2008) 31(4) West European Politics 806

Tison M, 'Challenging the Prudential Supervisor: Liability versus (Regulatory) Immunity' (2004) Gent University, Financial Law Institute Working Paper Series, WP 2003-04 2004

Tridimas T, *The General Principles of EU Law* (Oxford: Oxford University Press 2006)

Trillas F, 'The Institutional Architecture of Regulation and Competition: Spain's 2012 Reform' (2013) IESE Business School Working Paper No. WP-1067-E

van Cleynenbreugel P, 'From Shared Competences to Constitutional Heteronomy. The Institutional Architecture of Supranationally Structured Market Supervision' (dissertation, Leuven: Katholieke Universiteit Leuven 2013)

van Dam C, *Liability of Regulators* (British Institute of International and Competition Law, Report commissioned by the Research and Documentation Centre of the Netherlands Ministry of Justice 2006)

Van den Bergh R and Camesasca P D, *European Competition Law and Economics. A Comparative Perspective* (Antwerp: Intersentia 2001) 70

van Erp J, 'Reputational Sanctions in Private and Public Regulation' (2008) 1(5) Erasmus Law Review 145

van Gerven W, 'Two Twin-Principles of EU Law: Democracy and Accountability, Consistency and Convergence' in Bernitz U, Nergelius J, and Cardner C, *General Principles of EC Law in a Process of Development* (Alphen aan den Rijn: Wolters Kluwer 2008)

van Veldhoven B C J and van Wijck P W, *Recht en efficiëntie. Een inleiding in de economische analyse van het recht* (Deventer: Kluwer 2007)
Verhoest K, van Thiel S, Bouckaert G, and Laegreid P (eds), *Government Agencies: Practices and Lessons from 30 Countries* (London: Palgrave MacMillan 2012)
Vervaele J A E (ed), *Compliance and Enforcement of European Community Law* (The Hague: Kluwer Law International 1999)
Vesterdorf B, 'Standard of Proof in Merger Cases: Reflections in the Light of Recent Case Law of the Community Courts' (2005) 1(1) European Competition Journal 25
Viñals J and Fiechter J, 'The Making of Good Supervision: Learning to Say "No"' (2010) IMF Staff Position Note, SPN/10/08
Wade H W R and Forsyth C, *Administrative Law* (9th edn, Oxford: Oxford University Press 2004)
Weber Waller S, 'In Search of Economic Justice; Considering Competition and Consumer Protection Law' (2005) 36 Loyola University Chicago Law Journal 3
Westerman P, 'Pyramids and the Value of Generality' (2013) 7 Regulation & Governance 89
Wettenhall R, 'Agencies and Non-Departmental Public Bodies. The Hard and Soft Lenses of Agencification Theory' (2005) 7(4) Public Management Review 615
Whelan P, 'A Principled Argument for Personal Criminal Sanctions as Punishment Under EC Cartel Law' (2007) 4(1) The Competition Law Review 7
Whish R and Bailey D, *Competition Law* (Oxford: Oxford University Press 2012)
Wilks S and Bartle I 'The Unanticipated Consequences of Creating Independent Competition Agencies' (2002) 25(1) West European Politics 148
Williamson O E, *The New Institutional Economics: Taking Stock, Looking Ahead* (2000) 38(3) Journal of Economic Literature 595
Wils W P J, 'The Combination of the Investigative and Prosecutorial Function and the Adjudicative Function in EC Antitrust Enforcement: A Legal and Economic Analysis' (2004) 27(2) World Competition 201
Wils W P J, 'Is Criminalization of EU Competition Law the Answer?' (2005) 28(2) World Competition 117
Wils W P J, 'Antitrust Compliance Programmes and Optimal Antitrust Enforcement' (2013) 1(1) Journal of Antitrust Enforcement 52
Wils W P J, 'The Increased Level of EU Antitrust Fines, Judicial Review and the European Convention on Human Rights' (2013) 33(1) World Competition 5
Yesilkagit K and Van Thiel S, 'Political Influence and Bureaucratic Autonomy' (2008) 8(2) Public Organization Review 137
Yesilkagit K and Christensen J, 'Institutional Design and Formal Autonomy: Political versus Historical and Cultural Explanations' (2010) 20 Journal of Public Administration Research and Theory 53
Yeung K, 'Government by Publicity Management: Sunlight or Spin' (2005) 1 Public Law 360

Index

The manufacturer's authorised representative in the EU for product safety is Oxford University Press España S.A. of El Parque Empresarial San Fernando de Henares, Avenida de Castilla, 2 - 28830 Madrid (www.oup.es/en or product.safety@oup.com). OUP España S.A. also acts as importer into Spain of products made by the manufacturer.
Printed and bound by CPI Group (UK) Ltd, Croydon, CR0 4YY
14/09/2026
02216304-0006